5-12-60

B

D1302110

THE BOYS' LIFE OF
MARK TWAIN

The BOYS' LIFE of
MARK TWAIN

By
ALBERT BIGELOW PAINE

With an Introduction by
WALTER BARNES

HARPER'S MODERN CLASSICS

New York
HARPER & BROTHERS PUBLISHERS

THE BOYS' LIFE OF MARK TWAIN

CONTENTS

CONTENTS

vi

CONTENTS

vii

INTRODUCTION

UNLESS you are especially curious about authors and the details of their work, you may agree with that man, himself an author, who said: "The life of a writing man is monotonous and stupid—it consists of nothing more exciting than the eternal sitting bolt upright at a table and scratching down black marks on white paper." For even though that statement is a jocose exaggeration, perhaps it implies something of the truth, that many professional writers live necessarily a quiet, absorbed, somewhat isolated life.

However that may be, the life of Samuel L. Clemens the man and Mark Twain the writer is intensely interesting, full of variety, of action, of excitement, of drama. Perhaps that is because, as he said, he "stumbled into literature," because authorship seemed to be almost a side-line, a by-product. Perhaps it is because he lived so hard, so happily, so adventurously, and at so many trades and professions: printer, reporter, publisher, lecturer, steamboat pilot, miner, world traveler. Perhaps it is because his life was so typically and successfully American, because he rose from obscurity and poverty to world-wide fame and riches, without even the assistance of formal schooling. Perhaps it is rather because back of everything he wrote, glowing through it, is a rich, romantic, appealing personality; robust yet sensitive, independent yet considerate, capable of seeing the humor and at the same time the deep tragedy of existence, free, frank, candid, generous, wise: one of the most fascinating human beings that ever lived. And perhaps it is because,

INTRODUCTION

even though he appeared to reveal himself so openly and even after we are acquainted with all the details of his life, the man himself remains a mystery and his literary art a secret.

But whatever the reasons, the life of Mark Twain is most interesting. The story presented here is the one that Mr. Albert Bigelow Paine, Mark Twain's "official" biographer, himself made from the much longer story. Mr. Paine's friendship with Mark Twain is described in this book; and a brief sketch of Mr. Paine is presented on page 355.

It is the thought of the present editor that the book will bring most pleasure and reward if its readers plunge straightway into Mark Twain's story and follow eagerly and absorbedly its course, thus obtaining a clear, vivid, bird's-eye view of the life and adventures of this lovable, romantic figure. But though the story should be read rapidly, it should be read thoughtfully: with pauses now and then for reflection and for discussion with other readers, in order to think about and exchange views about the more important and significant events, in order to take looks backward and forward.

WALTER BARNES

PREFACE

THIS is the story of a boy, born in the humblest surroundings, reared almost without schooling, and amid benighted conditions such as to-day have no existence, yet who lived to achieve a world-wide fame; to attain honorary degrees from the greatest universities of America and Europe; to be sought by statesmen and kings; to be loved and honored by all men in all lands, and mourned by them when he died. It is the story of one of the world's very great men—the story of Mark Twain.

THE BOYS'
LIFE OF MARK TWAIN

I

THE FAMILY OF JOHN CLEMENS

A LONG time ago, back in the early years of another century, a family named Clemens moved from eastern Tennessee to eastern Missouri—from a small, unheard-of place called Pall Mall, on Wolf River, to an equally small and unknown place called Florida, on a tiny river named the Salt.

That was a far journey, in those days, for railway trains in 1835 had not reached the South and West, and John Clemens and his family traveled in an old two-horse barouche, with two extra riding-horses, on one of which rode the eldest child, Orion Clemens, a boy of ten, and on the other Jennie, a slave girl.

In the carriage with the parents were three other children—Pamela and Margaret, aged eight and five, and little Benjamin, three years old. The time was spring, the period of the Old South, and, while these youngsters did not realize that they were passing through a sort of Golden Age, they must have enjoyed the weeks of leisurely journeying toward what was then the Far West—the Promised Land.

The Clemens fortunes had been poor in Tennessee. John Marshall Clemens, the father, was a lawyer, a man of education; but he was a dreamer, too, full of schemes that usually failed. Born in Virginia, he had grown up in Kentucky, and married there Jane Lampton, of Columbia, a descendant of the English Lamptons and the belle of her region. They had left Kentucky for Tennessee, drifting from one small town to another that was always smaller, and with dwindling law-practice John Clemens in time had been obliged to open a poor little store, which in the end had failed to pay. Jennie was the last of several slaves he had inherited from his Virginia ancestors. Besides Jennie, his fortune now consisted of the horses and barouche, a very limited supply of money, and a large, unsalable tract of east Tennessee land, which John Clemens dreamed would one day bring his children fortune.

Readers of the *Gilded Age* will remember the journey of the Hawkins family from the "Knobs" of Tennessee to Missouri and the important part in that story played by the Tennessee land. Mark Twain wrote those chapters, and while they are not history, but fiction, they are based upon fact, and the picture they present of family hardship and struggle is not overdrawn. The character of Colonel Sellers, who gave the Hawkinses a grand welcome to the new home, was also real. In life he was James Lampton, cousin to Mrs. Clemens, a gentle and radiant merchant of dreams, who believed himself heir to an English earldom and was always on the verge of colossal fortune. With others of the Lampton kin, he was already settled in Missouri and had written back glowing accounts; though perhaps not more glowing than those which had come from another relative, John Quarles, brother-in-law to Mrs. Clemens, a jovial, whole-hearted optimist, well-loved by all who knew him.

It was a June evening when the Clemens family, with the barouche and the two outriders, finally arrived in Florida, and the place, no doubt, seemed attractive enough then, however it may have appeared later. It was the end of a long journey; relatives gathered with fond welcome; prospects seemed bright. Already John Quarles had opened a general store in the little town. Florida, he said, was certain to become a city. Salt River would be made navigable with a series of locks and dams. He offered John Clemens a partnership in his business.

Quarles, for that time and place, was a rich man. Besides his store he had a farm and thirty slaves. His brother-in-law's funds, or lack of them, did not matter. The two had married sisters. That was capital enough for his hearty nature. So, almost on the moment of arrival in the new land, John Clemens once more found himself established in trade.

The next thing was to find a home. There were twenty-one houses in Florida, and none of them large. The one selected by John and Jane Clemens had two main rooms and a lean-to kitchen—a small place and lowly—the kind of a place that so often has seen the beginning of exalted lives. Christianity began with a babe in a manger; Shakespeare first saw the light in a cottage at Stratford; Lincoln entered the world by way of a leaky cabin in Kentucky, and into the narrow limits of the Clemens home in Florida, on a bleak autumn day—November 30, 1835—there was born one who under the name of Mark Twain would live to cheer and comfort a tired world.

The name Mark Twain had not been thought of then, and probably no one prophesied favorably for the new-comer, who was small and feeble, and not over-welcome in that crowded household. They named him Samuel, after his paternal grandfather, and added Langhorne for an old friend—a goodly burden for so frail a wayfarer. But more appropriately they called him "Little Sam," or "Sammy," which clung to him through the years of his delicate childhood.

It seems a curious childhood, as we think of it now. Missouri was a slave State—Little Sam's companions were as often black as white. All the children of that time and locality had negroes for playmates, and were cared for by them. They were fond of their black companions and would have felt lost without them. The negro children knew all the best ways of doing things—how to work charms and spells, the best way to cure warts and heal stone-bruises, and to make it rain, and to find lost money. They knew what signs meant, and dreams, and how

4

to keep off hoodoo; and all negroes, old and young, knew any number of weird tales.

John Clemens must have prospered during the early years of his Florida residence, for he added another slave to his household—Uncle Ned, a man of all work—and he built a somewhat larger house, in one room of which, the kitchen, was a big fireplace. There was a wide hearth and always plenty of wood, and here after supper the children would gather, with Jennie and Uncle Ned, and the latter would tell hair-lifting tales of "ha'nts," and lonely roads, and witch-work that would make his hearers shiver with terror and delight, and look furtively over their shoulders toward the dark window-panes and the hovering shadows on the walls. Perhaps it was not the healthiest entertainment, but it was the kind to cultivate an imagination that would one day produce *Tom Sawyer* and *Huck Finn*.

True, Little Sam was very young at this period, but even a little chap of two or three would understand most of that fireside talk, and get impressions more vivid than if the understanding were complete. He was barely four when this earliest chapter of his life came to a close.

John Clemens had not remained satisfied with Florida and his undertakings there. The town had not kept its promises. It failed to grow, and the lock-and-dam scheme that would make Salt River navigable fell through. Then one of the children, Margaret, a black-eyed, rosy little girl of nine, suddenly died. This was in August, 1839. A month or two later the saddened family abandoned their Flor-

1da home and moved in wagons, with their household furnishings, to Hannibal, a Mississippi River town, thirty miles away. There was only one girl left now, Pamela, twelve years old, but there was another boy, baby Henry, three years younger than Little Sam—four boys in all.

THE NEW HOME, AND UNCLE JOHN QUARLES'S FARM

HANNIBAL was a town with prospects and considerable trade. It was slumbrous, being a slave town, but it was not dead. John Clemens believed it a promising place for business, and opened a small general store with Orion Clemens, now fifteen, a studious, dreamy lad, for clerk.

The little city was also an attractive place of residence. Mark Twain remembered it as "the white town drowsing in the sunshine of a summer morning, . . . the great Mississippi, the magnificent Mississippi, rolling its mile-wide tide along, . . . the dense forest away on the other side."

The "white town" was built against green hills, and abutting the river were bluffs—Holliday's Hill and Lover's Leap. A distance below the town was a cave—a wonderful cave, as every reader of *Tom Sawyer* knows—while out in the river, toward the Illinois shore, was the delectable island that was one day to be the meeting-place of Tom's pirate band, and later to become the hiding-place of Huck and Nigger Jim.

The river itself was full of interest. It was the

highway to the outside world. Rafts drifted by; smartly painted steamboats panted up and down, touching to exchange traffic and travelers, a never-ceasing wonder to those simple shut-in dwellers whom the telegraph and railway had not yet reached. That Hannibal was a pleasant place of residence we may believe, and what an attractive place for a boy to grow up in!

Little Sam, however, was not yet ready to enjoy the island and the cave. He was still delicate—the least promising of the family. He was queer and fanciful, and rather silent. He walked in his sleep and was often found in the middle of the night, fretting with the cold, in some dark corner. Once he heard that a neighbor's children had the measles, and, being very anxious to catch the complaint, slipped over to the house and crept into bed with an infected playmate. Some days later, Little Sam's relatives gathered about his bed to see him die. He confessed, long after, that the scene gratified him. However, he survived, and fell into the habit of running away, usually in the direction of the river.

"You gave me more uneasiness than any child I had," his mother once said to him, in her old age.

"I suppose you were afraid I wouldn't live," he suggested.

She looked at him with the keen humor which had been her legacy to him. "No, afraid you *would*," she said. Which was only her joke, for she had the tenderest of hearts, and, like all mothers, had a weakness for the child that demanded most of her mother's care. It was chiefly on his account that she returned each year to Florida to spend the summer on John Quarles's farm.

If Uncle John Quarles's farm was just an ordinary Missouri farm, and his slaves just average negroes, they certainly never seemed so to Little Sam. There was a kind of glory about everything that belonged to Uncle John, and it was not all imagination, for some of the spirit of that jovial, kindly hearted man could hardly fail to radiate from his belongings.

The farm was a large one for that locality, and the farm-house was a big double log building—that is, two buildings with a roofed-over passage between, where in summer the lavish Southern meals were served, brought in on huge dishes by the negroes, and left for each one to help himself. Fried chicken, roast pig, turkeys, ducks, geese, venison just killed, squirrels, rabbits, partridges, pheasants, prairie-chickens, green corn, watermelon—a little boy who did not die on that bill of fare would be likely to get well on it, and to Little Sam the farm proved a life-saver.

It was, in fact, a heavenly place for a little boy. In the corner of the yard there were hickory and black-walnut trees, and just over the fence the hill sloped past barns and cribs to a brook, a rare place to wade, though there were forbidden pools. Cousin Tabitha Quarles, called "Puss," his own age, was Little Sam's playmate, and a slave girl, Mary, who, being six years older, was supposed to keep them out of mischief. There were swings in the big, shady pasture, where Mary swung her charges and ran under them until their feet touched the branches. All the woods were full of squirrels and birds and blooming flowers; all the meadows were gay with clover and butterflies, and musical with singing grasshoppers and calling larks; the fence-rows were full of wild blackberries; there were apples and peaches in the orchard, and plenty of melons ripening in the corn. Certainly it was a glorious place!

Little Sam got into trouble once with the watermelons. One of them had not ripened quite enough when he ate several slices of it. Very soon after he was seized with such terrible cramps that some of the household did not think he could live.

But his mother said: "Sammy will pull through. He was not born to die that way." Which was a true prophecy. Sammy's slender constitution withstood the strain. It was similarly tested more than once during those early years. He was regarded as a curious child. At times dreamy and silent, again wild-headed and noisy, with sudden impulses that sent him capering and swinging his arms into the wind until he would fall with shrieks and spasms of laughter and madly roll over and over in the grass. It is not remembered that any one prophesied very well for his future at such times.

The negro quarters on Uncle John's farm were especially fascinating. In one cabin lived a bedridden old woman whom the children looked upon with awe. She was said to be a thousand years old, and to have talked with Moses. She had lost her health in the desert, coming out of Egypt. She had seen Pharaoh drown, and the fright had caused the bald spot on her head. She could ward off witches and dissolve spells.

Uncle Dan'l was another favorite, a kind-hearted, gentle soul, who long after, as Nigger Jim in the *Tom Sawyer* and *Huckleberry Finn* tales, would win world-wide love and sympathy.

Through that far-off, warm, golden summer-time Little Sam romped and dreamed and grew. He would return each summer to the farm during those early years. It would become a beautiful memory. His mother generally kept him there until the late fall, when the chilly evenings made them gather around the wide, blazing fireplace. Sixty years later he wrote:

I can see the room yet with perfect clearness. I can see all its belongings, all its details; the family-room of the house, w th the trundle-bed in one corner and the spinning-wheel in another—a wheel whose rising and falling wail, heard from a distance, was the mournfulest of all sound; to me and made me homesick and low-spirited and filled my atmosphere with the wandering spirits of the dead; the vast fireplace, piled high with flaming logs from whose end; a sugary ;ap bubbled out but did not go to waste, for we scraped it off and ate it; . . . the lazy cat spread out on the rough hearthstones, the drowsy dogs braced against the jambs, blinking; my aunt in one chimney-corner, and my uncle in the other, smoking his corn-cob pipe.

It is hard not to tell more of the farm, for the boy who was one day going to write of Tom and Huck and the rest learned there so many things that Tom and Huck would need to know.

III

B UT he must have "book-learning," too, Jane
Clemens said. On his return to Hannibal that
first summer, she decided that Little Sam was ready
for school. He was five years old and regarded as a
"stirring child."

"He drives me crazy with his didoes when he's
in the house," his mother declared, "and when he's
out of it I'm expecting every minute that some one
will bring him home half dead."

Mark Twain used to say that he had had nine
narrow escapes from drowning, and it was at this
early age that he was brought home one afternoon
in a limp state, having been pulled from a deep hole
in Bear Creek by a slave girl.

When he was restored, his mother said: "I guess
there wasn't much danger. People born to be
hanged are safe in water."

Mark Twain's mother was the original of Aunt
Polly in the story of *Tom Sawyer*, an outspoken,
keen-witted, charitable woman, whom it was good
to know. She had a heart full of pity, especially for
dumb creatures. She refused to kill even flies, and

punished the cat for catching mice. She would drown young kittens when necessary, but warmed the water for the purpose. She could be strict, however, with her children, if occasion required, and recognized their faults.

Little Sam was inclined to elaborate largely on fact. A neighbor once said to her: "You don't believe anything that child says, I hope."

"Oh yes, I know his average. I discount him ninety per cent. The rest is pure gold."

She declared she was willing to pay somebody to take him off her hands for a part of each day and try to teach him "manners." A certain Mrs. E. Horr was selected for the purpose.

Mrs. Horr's school on Main Street, Hannibal, was of the old-fashioned kind. There were pupils of all ages, and everything was taught up to the third reader and long division. Pupils who cared to go beyond those studies went to a Mr. Cross, on the hill, facing what is now the public square. Mrs. Horr received twenty-five cents a week for each pupil, and the rules of conduct were read daily. After the rules came the A-B-C class, whose recitation was a hand-to-hand struggle, requiring no study-time.

The rules of conduct that first day interested Little Sam. He wondered how nearly he could come to breaking them and escape. He experimented during the forenoon, and received a warning. Another experiment would mean correction. He did not expect to be caught again; but when he least expected it he was startled by a command to go out and bring a stick for his own punishment.

This was rather dazing. It was sudden, and, then, he did not know much about choosing sticks for such a purpose. Jane Clemens had commonly used her hand. A second command was needed to start him in the right direction, and he was still dazed when he got outside. He had the forests of Missouri to select from, but choice was not easy. Everything looked too big and competent. Even the smallest switch had a wiry look. Across the way was a cooper's shop. There were shavings outside, and one had blown across just in front of him. He picked it up, and, gravely entering the room, handed it to Mrs. Horr. So far as known, it is the first example of that humor which would one day make Little Sam famous before all the world.

It was a failure in this instance. Mrs. Horr's comic side may have prompted forgiveness, but discipline must be maintained.

"Samuel Langhorne Clemens," she said (he had never heard it all strung together in that ominous way), "I am ashamed of you! Jimmy Dunlap, go and bring a switch for Sammy." And the switch that Jimmy Dunlap brought was of a kind to give Little Sam a permanent distaste for school. He told his mother at noon that he did not care for education; that he did not wish to be a great man; that his desire was to be an Indian and scalp such persons as Mrs. Horr. In her heart Jane Clemens was sorry for him, but she openly said she was glad there was somebody who could take him in hand.

Little Sam went back to school, but he never learned to like it. A school was ruled with a rod in those days, and of the smaller boys Little Sam's back was sore as often as the next. When the days of early summer came again, when from his desk he could see the sunshine lighting the soft green of Holliday's Hill, with the glint of the river and the purple distance beyond, it seemed to him that to be shut up with a Webster spelling-book and a cross teacher was more than human nature could bear. There still exists a yellow slip of paper upon which, in neat, old-fashioned penmanship is written:

Miss Pamela Clemens

Has won the love of her teacher and schoolmates by her amiable deportment and faithful application to her various studies.

E. Horr, Teacher.

Thus we learn that Little Sam's sister, eight years older than himself, attended the same school, and that she was a good pupil. If any such reward of merit was ever conferred on Little Sam, it has failed to come to light. If he won the love of his teacher and playmates, it was probably for other reasons.

Yet he must have learned somehow, for he could read, presently, and was a good speller for his age.

IV

EDUCATION OUT OF SCHOOL

ON their arrival in Hannibal, the Clemens family had moved into a part of what was then the Pavey Hotel. They could not have remained there long, for they moved twice within the next few years, and again in 1844 into a new house which Judge Clemens, as he was generally called, had built on Hill Street—a house still standing, and known to-day as the Mark Twain home.

John Clemens had met varying fortunes in Hannibal. Neither commerce nor the practice of law had paid. The office of justice of the peace, to which he was elected, returned a fair income, but his business losses finally obliged him to sell Jennie, the slave girl. Somewhat later his business failure was complete. He surrendered everything to his creditors, even to his cow and household furniture, and relied upon his law practice and justice fees. However, he seems to have kept the Tennessee land, possibly because no one thought it worth taking. There had been offers for it earlier, but none that its owner would accept. It appears to have been not even considered by his creditors, though his own faith in it never died.

EDUCATION OUT OF SCHOOL

The struggle for a time was very bitter. Orion Clemens, now seventeen, had learned the printer's trade and assisted the family with his wages. Mrs. Clemens took a few boarders. In the midst of this time of hardship little Benjamin Clemens died. He was ten years old. It was the darkest hour.

Then conditions slowly improved. There was more law practice and better justice fees. By 1844 Judge Clemens was able to build the house mentioned above—a plain, cheap house, but a shelter and a home. Sam Clemens—he was hardly "Little Sam" any more—was at this time nine years old. His boyhood had begun.

Heretofore he had been just a child—wild and mischievous, often exasperating, but still a child— a delicate little lad to be worried over, mothered, or spanked and put to bed. Now at nine he had acquired health, with a sturdy ability to look out for himself, as boys in such a community will. "Sam," as they now called him, was "grown up" at nine and wise for his years. Not that he was old in spirit or manner—he was never that, even to his death—but he had learned a great number of things, many of them of a kind not taught at school.

He had learned a good deal of natural history and botany—the habits of plants, insects, and animals. Mark Twain's books bear evidence of this early study. His plants, bugs, and animals never do the wrong things. He was learning a good deal about men, and this was often less pleasant knowledge. Once Little Sam—he was still Little Sam then— saw an old man shot down on Main Street at noon-

17

day. He saw them carry him home, lay him on
the bed, and spread on his breast an open family
Bible, which looked as heavy as an anvil. He
thought if he could only drag that great burden
away the poor old dying man would not breathe so
heavily.

He saw a young emigrant stabbed with a bowie-
knife by a drunken comrade, and two young men try
to kill their uncle, one holding him while the other
snapped repeatedly an Allen revolver, which failed
to go off. Then there was the drunken rowdy who
proposed to raid the "Welshman's" house, one sul-
try, threatening evening—he saw that, too. With
a boon companion, John Briggs, he followed at a
safe distance behind. A widow with her one daughter lived there. They stood in the shadow of the
dark porch; the man had paused at the gate to
revile them. The boys heard the mother's voice
warning the intruder that she had a loaded gun and
would kill him if he stayed where he was. He replied with a tirade, and she warned him that she
would count ten—that if he remained a second
longer she would fire. She began slowly and counted
up to five, the man laughing and jeering. At six
he grew silent, but he did not go. She counted on:
seven, eight, nine—

The boys, watching from the dark roadside, felt
their hearts stop. There was a long pause, then the
final count, followed a second later by a gush of
flame. The man dropped, his breast riddled. At
the same instant the thunder-storm that had been
gathering broke loose. The boys fled wildly, be-

lieving that Satan himself had arrived to claim the lost soul.

That was a day and locality of violent impulse and sudden action. Happenings such as these were not infrequent in a town like Hannibal. And there were events connected with slavery. Sam once saw a slave struck down and killed with a piece of slag, for a trifling offense. He saw an Abolitionist attacked by a mob that would have lynched him had not a Methodist minister defended him on a plea that he must be crazy. He did not remember in later years that he had ever seen a slave auction, but he added:

"I am suspicious that it was because the thing was a commonplace spectacle and not an uncommon or impressive one. I do vividly remember seeing a dozen black men and women, chained together, lying in a group on the pavement, waiting shipment to a Southern slave-market. They had the saddest faces I ever saw."

Readers of Mark Twain's books—especially the stories of *Huck* and *Tom*, will hardly be surprised to hear of these early happenings that formed so large a portion of the author's early education. Sam, however, did not regard them as education—not at the time. They got into his dreams. He set them down as warnings, or punishments, intended to give him a taste for a better life. He felt that it was his conscience that made such things torture him. That was his mother's idea, and he had a high respect for her opinion in such matters. Among other things, he had seen her one day defy a vicious and

fierce Corsican—a common terror in the town—who had chased his grown daughter with a heavy rope in his hand, declaring he would wear it out on her. Cautious citizens got out of the way, but Jane Clemens opened her door to the fugitive; then, instead of rushing in and closing it, spread her arms across it, barring the way. The man raved, and threatened her with the rope, but she did not flinch or show any sign of fear. She stood there and shamed and defied him until he slunk off, crestfallen and conquered. Any one as brave as his mother must have a perfect conscience, Sam thought, and would know how to take care of it. In the darkness he would say his prayers, especially when a thunderstorm was coming, and vow to begin a better life. He detested Sunday-school as much as he did dayschool, and once his brother Orion, who was moral and religious, had threatened to drag him there by the collar, but, as the thunder got louder, Sam decided that he loved Sunday-school and would go the next Sunday without being invited.

Sam's days were not all disturbed by fierce events. They were mostly filled with pleasanter things. There were picnics sometimes, and ferryboat excursions, and any day one could roam the woods, or fish, alone or in company. The hills and woods around Hannibal were never disappointing. There was the cave with its marvels. There was Bear Creek, where he had learned to swim. He had seen two playmates drown; twice, himself, he had been dragged ashore, more dead than alive; once by a slave girl, another time by a slave man—Neal

Champ, of the Pavey Hotel. But he had persevered, and with success. He could swim better than any playmate of his age.

It was the river that he cared for most. It was the pathway that led to the great world outside. He would sit by it for hours and dream. He would venture out on it in a quietly borrowed boat, when he was barely strong enough to lift an oar. He learned to know all its moods and phases.

More than anything in the world he hungered to make a trip on one of the big, smart steamers that were always passing. "You can hardly imagine what it meant," he reflected, once, "to a boy in those days, shut in as we were, to see those steamboats pass up and down, and never take a trip on them."

It was at the mature age of nine that he found he could endure this no longer. One day when the big packet came down and stopped at Hannibal, he slipped aboard and crept under one of the boats on the upper deck. Then the signal-bells rang, the steamer backed away and swung into midstream; he was really going at last. He crept from beneath the boat and sat looking out over the water and enjoying the scenery. Then it began to rain—a regular downpour. He crept back under the boat, but his legs were outside, and one of the crew saw him. He was dragged out and at the next stop set ashore. It was the town of Louisiana, where there were Lampton relatives, who took him home. Very likely the home-coming was not entirely pleasant, though a "lesson," too, in his general education.

And always, each summer, there was the farm, where his recreation was no longer mere girl plays and swings, with a colored nurse following about, but sports with his older boy cousins, who went hunting with the men, for partridges by day and for 'coons and 'possums by night. Sometimes the little boy followed the hunters all night long, and returned with them through the sparkling and fragrant morning, fresh, hungry, and triumphant, just in time for breakfast. So it is no wonder that Little Sam, at nine, was no longer Little Sam, but plain Sam Clemens, and grown up. If there were doubtful spots in his education—matters related to smoking and strong words—it is also no wonder, and experience even in these lines was worth something in a book like *Tom Sawyer*.

The boy Sam Clemens was not a particularly attractive lad. He was rather undersized, and his head seemed too large for his body. He had a mass of light sandy hair, which he plastered down to keep from curling. His eyes were keen and blue and his features rather large. Still, he had a fair, delicate complexion when it was not blackened by grime and tan; a gentle, winning manner; a smile and a slow way of speaking that made him a favorite with his companions. He did not talk much, and was thought to be rather dull—was certainly so in most of his lessons—but, for some reason, he never spoke that every playmate in hearing did not stop, whatever he was doing, to listen. Perhaps it would be a plan for a new game or lark; perhaps it was something droll; perhaps it was just a casual remark that his peculiar

drawl made amusing. His mother always referred to his slow fashion of speech as "Sammy's long talk." Her own speech was even more deliberate, though she seemed not to notice it. Sam was more like his mother than the others. His brother, Henry Clemens, three years younger, was as unlike Sam as possible. He did not have the "long talk," and was a handsome, obedient little fellow whom the mischievous Sam loved to tease. Henry was to become the Sid of *Tom Sawyer*, though he was in every way a finer character than Sid. With the death of little Benjamin, Sam and Henry had been drawn much closer together, and, in spite of Sam's pranks, loved each other dearly. For the pranks were only occasional, and Sam's love for Henry was constant. He fought *for* him oftener than *with* him.

Many of the home incidents in the *Tom Sawyer* book really happened. Sam did clod Henry for getting him into trouble about the colored thread with which he sewed his shirt when he came home from swimming; he did inveigle a lot of boys into whitewashing a fence for him; he did give painkiller to Peter, the cat. As for escaping punishment for his misdeeds, as described in the book, this was a daily matter, and his methods suited the occasions. For, of course, Tom Sawyer was Sam Clemens himself, almost entirely, as most readers of that book have imagined. However, we must have another chapter for Tom Sawyer and his doings —the real Tom and his real doings with those graceless, lovable associates, Joe Harper and Huckleberry Finn.

V

TOM SAWYER AND HIS BAND

IN beginning *The Adventures of Tom Sawyer* the author says, "Most of the adventures recorded in this book really occurred," and he tells us that Huck Finn is drawn from life; Tom Sawyer also, though not from a single individual, being a composite of three boys whom Mark Twain had known.

The three boys were himself, almost entirely, with traces of two schoolmates, John Briggs and Will Bowen. John Briggs was also the original of Joe Harper, the "Terror of the Seas." As for Huck Finn, the "Red-Handed," his original was a village waif named Tom Blankenship, who needed no change for his part in the story.

The Blankenship family picked up an uncertain livelihood, fishing and hunting, and lived at first under a tree in a bark shanty, but later moved into a large, barn-like building, back of the Clemens home on Hill Street. There were three male members of the household: Old Ben, the father, shiftless and dissolute; young Ben, the eldest son—a doubtful character, with certain good traits; and Tom— that is to say, Huck, who was just as he is described in the book—a ruin of rags, a river-rat, kind of heart, and accountable for his conduct to nobody in the world. He could come and go as he chose; he never had to work or go to school; he could do all the things, good and bad, that other boys longed to do and were forbidden. To them he was the symbol of liberty; his knowledge of fishing, trapping, signs, and of the woods and river gave value to his society, while the fact that it was forbidden made it necessary to Sam Clemens's happiness.

The Blankenships being handy to the back gate of the Hill Street house, he adopted them at sight. Their free mode of life suited him. He was likely to be there at any hour of the day, and Tom made cat-call signals at night that would bring Sam out on the shed roof at the back and down a little trellis and flight of steps to the group of boon companions, which, besides Tom, usually included John Briggs, Will Pitts, and the two younger Bowen boys. They were not malicious boys, but just mischievous, fun-loving boys—little boys of ten or twelve—rather thoughtless, being mainly bent on having a good time.

They had a wide field of action: they ranged from Holliday's Hill on the north to the cave on the south, and over the fields and through all the woods between. They explored both banks of the river, the islands, and the deep wilderness of the Illinois shore. They could run like turkeys and swim like ducks; they could handle a boat as if born in one. No orchard or melon-patch was entirely safe from them. No dog or slave patrol was so watchful that they did not sooner or later elude it. They borrowed boats with or without the owner's consent—it did not matter.

Most of their expeditions were harmless enough. They often cruised up to Turtle Island, about two miles above Hannibal, and spent the day feasting. There were quantities of turtles and their eggs there, and mussels, and plenty of fish. Fishing and swimming were their chief pastimes, with incidental raiding, for adventure. Bear Creek was their swimming-place by day, and the river-front at night-fall—a favorite spot being where the railroad bridge now ends. It was a good distance across to the island where, in the book, Tom Sawyer musters his pirate band, and where later Huck found Nigger Jim, but quite often in the evening they swam across to it, and when they had frolicked for an hour or more on the sand-bar at the head of the island, they would swim back in the dusk, breasting the strong, steady Mississippi current without exhaustion or dread. They could swim all day, those little scamps, and seemed to have no fear. Once, during his boyhood, Sam Clemens swam across to the Illinois side, then turned and swam back again without landing, a distance of at least two miles as he had to go. He was seized with a cramp on the return trip. His legs became useless and he was obliged to make the remaining distance with his arms.

The adventures of Sam Clemens and his comrades would fill several books of the size of *Tom Sawyer*. Many of them are, of course, forgotten now, but those still remembered show that Mark Twain had plenty of real material.

It was not easy to get money in those days, and the boys were often without it. Once "Huck" Blankenship had the skin of a 'coon he had captured, and offered to sell it to raise capital. At Selms's store, on Wild Cat Corner, the 'coon-skin would bring ten cents. But this was not enough. The boys thought of a plan to make it bring more. Selms's back window was open, and the place where he kept his pelts was pretty handy. Huck went around to the front door and sold the skin for ten cents to Selms, who tossed it back on the pile. Then Huck came back and, after waiting a reasonable time, crawled in the open window, got the 'coon-skin, and sold it to Selms again. He did this several times that afternoon, and the capital of the band grew. But at last John Pierce, Selms's clerk, said:

"Look here, Mr. Selms, there's something wrong about this. That boy has been selling us 'coon-skins all the afternoon."

Selms went back to his pile of pelts. There were several sheep-skins and some cow-hides, but only one 'coon-skin—the one he had that moment bought.

Selms himself, in after years, used to tell this story as a great joke.

One of the boys' occasional pastimes was to climb Holliday's Hill and roll down big stones, to frighten the people who were driving by. Holliday's Hill above the road was steep; a stone once started would go plunging downward and bound across the road with the deadly momentum of a shell. The boys would get a stone poised, then wait until they saw a team approaching, and, calculating the distance, would give the boulder a start. Dropping behind the bushes, they would watch the sudden effect upon the party below as the great missile shot across the road a few yards before them. This was huge sport, but they carried it too far. For at last they planned a grand climax that would surpass anything before attempted in the stone-rolling line.

A monstrous boulder was lying up there in the right position to go down-hill, once started. It would be a glorious thing to see that great stone go smashing down a hundred yards or so in front of some peaceful-minded countryman jogging along the road. Quarrymen had been getting out rock not far away and had left their picks and shovels handy. The boys borrowed the tools and went to work to undermine the big stone. They worked at it several hours. If their parents had asked them to work like that, they would have thought they were being killed.

Finally, while they were still digging, the big stone suddenly got loose and started down. They were not ready for it at all. Nobody was coming but an old colored man in a cart; their splendid stone was going to be wasted.

One could hardly call it wasted, however; they had planned for a thrilling result, and there was certainly thrill enough while it lasted. In the first place the stone nearly caught Will Bowen when it started. John Briggs had that moment quit digging and handed Will the pick. Will was about to take his turn when Sam Clemens leaped aside with a yell:

"Look out, boys; she's coming!"

She came. The huge boulder kept to the ground at first, then, gathering momentum, it went bounding into the air. About half-way down the hill it struck a sapling and cut it clean off. This turned its course a little, and the negro in the cart, hearing the noise and seeing the great mass come crashing in his direction, made a wild effort to whip up his mule.

The boys watched their bomb with growing interest. It was headed straight for the negro, also for a cooper-shop across the road. It made longer leaps with every bound, and, wherever it struck, fragments and dust would fly. The shop happened to be empty, but the rest of the catastrophe would call for close investigation. They wanted to fly, but they could not move until they saw the rock land. It was making mighty leaps now, and the terrified negro had managed to get exactly in its path. The boys stood holding their breath, their mouths open.

Then, suddenly, they could hardly believe their eyes; a little way above the road the boulder struck a projection, made one mighty leap into the air, sailed clear over the negro and his mule, and landed in the soft dirt beyond the road, only a fragment striking the shop, damaging, but not wrecking it. Half buried in the ground, the great stone lay there for nearly forty years; then it was broken up. It was the last rock the boys ever rolled down. Nearly sixty years later John Briggs and Mark Twain walked across Holliday's Hill and looked down toward the river road.

Mark Twain said: "It was a mighty good thing, John, that stone acted the way it did. We might have had to pay a fancy price for that old darky— I can see him yet." [1]

It can be no harm, now, to confess that the boy Sam Clemens—a pretty small boy, a good deal less than twelve at the time, and by no means large for his years—was the leader of this unhallowed band. In any case, truth requires this admission. If the band had a leader, it was Sam, just as it was Tom Sawyer in the book. They were always ready to listen to him—they would even stop fishing to do that—and to follow his plans. They looked to him for ideas and directions, and he gloried in being a leader and showing off, just as Tom did in the book. It seems almost a pity that in those far-off barefoot days he could not have looked down the years and caught a glimpse of his splendid destiny.

But of literary fame he could never have dreamed. The chief ambition—the "permanent ambition"— of every Hannibal boy was to be a pilot. The pilot in his splendid glass perch with his supreme power and princely salary was to them the noblest of all human creatures. An elder Bowen boy was already a pilot, and when he came home, as he did now and then, his person seemed almost too sacred to touch.

[1] John Briggs died in 1907; earlier in the same year the writer of this memoir spent an afternoon with him and obtained from him most of the material for this chapter.

Next to being a pilot, Sam thought he would like to be a pirate or a bandit or a trapper-scout— something gorgeous and awe-inspiring, where his word, his nod, would still be law. The river kept his river ambition always fresh, and with the cave and the forest round about helped him to imagine those other things.

The cave was the joy of his heart. It was a real cave, not merely a hole, but a marvel of deep passages and vaulted chambers that led back into the bluffs and far down into the earth, even below the river, some said. Sam Clemens never tired of the cave. He was willing any time to quit fishing or swimming or melon-hunting for the three-mile walk, or pull, that brought them to its mystic door. With its long corridors, its royal chambers hung with stalactites, its remote hiding-places, it was exactly suitable, Sam thought, to be the lair of an outlaw, and in it he imagined and carried out adventures which his faithful followers may not always have understood, though enjoying them none the less for that reason.

In *Tom Sawyer*, Indian Joe dies in the cave. He did not die there in real life, but was lost there once and was very weak when they found him. He was not as bad as painted in the book, though he was dissolute and accounted dangerous; and when one night he died in reality, there came a thunder-storm so terrific that Sam Clemens at home, in bed, was certain that Satan had come in person for the half-breed's soul. He covered his head and said his prayers with fearful anxiety lest the evil one might decide to save another trip by taking him along then.

The treasure-digging adventure in the book had this foundation in fact: It was said that two French trappers had once buried a chest of gold about two miles above Hannibal, and that it was still there. Tom Blankenship (Huck) one morning said he had dreamed just where the treasure was, and that if the boys—Sam Clemens and John Briggs—would go with him and help dig, he would divide. The boys had great faith in dreams, especially in Huck's dreams. They followed him to a place with some shovels and picks, and he showed them just where to dig. Then he sat down under the shade of a pawpaw-bush and gave orders.

They dug nearly all day. Huck didn't dig any himself, because he had done the dreaming, which was his share. They didn't find the treasure that day, and next morning they took two long iron rods to push and drive into the ground until they should strike something. They struck a number of things, but when they dug down it was never the money they found. That night the boys said they wouldn't dig any more.

But Huck had another dream. He dreamed the gold was exactly under the little pawpaw-tree. This sounded so circumstantial that they went back and dug another day. It was hot weather, too—August —and that night they were nearly dead. Even Huck gave it up then. He said there was something wrong about the way they dug.

This differs a good deal from the treasure incident

in the book, but it shows us what respect the boys had for the gifts of the ragamuffin original of Huck Finn. Tom Blankenship's brother Ben was also used, and very importantly, in the creation of our beloved Huck. Ben was considerably older, but certainly no more reputable, than Tom. He tormented the smaller boys, and they had little love for him. Yet somewhere in Ben Blankenship's nature there was a fine, generous strain of humanity that provided Mark Twain with that immortal episode— the sheltering of Nigger Jim. This is the real story:

A slave ran off from Monroe County, Missouri, and got across the river into Illinois. Ben used to fish and hunt over there in the swamps, and one day found him. It was considered a most worthy act in those days to return a runaway slave; in fact, it was a crime not to do it. Besides, there was for this one a reward of fifty dollars—a fortune to ragged, outcast Ben Blankenship. That money, and the honor he could acquire, must have been tempting to the waif, but it did not outweigh his human sympathy. Instead of giving him up and claiming the reward, Ben kept the runaway over there in the marshes all summer. The negro fished, and Ben carried him scraps of other food. Then, by and by, the facts leaked out. Some wood-choppers went on a hunt for the fugitive and chased him to what was called Bird Slough. There, trying to cross a drift, he was drowned.

Huck's struggle in the book is between conscience and the law, on one side, and deep human sympathy on the other. Ben Blankenship's struggle, supposing there was one, would be between sympathy and the offered reward. Neither conscience nor law would trouble him. It was his native humanity that made him shelter the runaway, and it must have been strong and genuine to make him resist the lure of the fifty-dollar prize.

There was another chapter to this incident. A few days after the drowning of the runaway, Sam Clemens and his band made their way to the place and were pushing the drift about, when, all at once, the negro shot up out of the water, straight and terrible, a full half-length in the air. He had gone down foremost and had been caught in the drift. The boys did not stop to investigate, but flew in terror to report their tale.

Those early days seem to have been full of gruesome things. In *The Innocents Abroad*, the author tells how he once spent a night in his father's office and discovered there a murdered man. This was a true incident. The man had been stabbed that afternoon and carried into the house to die. Sam and John Briggs had been playing truant all day and knew nothing of the matter. Sam thought the office safer than his home, where his mother was probably sitting up for him. He climbed in by a window and lay down on the lounge, but did not sleep. Presently he noticed what appeared to be an unusual shape on the floor. He tried to turn his face to the wall and forget it, but that would not do. In agony he watched the thing until at last a square of moonlight gradually revealed a sight that he never forgot. In the book he says:

I went away from there. I do not say that I went in any sort of hurry, but I simply went—that is sufficient. I went out of the window, and I carried the sash along with me. I did not need the sash, but it was handier to take it than to leave it, and so I took it. I was not scared, but I was considerable agitated.

Sam was not yet twelve, for his father was no longer living when the boy had reached that age. And how many things had crowded themselves into his few brief years! We must be content here with only a few of them. Our chapter is already too long.

Ministers and deacons did not prophesy well for Sam Clemens and his mad companions. They spoke feelingly of state prison and the gallows. But the boys were a disappointing lot. Will Bowen became a fine river-pilot. Will Pitts was in due time a leading merchant and bank president. John Briggs grew into a well-to-do and highly respected farmer. Huck Finn—which is to say, Tom Blankenship— died an honored citizen and justice of the peace in a Western town. As for Sam Clemens, we shall see what he became as the chapters pass.

VI

CLOSING SCHOOL-DAYS

SAM was at Mr. Cross's school on the Square in due time, and among the pupils were companions that appealed to his gentler side. There were the RoBards boys—George, the best Latin scholar, and John, who always won the good-conduct medal, and would one day make all the other boys envious by riding away with his father to California, his curls of gold blowing in the wind.

There was Buck Brown, a rival speller, and John Garth, who would marry little Helen Kercheval, and Jimmy MacDaniel, whom it was well to know because his father kept a pastry-shop and he used to bring cakes and candy to school.

There were also a number of girls. Bettie Ormsley, Artemisia Briggs, and Jennie Brady were among the girls he remembered in later years, and Mary Miller, who was nearly double his age and broke his heart by getting married one day, a thing he had not expected at all.

Yet through it all he appears, like Tom Sawyer, to have had one faithful sweetheart. In the book it is Becky Thatcher—in real life she was Laura

Hawkins. The Clemens and Hawkins families lived opposite, and the children were early acquainted. The "Black Avenger of the Spanish Main" was very gentle when he was playing at house-building with little Laura, and once, when he dropped a brick on her finger, he cried the louder and longer of the two.

For he was a tender-hearted boy. He would never abuse an animal, except when his tendency to mischief ran away with him, as in the "pain-killer" incident. He had a real passion for cats. Each summer he carried his cat to the farm in a basket, and it always had a place by him at the table. He loved flowers—not as a boy botanist or gardener, but as a companion who understood their thoughts. He pitied dead leaves and dry weeds because their lives were ended and they would never know summer again or grow glad with another spring. Even in that early time he had that deeper sympathy which one day would offer comfort to humanity and make every man his friend.

But we are drifting away from Sam Clemens's school-days. They will not trouble us much longer now. More than anything in the world Sam detested school, and he made any excuse to get out of going. It is hard to say just why, unless it was the restraint and the long hours of confinement.

The Square in Hannibal, where stood the school of Mr. Cross, was a grove in those days, with plum-trees and hazel-bushes and grape-vines. When spring came, the children gathered flowers at recess, climbed trees, and swung in the vines. It was a happy place enough, only—it was school. To Sam

Clemens, the spelling-bee every Friday afternoon was the one thing that made it worth while. Sam was a leader at spelling—it was one of his gifts—he could earn compliments even from Mr. Cross, whose name, it would seem, was regarded as descriptive. Once in a moment of inspiration Sam wrote on his slate:

> Cross by name and Cross by nature,
> Cross jumped over an Irish potato.

John Briggs thought this a great effort, and urged the author to write it on the blackboard at noon. Sam hesitated.

"Oh, pshaw!" said John, "*I* wouldn't be afraid to do it."

"I *dare* you to do it," said Sam.

This was enough. While Mr. Cross was at dinner John wrote in a large hand the fine couplet. The teacher returned and called the school to order. He looked at the blackboard, then, searchingly, at John Briggs. The handwriting was familiar.

"Did you do that?" he asked, ominously.

It was a time for truth.

"Yes, sir," said John.

"Come here!" And John came and paid handsomely for his publishing venture. Sam Clemens expected that the author would be called for next; but perhaps Mr. Cross had exhausted himself on John. Sam did not often escape. His back kept fairly warm from one "flailing" to the next.

Yet he usually wore one of the two medals offered in that school—the medal for spelling. Once he lost

it by leaving the first "r" out of February. Laura
Hawkins was on the floor against him, and he was
a gallant boy. If it had only been Buck Brown he
would have spelled that and all the other months
backward, to show off. There were moments of
triumph that almost made school worth while; the
rest of the time it was prison and servitude.

But then one day came freedom. Judge Clemens,
who, in spite of misfortune, had never lost faith in
humanity, indorsed a large note for a neighbor, and
was obliged to pay it. Once more all his property
was taken away. Only a few scanty furnishings
were rescued from the wreck. A St. Louis cousin
saved the home, but the Clemens family could not
afford to live in it. They moved across the street
and joined housekeeping with another family.

Judge Clemens had one hope left. He was a candidate for the clerkship of the surrogate court, a
good office, and believed his election sure. His
business misfortunes had aroused wide sympathy.
He took no chances, however, and made a house-to-
house canvas of the district, regardless of the
weather, probably undermining his health. He believed he would be elected by a large majority, and
rejoiced that his worries would soon be at an end.
They were, indeed, nearly over. At the end of February he rode to Palmyra, the county seat. He returned through a drenching storm and reached home
nearly frozen. Pneumonia set in, and a few days
later he was dying. His one comfort now was the
Tennessee land. He said it would make them all
rich and happy. Once he whispered:

"Cling to the land; cling to the land and wait. Let nothing beguile it away from you."

He was a man who had rarely displayed affection for his children. But presently he beckoned to Pamela, now a lovely girl of nineteen, and, putting his arm around her neck, kissed her for the first time in years.

"Let me die," he said.

He did not speak again. A little more, and his worries had indeed ended. The hard struggle of an upright, impractical man had come to a close. This was in March, 1847. John Clemens had lived less than forty-nine years.

The children were dazed. They had loved their father and honored his nobility of purpose. The boy Sam was overcome with remorse. He recalled his wildness and disobedience—a thousand things trifling enough at the time, but heartbreaking now. Boy and man, Samuel Clemens was never spared by remorse. Leading him into the room where his father lay, his mother said some comforting words and asked him to make her a promise.

He flung himself into her arms, sobbing: "I will promise anything, if you won't make me go to school! Anything!"

After a moment his mother said: "No, Sammy, you need not go to school any more. Only promise me to be a better boy. Promise not to break my heart!"

He gave his promise to be faithful and industrious and upright, like his father. Such a promise was a serious matter, and Sam Clemens, underneath all, was a serious lad. He would not be twelve until

November, but his mother felt that he would keep his word.

Orion Clemens returned to St. Louis, where he was receiving a salary of ten dollars a week—high wages for those days—out of which he could send three dollars weekly to the family. Pamela, who played the guitar and piano very well, gave music lessons, and so helped the family fund. Pamela Clemens, the original of Cousin Mary, in *Tom Sawyer*, was a sweet and noble girl. Henry was too young to work, but Sam, about a year later, was apprenticed to a printer named Ament, who had moved to Hannibal and bought a weekly paper, *The Courier*. Sam agreed with his mother that the printing trade offered a chance for further education without attending school, and then, some day, there might be wages.

VII

THE APPRENTICE

THE terms of Samuel Clemens's apprenticeship were the usual thing for that day: board and clothes—"more board than clothes, and not much of either," Mark Twain used to say.

"I was supposed to get two suits of clothes a year, but I didn't get them. I got one suit and took the rest out in Ament's old garments, which didn't fit me in any noticeable way. I was only about half as big as he was, and when I had on one of his shirts I felt as if I had on a circus-tent. I had to turn the trousers up to my ears to make them short enough."

Another apprentice, a huge creature, named Wales McCormick, was so large that Ament's clothes were much too small for him. The two apprentices, fitted out with their employer's cast-off garments, were amusing enough, no doubt. Sam and Wales ate in the kitchen at first, but later at the family table with Mr. and Mrs. Ament and Pet McMurry, a journeyman printer. McMurry was a happy soul, as one could almost guess from his name. He had traveled far and learned much. What the two apprentices did not already know, Pet McMurry could teach them. Sam Clemens had promised to be a good boy, and he was so, by the standards of boyhood. He was industrious, regular at his work, quick to learn, kind, and truthful. Angels could hardly be more than that in a printing-office. But when food was scarce, even an angel—a young printer-angel—could hardly resist slipping down the cellar stairs at night, for raw potatoes, onions, and apples, which they cooked in the office, where the boys slept on a pallet on the floor. Wales had a wonderful way of cooking a potato which his fellow-apprentice never forgot.

How one wishes for a photograph of Sam Clemens at that period! But in those days there were only daguerreotypes, and they were expensive things. There is a letter, though, written long afterward, by Pet McMurry to Mark Twain, which contains this paragraph:

If your memory extends so far back, you will recall a little sandy-haired boy of nearly a quarter of a century ago, in the printing-office at Hannibal, over the Brittingham drug-store, mounted upon a little box at the case, who used to love to sing so well the expression of the poor drunken man who was supposed to have fallen by the wayside, "If ever I get up again, I'll stay up—if I kin."

And with this portrait we must be content—we cannot doubt its truth.

Sam was soon office favorite and in time became chief stand-by. When he had been at work a year, he could set type accurately, run the job press to the tune of "Annie Laurie," and he had charge of the circulation. That is to say, he carried the papers—a mission of real importance, for a long, sagging span of telegraph-wire had reached across the river to Hannibal, and Mexican-war news delivered hot from the front gave the messenger a fine prestige.

He even did editing, of a kind. That is to say, when Ament was not in the office and copy was needed, Sam hunted him up, explained the situation, and saw that the necessary matter was produced. He was not ambitious to write—not then. He wanted to be a journeyman printer, like Pet, and travel and see the world. Sometimes he thought he would like to be a clown, or "end man" in a minstrel troupe. Once for a week he served as subject for a traveling hypnotist—and was dazzled by his success.

But he stuck to printing, and rapidly became a neat, capable workman. Ament gave him a daily task, after which he was free. By three in the afternoon he was likely to finish his stint. Then he was off for the river or the cave, joining his old comrades. Or perhaps he would go with Laura Hawkins to gather wild columbine on the high cliff above the river, known as Lover's Leap. When winter came these two sometimes went to Bear Creek, skating; or together they attended parties, where the old-fashioned games "Ring-around-Rosy" and "Dusty Miller" were the chief amusements.

In *The Gilded Age*, Laura Hawkins at twelve is pictured "with her dainty hands propped into the ribbon-bordered pockets of her apron . . . a vision to warm the coldest heart and bless and cheer the saddest." That was the real Laura, though her story in that book in no way resembles the reality.

It was just at this time that an incident occurred which may be looked back upon now as a turning-point in Samuel Clemens's life. Coming home from the office one afternoon, he noticed a square of paper being swept along by the wind. He saw that it was printed—was interested professionally in seeing what it was like. He chased the flying scrap and overtook it. It was a leaf from some old history of Joan of Arc, and pictured the hard lot of the "maid" in the tower at Rouen, reviled and mistreated by her ruffian captors. There were some paragraphs of description, but the rest was pitiful dialogue.

Sam had never heard of Joan before—he knew nothing of history. He was no reader. Orion was fond of books, and Pamela; even little Henry had read more than Sam. But now, as he read, there awoke in him a deep feeling of pity and indignation, and with it a longing to know more of the tragic story. It was an interest that would last his life through, and in the course of time find expression in one of the rarest books ever written.

The first result was that Sam began to read. He hunted up everything he could find on the subject of Joan, and from that went into French history in general—indeed, into history of every kind. Samuel Clemens had suddenly become a reader—almost a student. He even began the study of languages, German and Latin, but was not able to go on for lack of time and teachers.

He became a hater of tyranny, a champion of the weak. Watching a game of marbles or tops, he would remark to some offender, in his slow. drawling way, "You mustn't cheat that boy."

And the cheating stopped, or trouble followed.

VIII

A HANNIBAL paper, the *Journal*, was for sale
under a mortgage of five hundred dollars, and
Orion Clemens, returning from St. Louis, borrowed
the money and bought it. Sam's two years' apprenticeship with Ament had been completed, and Orion
felt that together they could carry on the paper and
win success. Henry Clemens, now eleven, was also
taken out of school to learn type-setting.

Orion was a better printer than proprietor. Like
so many of his family, he was a visionary, gentle and
credulous, ready to follow any new idea. Much
advice was offered him, and he tried to follow it all.

He began with great hopes and energy. He worked
like a slave and did not spare the others. The
paper was their hope of success. Sam, especially,
was driven. There were no more free afternoons.
In some chapters written by Orion Clemens in later
life, he said:

I was tyrannical and unjust to Sam. He was swift
and clean as a good journeyman. I gave him "takes,"
and, if he got through well, I begrudged him the time and
made him work more.

47

Orion did not mean to be unjust. The struggle against opposition and debt was bitter. He could not be considerate.

The paper for a time seemed on the road to success, but Orion worked too hard and tried too many schemes. His enthusiasm waned and most of his schemes turned out poorly. By the end of the year the *Journal* was on the down grade.

In time when the need of money became great, Orion made a trip to Tennessee to try to raise something on the land which they still held there. He left Sam in charge of the paper, and, though its proprietor returned empty-handed, his journey was worth while, for it was during his absence that Samuel Clemens began the career that would one day make him Mark Twain.

Sam had concluded to edit the paper in a way that would liven up the circulation. He had never written anything for print, but he believed he knew what the subscribers wanted. The editor of a rival paper had been crossed in love, and was said to have tried to drown himself. Sam wrote an article telling all the history of the affair, giving names and details. Then on the back of two big wooden letters, used for bill-printing, he engraved illustrations of the victim wading out into the river, testing the depth of the water with a stick.

The paper came out, and the demand for it kept the Washington hand-press busy. The injured editor sent word that he was coming over to thrash the whole *Journal* staff, but he left town, instead, for the laugh was too general.

ORION'S PAPER

Sam also wrote a poem which startled orthodox readers. Then Orion returned and reduced him to the ranks. In later years Orion saw his mistake.

"I could have distanced all competitors, even then," he wrote, "if I had recognized Sam's ability and let him go ahead, merely keeping him from offending worthy persons."

Sam was not discouraged. He liked the taste of print. He sent two anecdotes to the Philadelphia *Saturday Evening Post*. Both were accepted—without payment, of course, in those days—and when they appeared he walked on air. This was in 1851. Nearly sixty years later he said:

"Seeing them in print was a joy which rather exceeded anything in that line I have ever experienced since."

However, he wrote nothing further for the *Post*. Orion printed two of his sketches in the *Journal*, which was the extent of his efforts at this time. None of this early work has been preserved. Files of the *Post* exist, but the sketches were unsigned and could hardly be identified.

The Hannibal paper dragged along from year to year. Orion could pay nothing on the mortgage—financial matters becoming always worse. He could barely supply the plainest food and clothing for the family. Sam and Henry got no wages, of course. Then real disaster came. A cow got into the office one night, upset a type-case, and ate up two composition rollers. Somewhat later a fire broke out and did considerable damage. There was partial insurance, with which Orion replaced a few necessary articles; then, to save rent, he moved the office into the front room of the home on Hill Street, where they were living again at this time.

Samuel Clemens, however, now in his eighteenth year, felt that he was no longer needed in Hannibal. He was a capable workman, with little to do and no reward. Orion, made irritable by his misfortunes, was not always kind. Pamela, who, meantime, had married well, was settled in St. Louis. Sam told his mother that he would visit Pamela and look about the city. There would be work in St. Louis at good wages.

He was going farther than St. Louis, but he dared not tell her. Jane Clemens, consenting, sighed as she put together his scanty belongings. Sam was going away. He had been a good boy of late years, but her faith in his resisting powers was not strong. Presently she held up a little Testament.

"I want you to take hold of the other end of this, Sam," she said, "and make me a promise."

The slim, wiry woman of forty-nine, gray-eyed, tender, and resolute, faced the fair-cheeked youth of seventeen, his eyes as piercing and unwavering as her own. How much alike they were!

"I want you," Jane Clemens said, "to repeat after me, Sam, these words: I do solemnly swear that I will not throw a card or drink a drop of liquor while I am gone."

He repeated the vow after her, and she kissed him.

"*Remember* that, Sam, and write to us," she said.

ORION'S PAPER

"And so," writes Orion, "he went wandering in search of that comfort and advancement, and those rewards of industry, which he had failed to find where I was—gloomy, taciturn, and selfish. I not only missed his labor; we all missed his abounding activity and merriment."

IX

THE OPEN ROAD

SAMUEL CLEMENS went to visit his sister Pamela in St. Louis and was presently at work, setting type on the *Evening News*. He had no intention, however, of staying there. His purpose was to earn money enough to take him to New York City. The railroad had by this time reached St. Louis, and he meant to have the grand experience of a long journey "on the cars." Also, there was a Crystal Palace in New York, where a world's exposition was going on.

Trains were slow in 1853, and it required several days and nights to go from St. Louis to New York City, but to Sam Clemens it was a wonderful journey. All day he sat looking out of the window, eating when he chose from the food he carried, curling up in his seat at night to sleep. He arrived at last with a few dollars in his pocket and a ten-dollar bill sewed into the lining of his coat.

New York was rather larger than he expected. All of the lower end of Manhattan Island was covered by it. The Crystal Palace—some distance out—stood at Forty-second Street and Sixth Avenue

·—the present site of Bryant Park. All the world's newest wonders were to be seen there—a dazzling exhibition. A fragment of the letter which Sam Clemens wrote to his sister Pamela—the earliest piece of Mark Twain's writing that has been preserved—expresses his appreciation of the big fair:

From the gallery (second floor) you have a glorious sight—the flags of the different countries represented, the lofty dome, glittering jewelry, gaudy tapestry, etc., with the busy crowd passing to and fro—'tis a perfect fairy palace—beautiful beyond description.

The machinery department is on the main floor, but I cannot enumerate any of it on account of the lateness of the hour (past one o'clock). It would take more than a week to examine everything on exhibition, and I was only in a little over two hours to-night. I only glanced at about one-third of the articles; and, having a poor memory, I have enumerated scarcely any of even the principal objects. The visitors to the Palace average 6,000 daily —double the population of Hannibal. The price of admission being fifty cents, they take in about $3,000.

The Latting Observatory (height about 280 feet) is near the Palace. From it you can obtain a grand view of the city and the country around. The Croton Aqueduct, to supply the city with water, is the greatest wonder yet. Immense pipes are laid across the bed of the Harlem River, and pass through the country to Westchester County, where a whole river is turned from its course and brought to New York. From the reservoir in the city to Westchester County reservoir the distance is thirty-eight miles, and, if necessary, they could easily supply every family in New York with one hundred barrels of water a day!

I am very sorry to learn that Henry has been sick. He

5

ought to go to the country and take exercise, for he is not half so healthy as Ma thinks he is. If he had my walking to do, he would be another boy entirely. Four times every day I walk a little over a mile; and working hard all day and walking four miles is exercise. I am used to it now, though, and it is no trouble. Where is it Orion's going to? Tell Ma my promises are faithfully kept; and if I have my health I will take her to Ky. in the spring. I shall save money for this.

(It has just struck 2 A.M., and I always get up at six and am at work at 7.) You ask where I spend my evenings. Where would you suppose, with a free printers' library containing more than 4,000 volumes within a quarter of a mile of me, and nobody at home to talk to? I shall write to Ella soon. Write soon.

Truly your Brother

SAMY.

P. S.—I have written this by a light so dim that you nor Ma could not read by it.

We get a fair idea of Samuel Clemens at seventeen from this letter. For one thing, he could write good, clear English, full of interesting facts. He is enthusiastic, but not lavish of words. He impresses us with his statement that the visitors to the Palace each day are in number double the population of Hannibal; a whole river is turned from its course to supply New York City with water; the water comes thirty-eight miles, and each family could use a hundred barrels a day! The letter reveals his personal side—his kindly interest in those left behind, his anxiety for Henry, his assurance that the promise to his mother was being kept, his memory of her longing to visit her old home. And the boy who

THE OPEN ROAD

hated school has become a reader—he is reveling in a printers' library of thousands of volumes. We feel, somehow, that Samuel Clemens has suddenly become quite a serious-minded person, that he has left Tom Sawyer and Joe Harper and Huck Finn somewhere in a beautiful country a long way behind.

Where would you suppose, with a free printers' library containing more than 4,000 volumes within a quarter of a mile of me, and nobody at home to talk to? I shall write to Ella soon. Write soon.

Truly your Brother

Sam

P.S. I have written this by a light so dim that you nor Ma could not read by it.

EARLIEST SPECIMEN OF MARK TWAIN'S HANDWRITING

He found work with the firm of John A. Gray & Green, general printers, in Cliff Street. His pay was four dollars a week, in wild-cat money—that is, money issued by private banks—rather poor money, being generally at a discount and sometimes worthless. But if wages were low, living was cheap in those days, and Sam Clemens, lodging in a mechanics' boarding-house in Duane Street, sometimes had fifty cents left on Saturday night when his board and washing were paid.

Luckily, he had not set out to seek his fortune, but only to see something of the world. He lingered in New York through the summer of 1853, never

55

expecting to remain long. His letters of that period were few. In October he said, in a letter to Pamela, that he did not write to the family because he did not know their whereabouts, Orion having sold the paper and left Hannibal.

"I have been fooling myself with the idea that I was going to leave New York every day for the last two weeks," he adds, which sounds like the Mark Twain of fifty years later. Farther along, he tells of going to see Edwin Forrest, then playing at the Broadway Theater:

The play was the "Gladiator." I did not like parts of it much, but other portions were really splendid. In the latter part of the last act . . . the man's whole soul seems absorbed in the part he is playing; and it is really startling to see him. I am sorry I did not see him play "Damon and Pythias," the former character being the greatest. He appears in Philadelphia on Monday night.

A little farther along he says:

If my letters do not come often, you need not bother yourself about me; for if you have a brother nearly eighteen years old who is not able to take care of himself a few miles from home, such a brother is not worth one's thoughts.

Sam Clemens may have followed Forrest to Philadelphia. At any rate, he was there presently, "subbing" in the composing-rooms of the *Inquirer*, setting ten thousand ems a day, and receiving pay accordingly. When there was no vacancy for him to fill, he put in the time visiting the Philadelphia libraries, art galleries, and historic landmarks. After all, his chief business was sight-seeing. Work was only a means to this end. Chilly evenings, when he returned to his boarding-house, his room-mate, an Englishman named Sumner, grilled a herring over their small open fire, and this was a great feast. He tried writing—obituary poetry, for the Philadelphia *Ledger*—but it was not accepted.

"My efforts were not received with approval" was his comment long after.

In the *Inquirer* office there was a printer named Frog, and sometimes, when he went out, the office "devils" would hang over his case a line with a hook on it baited with a piece of red flannel. They never got tired of this joke, and Frog never failed to get fighting mad when he saw that dangling string with the bit of red flannel at the end. No doubt Sam Clemens had his share in this mischief.

Sam found that he liked Philadelphia. He could save a little money and send something to his mother —small amounts, but welcome. Once he inclosed a gold dollar, "to serve as a specimen of the kind of stuff we are paid with in Philadelphia." Better than doubtful "wild-cat," certainly. Of his work he writes:

One man has engaged me to work for him every Sunday till the first of next April, when I shall return home to take Ma to Ky. . . . If I want to, I can get subbing every night of the week. I go to work at seven in the evening and work till three the next morning. . . . The type is mostly agate and minion, with some bourgeois, and when one gets a good agate "take," he is sure to make money. I made $2.50 last Sunday.

There is a long description of a trip on the Fair-mount stage in this letter, well-written and interesting, but too long to have place here. In the same letter he speaks of the graves of Benjamin Franklin and his wife, which he had looked at through the iron railing of the locked inclosure. Probably it did not occur to him that there might be points of similarity between Franklin's career and his own. Yet in time these would be rather striking: each learned the printer's trade; each worked in his brother's office and wrote for the paper; each left quietly and went to New York, and from New York to Philadelphia, as a journeyman printer; each in due season became a world figure, many-sided, human, and of incredible popularity.

Orion Clemens, meantime, had bought a paper in Muscatine, Iowa, and located the family there. Evidently by this time he had realized the value of his brother as a contributor, for Sam, in a letter to Orion, says, "I will try to write for the paper occasionally, but I fear my letters will be very uninteresting, for this incessant night work dulls one's ideas amazingly."

Meantime, he had passed his eighteenth birthday, winter was coming on, he had been away from home half a year, and the first attack of homesickness was due. "One only has to leave home to learn how to write interesting letters to an absent friend," he wrote; and again, "I don't like our present prospect for cold weather at all."

He declared he only wanted to get back to avoid night work, which was injuring his eyes, but we may guess there was a stronger reason, which perhaps he did not entirely realize. The novelty of wandering had worn off, and he yearned for familiar faces, the comfort of those he loved.

But he did not go. He made a trip to Washington in January—a sight-seeing trip—returning to Philadelphia, where he worked for the *Ledger* and *North American*. Eventually he went back to New York, and from there took ticket to St. Louis. This was in the late summer of 1854; he had been fifteen months away from his people when he stepped aboard the train to return.

Sam was worn out when he reached St. Louis; but the Keokuk packet was leaving, and he stopped only long enough to see Pamela, then went aboard and, flinging himself into his berth, did not waken until the boat reached Muscatine, Iowa, thirty-six hours later.

It was very early when he arrived, too early to rouse the family. He sat down in the office of a little hotel to wait for morning, and picked up a small book that lay on the writing-table. It contained pictures of the English rulers with the brief facts of their reigns. Sam Clemens entertained himself learning these data by heart. He had a fine memory for such things, and in an hour or two had those details so perfectly committed that he never forgot one of them as long as he lived. The knowledge acquired in this stray fashion he found invaluable in later life. It was his groundwork for all English history.

X

A WIND OF CHANCE

ORION could not persuade his brother to remain in Muscatine. Sam returned to his old place on the *Evening News*, in St. Louis, where he remained until the following year, rooming with a youth named Burrough, a journeyman chair-maker with literary taste, a reader of the English classics, a companionable lad, and for Samuel Clemens a good influence.

By spring, Orion Clemens had married and had sold out in Muscatine. He was now located in Keokuk, Iowa. When presently Brother Sam came visiting to Keokuk, Orion offered him five dollars a week and his board to remain. He accepted. Henry Clemens, now seventeen, was also in Orion's employ, and a lad named Dick Hingham. Henry and Sam slept in the office; Dick and a young fellow named Brownell, who roomed above, came in for social evenings.

They were pretty lively evenings. A music-teacher on the floor below did not care for them—they disturbed his class. He was furious, in fact, and assailed the boys roughly at first, with no result but to make matters worse. Then he tried gentleness, and succeeded. The boys stopped their capers and joined his class. Sam, especially, became a distinguished member of that body. He was never a great musician, but with his good nature, his humor, his slow, quaint speech and originality, he had no rival in popularity. He was twenty now, and much with young ladies, yet he was always a beau rather than a suitor, a good comrade to all, full of pranks and pleasantries, ready to stop and be merry with any that came along. If they prophesied concerning his future, it is not likely that they spoke of literary fame. They thought him just easy-going and light-minded. True, they noticed that he often carried a book under his arm—a history, a volume of Dickens, or the tales of Poe.

He read more than any one guessed. At night, propped up in bed—a habit continued until his death—he was likely to read until a late hour. He enjoyed smoking at such times, and had made himself a pipe with a large bowl which stood on the floor and had a long rubber stem, something like the Turkish hubble-bubble. He liked to fill the big bowl and smoke at ease through the entire evening. But sometimes the pipe went out, which meant that he must strike a match and lean far over to apply it, just when he was most comfortable. Sam Clemens never liked unnecessary exertion. One night, when the pipe had gone out for the second time, he happened to hear the young book-clerk, Brownell, passing up to his room on the top floor. Sam called to him:

"Ed, come here!"

Brownell poked his head in the door. The two were great chums.

"What will you have, Sam?" he asked.

"Come in, Ed; Henry's asleep, and I'm in trouble. I want somebody to light my pipe."

"Why don't you light it yourself?" Brownell asked.

"I would, only I knew you'd be along in a few minutes and would do it for me."

Brownell scratched a match, stooped down, and applied it.

"What are you reading, Sam?"

"Oh, nothing much—a so-called funny book. One of these days I'll write a funnier book myself."

Brownell laughed. "No, you won't, Sam," he said. "You're too lazy ever to write a book."

Years later, in the course of a lecture which he delivered in Keokuk, Mark Twain said that he supposed the most untruthful man in the world lived right there in Keokuk and that his name was Ed Brownell.

Orion Clemens did not have the gift of prosperity, and his printing-office did not flourish. When he could no longer pay Sam's wages he took him into partnership, which meant that Sam got no wages at all, though this was of less consequence, since his mother, now living with Pamela, was well provided for. The disorder of the office, however, distressed him. He wrote home that he could not work without system, and, a little later, that he was going to leave Keokuk, that, in fact, he was planning a great adventure—a trip to the upper Amazon!

A WIND OF CHANCE

His interest in the Amazon had been awakened by a book. Lynch and Herndon had surveyed the upper river, and Lieutenant Herndon's book was widely read. Sam Clemens, propped up in bed, pored over it through long evenings, and nightly made fabulous fortunes collecting cocoa and other rare things— resolving, meantime, to start in person for the upper Amazon with no unnecessary delay. Boy and man, Samuel Clemens was the same. His vision of grand possibilities ahead blinded him to the ways and means of arrival. It was an inheritance from both sides of his parentage. Once, in old age, he wrote:

I have been punished many and many a time, and bitterly, for doing things and reflecting afterward. . . . When I am reflecting on these occasions, even deaf persons can hear me think.

He believed, however, that he had reflected carefully concerning the Amazon, and that in a brief time he should be there at the head of an expedition, piling up untold wealth. He even stirred the imaginations of two other adventurers, a Dr. Martin and a young man named Ward. To Henry, then in St. Louis, he wrote, August 5, 1856:

Ward and I held a long consultation Sunday morning, and the result was that we two have determined to start to Brazil, if possible, in *six weeks* from now, in order to look carefully into matters there and report to Dr. Martin in time for him to follow on the first of March.

The matter of finance troubled him. Orion could not be depended on for any specified sum, and the

63

fare to the upper Amazon would probably be considerable. Sam planned different methods of raising it. One of them was to go to New York or Cincinnati and work at his trade until he saved the amount. He would then sail from New York direct, or take boat for New Orleans and sail from there. Of course there would always be vessels clearing for the upper Amazon. After Lieutenant Herndon's book the ocean would probably be full of them.

He did not make the start with Ward, as planned, and Ward and Martin seem to have given up the Amazon idea. Not so with Samuel Clemens. He went on reading Herndon, trying meantime to raise money enough to get him out of Keokuk. Was it fate or Providence that suddenly placed it in his hands? Whatever it was, the circumstance is so curious that it must be classed as one of those strange facts that have no place in fiction.

The reader will remember how, one day in Hannibal, the wind had brought to Sam Clemens, then printer's apprentice, a stray leaf from a book about Joan of Arc, and how that incident marked a turning-point in his mental life. Now, seven years later, it was the wind again that directed his fortune. It was a day in early November—bleak, bitter, and gusty, with whirling snow; most persons were indoors. Samuel Clemens, going down Main Street, Keokuk, saw a flying bit of paper pass him and lodge against a building. Something about it attracted him and he captured it. It was a fifty-dollar bill! He had never seen one before, but he recognized it. He thought he must be having a pleasant dream.

64

A WIND OF CHANCE

He was tempted to pocket his good fortune and keep still. But he had always a troublesome conscience. He went to a newspaper office and advertised that he had found a sum of money, a large bill.

Once, long after, he said: "I didn't describe it very particularly, and I waited in daily fear that the owner would turn up and take away my fortune. By and by I couldn't stand it any longer. My conscience had gotten all that was coming to it. I felt that I must take that money out of danger."

Another time he said, "I advertised the find and left for the Amazon the same day." All of which we may take with his usual literary discount—the one assigned to him by his mother in childhood. As a matter of fact, he remained for an ample time, and nobody came for the money. What was its origin? Was it swept out of a bank, or caught up by the wind from some counting-room table? Perhaps it materialized out of the unseen. Who knows?

XI

THE LONG WAY TO THE AMAZON

SAM decided on Cincinnati as his base. From there he could go either to New York or New Orleans to catch the Amazon boat. He paid a visit to St. Louis, where his mother made him renew his promise as to drink and cards. Then he was seized with a literary idea, and returned to Keokuk, where he proposed to a thriving weekly paper, the *Saturday Post*, to send letters of travel, which might even be made into a book later on. George Reese, owner of the *Post*, agreed to pay five dollars each for the letters, which speaks well for his faith in Samuel Clemens's talent, five dollars being good pay for that time and place—more than the letters were worth, judged by present standards. The first was dated Cincinnati, November 14, 1856, and was certainly not promising literature. It was written in the ridiculous dialect which was once thought to be the dress of humor; and while here and there is a comic flash, there is in it little promise of the future Mark Twain. One extract is enough:

When we got to the depo', I went around to git a look at the iron hoss. Thunderation! It wasn't no more like

a hoss than a meetin'-house. If I was goin' to describe
the animule, I'd say it looked like—well, it looked like—
blamed if I know *what* it looked like, snor ng fire and
brimstone out of his nostrils, and puffin' out black smoke
all 'round, and pantin', and heavin', and swellin', and
chawin' up red-hot coals like they was good. A feller
stood in a little house like, feedin' him all the time; but
the more he got, the more he wanted and the more he
blowed and snorted. After a spell the feller ketched him
by the tail, and great Jericho! he set up a yell that split
the ground for more'n a mile and a half, and the next
minit I felt my legs a-waggin', and found myself at t'other
end of the string o' vehickles. I wasn't *skeered*, but I
had three chills and a stroke of palsy in less than five
minits, and my face had a cur'us brownish-yaller-green-
bluish color in it, which was perfectly unaccountable.
"Well," say I, "comment is super-flu-ous."

How Samuel Clemens could have written that.
and worse, at twenty-one, and a little more than
ten years later have written *The Innocents Abroad*,
is one of the mysteries of literature. The letters were
signed "Snodgrass," and there are but two of them.
Snodgrass seems to have found them hard work, for
it is said he raised on the price, which, fortunately,
brought the series to a close. Their value to-day
lies in the fact that they are the earliest of Mark
Twain's newspaper contributions that have been
preserved—the first for which he received a cash
return.

Sam remained in Cincinnati until April of the following year, 1857, working for Wrightson & Co.,
general printers, lodging in a cheap boarding-house
saving every possible penny for his great adventure.

He had one associate at the boarding-house, a lank, unsmiling Scotchman named Macfarlane, twice young Clemens's age, and a good deal of a mystery. Sam never could find out what Macfarlane did. His hands were hardened by some sort of heavy labor; he left at six in the morning and returned in the evening at the same hour. He never mentioned his work, and young Clemens had the delicacy not to inquire.

For Macfarlane was no ordinary person. He was a man of deep knowledge, a reader of many books, a thinker; he was versed in history and philosophy, he knew the dictionary by heart. He made but two statements concerning himself: one, that he had acquired his knowledge from reading, and not at school; the other, that he knew every word in the English dictionary. He was willing to give proof of the last, and Sam Clemens tested him more than once, but found no word that Macfarlane could not define.

Macfarlane was not silent—he would discuss readily enough the deeper problems of life and had many startling theories of his own. Darwin had not yet published his *Descent of Man*, yet Macfarlane was already advancing ideas similar to those in that book. He went further than Darwin. He had startling ideas of the moral evolution of man, and these he would pour into the ears of his young listener until ten o'clock, after which, like the English Sumner in Philadelphia, he would grill a herring, and the evening would end. Those were fermenting discourses that young Samuel Clemens listened to that winter in Macfarlane's room, and they did not fail to influence his later thought.

It was the high-tide of spring, late in April, when the prospective cocoa-hunter decided that it was time to set out for the upper Amazon. He had saved money enough to carry him at least as far as New Orleans, where he would take ship, it being farther south and therefore nearer his destination. Furthermore, he could begin with a lazy trip down the Mississippi, which, next to being a pilot, had been one of his most cherished dreams. The Ohio River steamers were less grand than those of the Mississippi, but they had a home-like atmosphere and did not hurry. Samuel Clemens had the spring fever and was willing to take his time.

In *Life on the Mississippi* we read that the author ran away, vowing never to return until he could come home a pilot, shedding glory. But this is the fiction touch. He had always loved the river, and his boyhood dream of piloting had time and again returned, but it was not uppermost when he bade good-by to Macfarlane and stepped aboard the *Paul Jones*, bound for New Orleans, and thus conferred immortality on that ancient little craft.

Now he had really started on his voyage. But it was a voyage that would continue not for a week or a fortnight, but for four years—four marvelous, sun-lit years, the glory of which would color all that followed them.

6

XII

RENEWING AN OLD AMBITION

A READER of Mark Twain's Mississippi book gets the impression that the author was a boy of about seventeen when he started to learn the river, and that he was painfully ignorant of the great task ahead. But this also is the fiction side of the story. Samuel Clemens was more than twenty-one when he set out on the *Paul Jones*, and in a way was familiar with the trade of piloting. Hannibal had turned out many pilots. An older brother of the Bowen boys was already on the river when Sam Clemens was rolling rocks down Holliday's Hill. Often he came home to air his grandeur and hold forth on the wonder of his work. That learning the river was no light task Sam Clemens would know as well as any one who had not tried it.

Nevertheless, as the drowsy little steamer went puffing down into softer, sunnier lands, the old dream, the "permanent ambition" of boyhood, returned, while the call of the far-off Amazon and cocoa grew faint.

RENEWING AN OLD AMBITION

Horace Bixby,[1] pilot of the *Paul Jones*, a man of thirty-two, was looking out over the bow at the head of Island No. 35 when he heard a slow, pleasant voice say, "Good morning."

Bixby was a small, clean-cut man. "Good morning, sir," he said, rather briskly, without looking around.

He did not much care for visitors in the pilot-house. This one entered and stood a little behind him.

"How would you like a young man to learn the river?" came to him in that serene, deliberate speech.

The pilot glanced over his shoulder and saw a rather slender, loose-limbed youth with a fair, girlish complexion and a great mass of curly auburn hair.

"I wouldn't like it. Cub pilots are more trouble than they're worth. A great deal more trouble than profit."

"I am a printer by trade," the easy voice went on. "It doesn't agree with me. I thought I'd go to South America."

Bixby kept his eye on the river, but there was interest in his voice when he spoke. "What makes you pull your words that way?" he asked—"pulling" being the river term for drawling.

The young man, now seated comfortably on the visitors' bench, said more slowly than ever: "You'll have to ask my mother—she pulls hers, too."

[1] Horace Bixby lived until 1912 and remained at the wheel until within a short time of his death, in his eighty-seventh year. The writer of this memoir visited him in 1910 and took down from his dictation the dialogue that follows.

Pilot Bixby laughed. The manner of the reply amused him. His guest was encouraged.

"Do you know the Bowen boys?" he asked, "pilots in the St. Louis and New Orleans trade?"

"I know them well—all three of them. William Bowen did his first steering for me; a mighty good boy. I know Sam, too, and Bart."

"Old schoolmates of mine in Hannibal. Sam and Will, especially, were my chums."

Bixby's tone became friendly. "Come over and stand by me," he said. "What is your name?"

The applicant told him, and the two stood looking out on the sunlit water.

"Do you drink?"

"No."

"Do you gamble?"

"No, sir."

"Do you swear?"

"N-not for amusement; only under pressure."

"Do you chew?"

"No, sir, never; but I must—smoke."

"Did you ever do any steering?"

"I have steered everything on the river but a steamboat, I guess."

"Very well. Take the wheel and see what you can do with a steamboat. Keep her as she is—toward that lower cottonwood snag."

Bixby had a sore foot and was glad of a little relief. He sat on the bench where he could keep a careful eye on the course. By and by he said: "There is just one way I would take a young man to learn the river—that is, for money."

72

"What—do you—charge?"

"Five hundred dollars, and I to be at no expense whatever."

In those days pilots were allowed to carry a learner, or "cub," board free. Mr. Bixby meant that he was to be at no expense in port or for incidentals. His terms seemed discouraging.

"I haven't got five hundred dollars in money," Sam said. "I've got a lot of Tennessee land worth two bits an acre. I'll give you two thousand acres of that."

Bixby shook his head. "No," he said, "I don't want any unimproved real estate. I have too much already."

Sam reflected. He thought he might be able to borrow one hundred dollars from William Moffett, Pamela's husband, without straining his credit.

"Well, then," he proposed, "I'll give you one hundred dollars cash, and the rest when I earn it."

Something about this young man had won Horace Bixby's heart. His slow, pleasant speech, his unhurried, quiet manner at the wheel, his evident simplicity and sincerity—the inner qualities of mind and heart which would make the world love Mark Twain. The terms proposed were accepted. The first payment was to be in cash; the others were to begin when the pupil had learned the river and was earning wages. During the rest of the trip to New Orleans the new pupil was often at the wheel, while Mr. Bixby nursed his sore foot and gave directions. Any literary ambitions that Samuel Clemens still nourished waned rapidly. By the time he had reached New Orleans he had almost forgotten he had ever been a printer. As for the Amazon and cocoa, why, there had been no ship sailing in that direction for years, and it was unlikely that any would ever sail again, a fact that rather amused the would-be adventurer now, since Providence had regulated his affairs in accordance with his oldest and longest-cherished dream.

At New Orleans Bixby left the *Paul Jones* for a fine St. Louis boat, taking his cub with him. This was a sudden and happy change, and Sam was a good deal impressed with his own importance in belonging to so imposing a structure, especially when, after a few days' stay in New Orleans, he stood by Bixby's side in the big glass turret while they backed out of the line of wedged-in boats and headed up the great river.

This was glory, but there was sorrow ahead. He had not really begun learning the river as yet—he had only steered under directions. He had known that to learn the river would be hard, but he had never realized quite how hard. Serenely he had undertaken the task of mastering twelve hundred miles of the great, changing, shifting river as exactly and as surely by daylight or darkness as one knows the way to his own features. Nobody could realize the full size of that task—not till afterward.

XIII

LEARNING THE RIVER

IN that early day, to be a pilot was to be "greater than a king." The Mississippi River pilot was a law unto himself—there was none above him. His direction of the boat was absolute; he could start or lay up when he chose; he could pass a landing regardless of business there, consulting nobody, not even the captain; he could take the boat into what seemed certain destruction, if he had that mind, and the captain was obliged to stand by, helpless and silent, for the law was with the pilot in everything.

Furthermore, the pilot was a gentleman. His work was clean and physically light. It ended the instant the boat was tied to the landing, and did not begin again until it was ready to back into the stream. Also, for those days his salary was princely—the Vice-President of the United States did not receive more. As for prestige, the Mississippi pilot, perched high in his glass inclosure, fashionably dressed, and commanding all below him, was the most conspicuous and showy, the most observed and envied creature in the world. No wonder Sam Clemens, with his love of the river and his boyish fondness for honors, should aspire to that stately rank. Even at twenty-one he was still just a boy—as, indeed, he was till his death—and we may imagine how elated he was, starting up the great river as a real apprentice pilot, who in a year or two would stand at the wheel, as his chief was now standing, a monarch with a splendid income and all the great river packed away in his head.

In that last item lay the trouble. In the Mississippi book he tells of it in a way that no one may hope to equal, and if the details are not exact, the truth is there—at least in substance.

For a distance above New Orleans Mr. Bixby had volunteered information about the river, naming the points and crossings, in what seemed a casual way, all through his watch of four hours. Their next watch began in the middle of the night, and Mark Twain tells how surprised and disgusted he was to learn that pilots must get up in the night to run their boats, and his amazement to find Mr. Bixby plunging into the blackness ahead as if it had been daylight. Very likely this is mainly fiction, but hardly the following:

Presently he turned to me and said: "What's the name of the first point above New Orleans?"

I was gratified to be able to answer promptly, and I did. I said I didn't know.

"Don't *know!*"

His manner jolted me. I was down at the foot again, in a moment. But I had to say just what I had said before.

"Well, you're a smart one," said Mr. Bixby. "What's the name of the *next* point?"

LEARNING THE RIVER

Once more I didn't know.

"Well, this beats anything! Tell me the name of any point or place I told you."

I studied awhile and decided that I couldn't.

"Look here! What do you start from, above Twelve-Mile Point, to cross over?"

"I—I—don't know."

"'You—you don't know,'" mimicking my drawling manner of speech. "What do you know?"

"I—I— Nothing, for certain."

Bixby was a small, nervous man, hot and quick-firing. He went off now, and said a number of severe things. Then:

"Look here, what do you suppose I told you the names of those points for?"

I tremblingly considered a moment—then the devil of temptation provoked me to say: "Well—to—to—be entertaining, I thought."

This was a red flag to the bull. He raged and stormed so (he was crossing the river at the time) that I judged it made him blind, because he ran over the steering-oar of a trading-scow. Of course the traders sent up a volley of red-hot profanity. Never was a man so grateful as Mr. Bixby was, because he was brimful, and here were subjects who would *talk back*. He threw open a window, thrust his head out, and such an irruption followed as I had never heard before. . . . When he closed the window he was empty. Presently he said to me, in the gentlest way:

"My boy, you must get a little memorandum-book, and every time I tell you a thing, put it down right away. There's only one way to be a pilot, and that is to get this entire river by heart. You have to know it just like A-B-C."

The little memorandum-book which Sam Clemens bought, probably at the next daylight landing, still exists—the same that he says "fairly bristled with the names of towns, points, bars, islands, bends, reaches, etc."; but it made his heart ache to think he had only half the river set down, for, as the watches were four hours off and four hours on, there were the long gaps where he had slept.

It is not easy to make out the penciled notes to-day. The small, neat writing is faded, and many of them are in an abbreviation made only for himself. It is hard even to find these examples to quote:

Meriwether's Bend

One-fourth less 3[1]—run shape of upper bar and go into the low place in the willows about 200 (ft.) lower down than last year.

Outside of Montezuma

Six or eight feet more water. Shape bar till high timber on towhead gets nearly even with low willows. Then hold a little open on right of low willows—run 'em close if you want to, but come out 200 yards when you get nearly to head of towhead.

The average mind would not hold a single one of these notes ten seconds, yet by the time he reached St. Louis he had set down pages that to-day make one's head weary even to contemplate. And those long four-hour gaps where he had been asleep—they are still there; and now, after nearly sixty years, the old heartache is still in them. He must have

[1] Depth of water. One-quarter less than three fathoms.

78

bought a new book for the next trip and laid this one away.

To the new "cub" it seemed a long way to St. Louis that first trip, but in the end it was rather grand to come steaming up to the big, busy city, with its thronging waterfront flanked with a solid mile of steamboats, and to nose one's way to a place in that stately line.

At St. Louis, Sam borrowed from his brother-in-law the one hundred dollars he had agreed to pay, and so closed his contract with Bixby. A few days later his chief was engaged to go on a very grand boat indeed—a "sumptuous temple," he tells us, all brass and inlay, with a pilot-house so far above the water that he seemed perched on a mountain. This part of learning the river was worth while; and when he found that the regiment of natty servants respectfully "sir'd" him, his happiness was complete.

But he was in the depths again, presently, for when they started down the river and he began to take account of his knowledge, he found that he had none. Everything had changed—that is, he was seeing it all from the other direction. What with the four-hour gaps and this transformation, he was lost completely.

How could the easy-going, dreamy, unpractical man whom the world knew as Mark Twain ever have persisted against discouragement like that to acquire the vast, the absolute, limitless store of information necessary to Mississippi piloting? The answer is that he loved the river, the picturesqueness and poetry of a steamboat, the ease and glory of a pilot's life; and then, in spite of his own later claims to the contrary, Samuel Clemens, boy and man, in the work suited to his tastes and gifts, was the most industrious of persons. Work of the other sort he avoided, overlooked, refused to recognize, but never any labor for which he was qualified by his talents or training. Piloting suited him exactly, and he proved an apt pupil.

Horace Bixby said to the writer of this memoir: "Sam was always good-natured, and he had a natural taste for the river. He had a fine memory and never forgot what I told him."

Yet there must have been hard places all along, for to learn every crook and turn and stump and snag and bluff and bar and sounding of that twelve hundred miles of mighty, shifting water was a gigantic task. Mark Twain tells us how, when he was getting along pretty well, his chief one day turned on him suddenly with this "settler":

"What is the shape of Walnut Bend?"

He might as well have asked me my grandmother's opinion of protoplasm. I replied respectfully and said I didn't know it had any particular shape. My gunpowdery chief went off with a bang, of course, and then went on loading and firing until he was out of adjectives. . . . I waited. By and by he said:

"My boy, you've got to know the shape of the river perfectly. It is all that is left to steer by on a very dark night. Everything else is blotted out and gone. But mind you, it hasn't got the same shape in the night that it has in the daytime."

LEARNING THE RIVER

"How on earth am I going to learn it, then?"

"How do you follow a hall at home in the dark? Because you know the shape of it. You can't see it."

"Do you mean to say that I've got to know all the million trifling variations of shape in the banks of this interminable river as well as I know the shape of the front hall at home?"

"On my honor, you've got to know them *better* than any man ever did know the shapes of the halls in his own house."

"I wish I was dead!"

But the reader must turn to Chapter VIII of *Life on the Mississippi* and read, or reread, the pages which follow this extract—nothing can better convey the difficulties of piloting. That Samuel Clemens had the courage to continue is the best proof, not only of his great love of the river, but of that splendid gift of resolution that one rarely fails to find in men of the foremost rank.

XIV

PILOTING was only a part of Sam Clemens's education on the Mississippi. He learned as much of the reefs and shallows of human nature as of the river-bed. In one place he writes:

> In that brief, sharp schooling I got personally and familiarly acquainted with all the different types of human nature that are to be found in fiction, biography, or history.

All the different types, but most of them in the rough. That Samuel Clemens kept the promise made to his mother as to drink and cards during those apprentice days is well worth remembering.

Horace Bixby, answering a call for pilots from the Missouri River, consigned his pupil, as was customary, to one of the pilots of the *John J. Roe*, a freight-boat, owned and conducted by some retired farmers, and in its hospitality reminding Sam of his Uncle John Quarles's farm. The *Roe* was a very deliberate boat. It was said that she could beat an island to St. Louis, but never quite overtake the current going down-stream. Sam loved the *Roe*. She was not licensed to carry passengers, but she always had a family party of the owners' relations aboard, and there was a big deck for dancing and a piano in the cabin. The young pilot could play the chords, and sing, in his own fashion, about a grasshopper that sat on a sweet-potato vine, and about—

> An old, old horse whose name was Methusalem,
> Took him down and sold him in Jerusalem,
>   A long time ago.

The *Roe* was a heavenly place, but Sam's stay there did not last. Bixby came down from the Missouri, and perhaps thought he was doing a fine thing for his pupil by transferring him to a pilot named Brown, then on a large passenger-steamer, the *Pennsylvania*. The *Pennsylvania* was new and one of the finest boats on the river. Sam Clemens, by this time, was accounted a good steersman, so it seemed fortunate and a good arrangement for all parties.

But Brown was a tyrant. He was illiterate and coarse, and took a dislike to Sam from the start. His first greeting was a question, harmless enough in form but offensive in manner.

"Are you Horace Bigsby's cub?"—Bixby being usually pronounced "Bigsby" in river parlance.

Sam answered politely enough that he was, and Brown proceeded to comment on the "style" of his clothes and other personal matters.

He had made an effort to please Brown, but it was no use. Brown was never satisfied. At a moment when Sam was steering, Brown, sitting on the bench, would shout: "Here! Where are you going now? Pull her *down!* Pull her *down!* Do you *hear* me? *Blamed mud-cat!"*

The young pilot soon learned to detest his chief, and presently was putting in a good deal of his time inventing punishments for him.

I could imagine myself killing Brown; there was no law against that, and that was the thing I always used to do the moment I was abed. Instead of going over the river in my mind, as was my duty, I threw business aside for pleasure, and killed Brown.

He gave up trying to please Brown, and was even willing to stir him up upon occasion. One day when the cub was at the wheel his chief noticed that the course seemed peculiar.

"Here! Where you headin' for now?" he yelled. "What in the nation you steerin' at, anyway? *Blamed numskull!"*

"Why," said Sam in his calm, slow way, "I didn't see much else I could steer for, so I was heading for that white heifer on the bank."

"Get away from that wheel! And get outen this pilot-house!" yelled Brown. "You ain't fitten to become no pilot!" An order that Sam found welcome enough. The other pilot, George Ealer, was a lovable soul who played the flute and chess during his off watch, and read aloud to Sam from Goldsmith and Shakespeare. To be with George Ealer was to forget the persecutions of Brown.

Young Clemens had been on the river nearly a year at this time, and, though he had learned a good deal and was really a fine steersman, he received no wages. He had no board to pay, but there were things he must buy, and his money supply had become limited. Each trip of the *Pennsylvania* she remained about two days and nights in New Orleans, during which time the young man was free. He found he could earn two and a half to three dollars a night watching freight on the levee, and, as this opportunity came around about once a month, the amount was useful. Nor was this the only return; many years afterward he said:

"It was a desolate experience, watching there in the dark, among those piles of freight; not a sound, not a living creature astir. But it was not a profitless one. I used to have inspirations as I sat there alone those nights. I used to imagine all sorts of situations and possibilities. These things got into my books by and by, and furnished me with many a chapter. I can trace the effects of those nights through most of my books, in one way and another."

Piloting, even with Brown, had its pleasant side. In St. Louis, young Clemens stopped with his sister, and often friends were there from Hannibal. At both ends of the line he visited friendly boats, especially the *Roe*, where a grand welcome was always waiting. Once among the guests of that boat a young girl named Laura so attracted him that he forgot time and space until one of the *Roe* pilots, Zeb Leavenworth, came flying aft, shouting:

"The *Pennsylvania* is backing out!"

A hasty good-by, a wild flight across the decks of several boats, and a leap across several feet of open water closed the episode. He wrote to Laura, but there was no reply. He never saw her again, never heard from her for nearly fifty years, when both were widowed and old. She had not received his letter.

Occasionally there were stirring adventures aboard the *Pennsylvania*. In a letter written in March, 1858, the young pilot tells of an exciting night search in the running ice for Hat Island soundings:

Brown, the pilot, stood in the bow with an oar, to keep her head out, and I took the tiller. We would start the men, and all would go well until the yawl would bring us on a heavy cake of ice, and then the men would drop like so many tenpins, while Brown assumed the horizontal in the bottom of the boat. After an hour's hard work we got back, with ice half an inch thick on the oars. . . . The next day was colder still. I was out in the yawl twice, and then we got through, but the infernal steamboat came near running over us. . . . The *Maria Denning* was aground at the head of the island; they hailed us; we ran alongside, and they hoisted us in and thawed us out. We had been out in the yawl from four in the morning until half-past nine without being near a fire. There was a thick coating of ice over men and yawl, ropes, and everything, and we looked like rock-candy statuary.

He was at the right age to enjoy such adventures, and to feel a pride in them. In the same letter he tells how he found on the *Pennsylvania* a small clerkship for his brother Henry, who was now nearly twenty, a handsome, gentle boy of whom Sam was lavishly fond and proud. The young pilot was eager to have Henry with him—to see him started in life. How little he dreamed what sorrow would come of his well-meant efforts in the lad's behalf! Yet he always believed, later, that he had a warning, for one night at the end of May, in St. Louis, he had a vivid dream, which time would presently fulfil.

An incident now occurred on the *Pennsylvania* that closed Samuel Clemens's career on that boat. It was the down trip, and the boat was in Eagle Bend when Henry Clemens appeared on the hurricane deck with an announcement from the captain of a landing a little lower down. Brown, who would never own that he was rather deaf, probably misunderstood the order. They were passing the landing when the captain appeared on the deck.

"Didn't Henry tell you to land here?" he called to Brown.

"No, sir."

Captain Klinefelter turned to Sam. Didn't you hear him?"

"Yes, sir!"

Brown said: "Shut your mouth! You never heard anything of the kind!"

Henry appeared, not suspecting any trouble.

Brown said, fiercely, "Here, why didn't you tell me we had got to land at that plantation?"

"I did tell you, Mr. Brown," Henry said, politely.

"It's a lie!"

Sam Clemens could stand Brown's abuse of himself, but not of Henry. He said: "You lie yourself. He *did* tell you!"

For a cub pilot to defy his chief was unheard of. Brown was dazed, then he shouted:

"I'll attend to your case in half a minute!" And to Henry, "Get out of here!"

Henry had started when Brown seized him by the collar and struck him in the face. An instant later Sam was upon Brown with a heavy stool and stretched him on the floor. Then all the repressed fury of months broke loose; and, leaping upon Brown and holding him down with his knees, Samuel Clemens pounded the tyrant with his fists till his strength gave out. He let Brown go then, and the latter, with pilot instinct, sprang to the wheel, for the boat was drifting. Seeing she was safe, he seized a spy-glass as a weapon and ordered his chastiser out of the pilot-house. But Sam lingered. He had become very calm, and he openly corrected Brown's English.

"Don't give me none of your airs!" yelled Brown. "I ain't goin' to stand nothin' more from you!"

"You should say, 'Don't give me any of your airs,'" Sam said, sweetly, "and the last half of your sentence almost defies correction."

A group of passengers and white-aproned servants, assembled on the deck forward, applauded the victor. Sam went down to find Captain Klinefelter. He expected to be put in irons, for it was thought to be mutiny to strike a pilot.

The captain took Sam into his private room and made some inquiries. Mark Twain, in the *Mississippi* book, remembers them as follows:

"Did you strike him first?" Captain Klinefelter asked.
"Yes, sir."
"What with?"
"A stool, sir."
"Hard?"

"Middling, sir."

"Did it knock him down?"

"He—he fell, sir."

"Did you follow it up?   Did you do anything further?"

"Yes, sir."

"What did you do?"

"Pounded him, sir."

"Pounded him?"

"Yes, sir."

"Did you pound him much—that is, severely?"

"One might call it that, sir, maybe."

"I am mighty glad of it! Hark ye—never mention that I said that! You have been guilty of a great crime; and don't ever be guilty of it again on this boat, but—lay for him ashore! Give him a good, sound thrashing, do you hear?   I'll pay the expenses."

In a letter which Samuel Clemens wrote to Orion's wife, immediately after this incident, he gives the details of the encounter with Brown and speaks of Captain Klinefelter's approval.[1] Brown declared he would leave the boat at New Orleans if Sam Clemens remained on it, and the captain told him to go, offering to let Sam himself run the daylight watches back to St. Louis, thus showing his faith in the young steersman. The "cub," however, had less confidence, and advised that Brown be kept for the up trip, saying he would follow by the next boat. It was a decision that probably saved his life.

That night, watching on the levee, Henry joined him, when his own duties were finished, and the

---

[1] In the Mississippi book the author says that Brown was about to strike Henry with a lump of coal, but in the letter above mentioned the details are as here given.

brothers made the round together. It may have been some memory of his dream that made Samuel Clemens say:

"Henry, in case of accident, whatever you do, don't lose your head — the passengers will do that. Rush for the hurricane-deck and to the life-boat, and obey the mate's orders. When the boat is launched, help the women and children into it. Don't get in yourself. The river is only a mile wide. You can swim ashore easily enough."

It was good, manly advice, but a long grief lay behind it.

XV

THE WRECK OF THE "PENNSYLVANIA"

THE *A. T. Lacy*, that brought Samuel Clemens up the river, was two days behind the *Pennsylvania*. At Greenville, Mississippi, a voice from the landing shouted:

"The *Pennsylvania* is blown up just below Memphis, at Ship Island. One hundred and fifty lives lost!"

It proved a true report. At six o'clock that warm mid-June morning, while loading wood, sixty miles below Memphis, four out of eight of the *Pennsylvania's* boilers had suddenly exploded, with fearful results. Henry Clemens had been one of the victims. He had started to swim for the shore, only a few hundred yards away, but had turned back to assist in the rescue of others. What followed could not be clearly learned. He was terribly injured, and died on the fourth night after the catastrophe. His brother was with him by that time, and believed he recognized the exact fulfilment of his dream.

The young pilot's grief was very great. In a letter home he spoke of the dying boy as "My darling, my pride, my glory, my all." His heavy sorrow, and the fact that with unsparing self-blame he held himself in a measure responsible for his brother's tragic death, saddened his early life. His early gaiety came back, but his face had taken on the serious, pathetic look which from that time it always wore in repose. Less than twenty-three, he had suddenly the look of thirty, and while Samuel Clemens in spirit, temperament, and features never would become really old, neither would he ever look really young again.

He returned to the river as steersman for George Ealer, whom he loved, and in September of that year obtained a full license as Mississippi River pilot from St. Louis to New Orleans. In eighteen months he had packed away in his head all those wearisome details and acquired that confidence that made him one of the elect. He knew every snag and bank and dead tree and depth in all those endless miles of shifting current, every cut-off and crossing. He could read the surface of the water by day, he could smell danger in the dark. To the writer of these chapters, Horace Bixby said:

"In a year and a half from the time he came to the river, Sam was not only a pilot, but a good one. Sam was a *fine* pilot, and in a day when piloting on the Mississippi required a great deal more brains and skill and application than it does now. There were no signal-lights along the shore in those days, and no search-lights on the vessels; everything was blind; and on a dark, misty night, in a river full of snags and shifting sandbars and changing shores, a pilot's judgment had to be founded on *absolute certainty*."

Bixby had returned from the Missouri by the time his pupil's license was issued, and promptly took him as full partner on the *Crescent City*, and later on a fine new boat, the *New Falls City*. Still later, they appear to have been together on a very large boat, the *City of Memphis*, and again on the *Alonzo Child*.

XVI

THE PILOT

FOR Samuel Clemens these were happy days—the happiest, in some respects, he would ever know. He had plenty of money now. He could help his mother with a liberal hand, and could put away fully a hundred dollars a month for himself. He had few cares, and he loved the ease and romance and independence of his work as he would never quite love anything again.

His popularity on the river was very great. His humorous stories and quaint speech made a crowd collect wherever he appeared. There were pilot-association rooms in St. Louis and New Orleans, and his appearance at one of these places was a signal for the members to gather.

A friend of those days writes: "He was much given to spinning yarns so funny that his hearers were convulsed, and yet all the time his own face was perfectly sober. Occasionally some of his droll yarns got into the papers. He may have written them himself."

Another old river-man remembers how, one day, at the association, they were talking of presence of mind in an accident, when Pilot Clemens said:

THE PILOT

"Boys, I had great presence of mind once. It was at a fire. An old man leaned out of a four-story building, calling for help. Everybody in the crowd below looked up, but nobody did anything. The ladders weren't long enough. Nobody had any presence of mind—nobody but me. I came to the rescue. I yelled for a rope. When it came I threw the old man the end of it. He caught it, and I told him to tie it around his waist. He did so, and I *pulled him down*."

This was a story that found its way into print, probably his own contribution.

"Sam was always scribbling when not at the wheel," said Bixby, "but the best thing he ever did was the burlesque of old Isaiah Sellers. He didn't write it for print, but only for his own amusement and to show to a few of the boys. Bart Bowen, who was with him on the *Edward J. Gay* at the time, got hold of it, and gave it to one of the New Orleans papers."

The burlesque on Captain Sellers would be of little importance if it were not for its association with the origin, or, at least, with the originator, of what is probably the best known of literary names—the name Mark Twain.

This strong, happy title—a river term indicating a depth of two fathoms on the sounding-line—was first used by the old pilot, Isaiah Sellers, who was a sort of "oldest inhabitant" of the river, with a passion for airing his ancient knowledge before the younger men. Sellers used to send paragraphs to the papers, quaint and rather egotistical in tone, usually beginning, "My opinion for the citizens of New Orleans," etc., prophesying river conditions and recalling memories as far back as 1811. These he generally signed "Mark Twain."

Naturally, the younger pilots amused themselves by imitating Sellers, and when Sam Clemens wrote a broad burlesque of the old man's contributions, relating a perfectly impossible trip, supposed to have been made in 1763 with a Chinese captain and a Choctaw crew, it was regarded as a masterpiece of wit.

It appeared in the *True Delta* in May, 1859, and broke Captain Sellers's literary heart. He never wrote another paragraph. Clemens always regretted the whole matter deeply, and his own revival of the name afterward was a sort of tribute to the old man he had thoughtlessly and unintentionally wounded.

Old pilots of that day remembered Samuel Clemens as a slender, fine-looking man, well dressed, even dandified, generally wearing blue serge, with fancy shirts, white duck trousers, and patent-leather shoes. A pilot could do that, for his surroundings were speckless.

The pilots regarded him as a great reader—a student of history, travels, and the sciences. In the association rooms they often saw him poring over serious books. He began the study of French one day in New Orleans, when he had passed a school of languages where French, German, and Italian were taught, one in each of three rooms. The price was twenty-five dollars for one language, or three for fifty. The student was provided with a set of conversation cards for each, and was supposed to walk from one apartment to another, changing his nationality at each threshold. The young pilot, with his usual enthusiasm, invested in all three languages, but after a few round trips decided that French would do. He did not return to the school, but kept the cards and added text-books. He studied faithfully when off watch and in port, and his old river note-book, still preserved, contains a number of advanced exercises, neatly written out.

Still more interesting are the river notes themselves. They are not the timid, hesitating memoranda of the "little book" which, by Bixby's advice, he bought for his first trip. They are quick, vigorous records that show confidence and knowledge. Under the head of "Second high-water trip—Jan., 1861 —Alonzo Child," the notes tell the story of a rising river, with overflowing banks, blind passages, and cut-offs—a new river, in fact, that must be judged by a perfect knowledge of the old—guessed, but guessed right.

Good deal of water all over Cole's Creek Chute, 12 or 15 ft. bank—could have gone up above General Taylor's—too much drift. . . .

Night—didn't run either 77 or 76 towheads—8-ft. bank on main shore Ozark chute.

To the reader to-day it means little enough, but one may imagine, perhaps, a mile-wide sweep of boiling water, full of drift, shifting currents with newly forming bars, and a lone figure in the dark pilot-house, peering into the night for blind and disappearing landmarks.

But such nights were not all there was of piloting. There were glorious nights when the stars were blazing out, and the moon was on the water, and the young pilot could follow a clear channel and dream long dreams. He was very serious at such times—he reviewed the world's history he had read, he speculated on the future, he considered philosophies, he lost himself in a study of the stars. Mark Twain's love of astronomy, which never waned until his last day, began with those lonely river watches. Once a great comet blazed in the sky, a "wonderful sheaf of light," and glorified his long hours at the wheel.

Samuel Clemens was now twenty-five, full of health and strong in his courage. In the old note-book there remains a well-worn clipping, the words of some unknown writer, which he may have kept as a sort of creed:

How to Take Life.—Take it just as though it was—as it is—an earnest, vital, and important affair. Take it as though you were born to the task of performing a merry part in it—as though the world had awaited for your coming. Take it as though it was a grand opportunity to do and achieve, to carry forward great and good schemes to help and cheer a suffering, weary, it may be heart-broken, brother. Now and then a man stands aside from the crowd, labors earnestly, steadfastly, confidently, and straightway becomes famous for wisdom, intellect, skill, greatness of some sort. The world wonders, admires, idolizes, and it only illustrates what others may do if they take hold of life with a purpose. The miracle, or the power that elevates the few, is to be found in their industry, application, and perseverance under the promptings of a brave, determined spirit.

Bixby and Clemens were together that winter on the *Child*, and were the closest friends. Once the young pilot invited his mother to make the trip to New Orleans, and the river journey and a long drive about the beautiful Southern city filled Jane Clemens with wonder and delight. She no longer had any doubts of Sam. He had long since become the head of the family. She felt called upon to lecture him, now and then, but down in her heart she believed that he could really do no wrong. They joked each other unmercifully, and her wit, never at a loss, was quite as keen as his.

XVII

THE END OF PILOTING

WHEN one remembers how much Samuel Clemens loved the river, and how perfectly he seemed suited to the ease and romance of the pilot life, one is almost tempted to regret that it should so soon have come to an end.

Those trips of early '61, which the old note-book records, were the last he would ever make. The golden days of Mississippi steamboating were growing few.

Nobody, however, seemed to suspect it. Even a celebrated fortune-teller in New Orleans, whom the young pilot one day consulted as to his future, did not mention the great upheaval then close at hand. She told him quite remarkable things, and gave him some excellent advice, but though this was February, 1861, she failed to make any mention of the Civil War! Yet, a month later, Abraham Lincoln was inaugurated and trouble was in the air. Then in April Fort Sumter was fired upon and the war had come.

It was a feverish time among the pilots. Some were for the Union—others would go with the Corfederacy. Horace Bixby stood for the North, and in time was chief of the Union river-service. A pilot named Montgomery (Clemens had once steered for him) went with the South and by and by commanded the Confederate Mississippi fleet. In the beginning a good many were not clear as to their opinions. Living both North and South, as they did, they divided their sympathies. Samuel Clemens was thoughtful, and far from bloodthirsty. A pilot-house, so fine and showy in times of peace, seemed a poor place to be in when fighting was going on. He would consider the matter.

"I am not anxious to get up into a glass perch and be shot at by either side," he said. "I'll go home and reflect."

He went up the river as a passenger on a steamer named the *Uncle Sam*. Zeb Leavenworth, formerly of the *John J. Roe*, was one of the pilots, and Clemens usually stood the watch with him. At Memphis they barely escaped the blockade. At Cairo they saw soldiers drilling—troops later commanded by Grant.

The *Uncle Sam* came steaming up to St. Louis, glad to have slipped through safely. They were not quite through, however. Abreast of Jefferson Barracks they heard the boom of a cannon, and a great ring of smoke drifted in their direction. They did not recognize it as a thunderous "Halt!" and kept on. Less than a minute later, a shell exploded directly in front of the pilot-house, breaking a lot of glass and damaging the decoration. Zeb Leavenworth tumbled into a corner.

"Gee-mighty, Sam!" he said. "What do they mean by that?"

Clemens stepped from the visitors' bench to the wheel and brought the boat around.

"I guess—they want us—to wait a minute—Zeb," he said.

They were examined and passed. It was the last steamboat to make the trip through from New Orleans to St. Louis. Mark Twain's pilot days were over. He would have grieved had he known this fact.

"I loved the profession far better than any I have followed since," he long afterward declared, "and I took a measureless pride in it."

At the time, like many others, he expected the war to be brief, and his life to be only temporarily interrupted. Within a year, certainly, he would be back in the pilot-house. Meantime the war must be settled; he would go up to Hannibal to see about it.

XVIII

THE SOLDIER

WHEN he reached Hannibal, Samuel Clemens found a very mixed condition of affairs. The country was in an uproar of war preparation; in a border State there was a confusion of sympathies, with much ignorance as to what it was all about. Any number of young men were eager to enlist for a brief camping-out expedition, and small private companies were formed, composed about half-and-half of Union and Confederate men, as it turned out later.

Missouri, meantime, had allied herself with the South, and Samuel Clemens, on his arrival in Hannibal, decided that, like Lee, he would go with his State. Old friends, who were getting up a company "to help Governor 'Claib' Jackson repel the invader," offered him a lieutenancy if he would join. It was not a big company; it had only about a dozen members, most of whom had been schoolmates, some of them fellow-pilots, and Sam Clemens was needed to make it complete. It was just another *Tom Sawyer* band, and they met in a secret place above Bear Creek Hill and planned how they would sell their lives on the field of glory, just as years before fierce raids had been arranged on peach-orchards and melon-patches. Secrecy was necessary, for the Union militia had a habit of coming over from Illinois and arresting suspicious armies on sight. It would humiliate the finest army in the world to spend a night or two in the calaboose.

So they met secretly at night, and one mysterious evening they called on girls who either were their sweethearts or were pretending to be for the occasion, and when the time came for good-by the girls were invited to "walk through the pickets" with them, though the girls didn't notice any pickets, because the pickets were calling on their girls, too, and were a little late getting to their posts.

That night they marched, through brush and vines, because the highroad was thought to be dangerous, and next morning arrived at the home of Colonel Ralls, of Ralls County, who had the army form in dress parade and made it a speech and gave it a hot breakfast in good Southern style. Then he sent out to Col. Bill Splawn and Farmer Nuck Matson a requisition for supplies that would convert this body of infantry into cavalry—rough-riders of that early day. The community did not wish to keep an army on its hands, and were willing to send it along by such means as they could spare handily. When the outfitting was complete, Lieutenant Samuel Clemens, mounted on a small yellow mule whose tail had been trimmed in the paint-brush pattern then much worn by mules, and surrounded by variously attached articles—such as an extra pair of cowhide boots, a pair of gray blankets, a home-made quilt, a frying-pan, a carpet-sack, a small valise, an overcoat, an old-fashioned Kentucky rifle, twenty yards of rope, and an umbrella—was a fair sample of the brigade.

An army like that, to enjoy itself, ought to go into camp; so it went over to Salt River, near the town of Florida, and took up headquarters in a big log stable. Somebody suggested that an army ought to have its hair cut, so that in a hand-to-hand conflict the enemy could not get hold of it. There was a pair of sheep-shears in the stable, and Private Tom Lyons acted as barber. They were not sharp shears, and a group of little darkies gathered from the farm to enjoy the torture.

Regular elections were now held—all officers, down to sergeants and orderlies, being officially chosen. There were only three privates, and you couldn't tell them from officers. The discipline in that army was very bad.

It became worse soon. Pouring rain set in. Salt River rose and overflowed the bottoms. Men ordered on picket duty climbed up into the stable-loft and went to bed. Twice, on black, drenching nights, word came from the farm-house that the enemy, commanded by a certain Col. Ulysses Grant, was in the neighborhood, and the Hannibal division went hastily slopping through mud and brush in the other direction, dragging wearily back when the alarm was over. Military ardor was bound to cool under such treatment. Then Lieutenant Clemens developed a very severe boil, and was obliged to lie most of the day on some hay in a horse-trough, where he spent his time denouncing the war and the mistaken souls who had invented it. When word that "General" Tom Harris, commander of the district— formerly telegraph-operator in Hannibal—was at a near-by farm-house, living on the fat of the land, the army broke camp without further ceremony. Half-way there they met General Harris, who ordered them back to quarters. They called him familiarly "Tom," and told him they were through with that camp forever. He begged them, but it was no use. A little farther on they stopped at a farm-house for supplies. A tall, bony woman came to the door.

"You're Secesh, ain't you?"

Lieutenant Clemens said: "We are, madam, defenders of the noble cause, and we should like to buy a few provisions."

The request seemed to inflame her.

"Provisions!" she screamed. "Provisions for Secesh, and my husband a colonel in the Union Army. You get out of here!"

She reached for a hickory hoop-pole [1] that stood by the door, and the army moved on. When they reached the home of Col. Bill Splawn it was night and the family had gone to bed. So the hungry army camped in the barn-yard and crept into the hay-loft to sleep. Presently somebody yelled "Fire!" One of the boys had been smoking and had ignited the hay.

[1] In an earlier day, barrel hoops were made of small hickory trees, split and shaved. The hoop-pole was a very familiar article of commerce, and of household defense.

THE SOLDIER

Lieutenant Clemens, suddenly wakened, made a quick rotary movement away from the blaze, and rolled out of a big hay-window into the barn-yard below. The rest of the brigade seized the burning hay and pitched it out of the same window. The lieutenant had sprained his ankle when he struck, and his boil was still painful, but the burning hay cured him—for the moment. He made a spring from under it; then, noticing that the rest of the army, now that the fire was out, seemed to think his performance amusing, he rose up and expressed himself concerning the war, and military life, and the human race in general. They helped him in, then, for his ankle was swelling badly.

In the morning, Colonel Splawn gave the army a good breakfast, and it moved on. Lieutenant Clemens, however, did not get farther than Farmer Nuck Matson's. He was in a high fever by that time from his injured ankle, and Mrs. Matson put him to bed. So the army left him, and presently disbanded. Some enlisted in the regular service, North or South, according to preference. Properly officered and disciplined, that *Tom Sawyer* band would have made as good soldiers as any.

Lieutenant Clemens did not enlist again. When he was able to walk, he went to visit Orion in Keokuk. Orion was a Union Abolitionist, but there would be no unpleasantness on that account. Samuel Clemens was beginning to have leanings in that direction himself.

XIX

THE PIONEER

HE arrived in Keokuk at what seemed a lucky moment. Through Edward Bates, a member of Lincoln's Cabinet, Orion Clemens had received an appointment as territorial secretary of Nevada, and only needed the money to carry him to the seat of his office at Carson City. Out of his pilot's salary his brother had saved more than enough for the journey, and was willing to pay both their fares and go along as private secretary to Orion, whose position promised something in the way of adventure and a possible opportunity for making a fortune.

The brothers went at once to St. Louis for final leave-taking, and there took boat for "St. Jo," Missouri, terminus of the great Overland Stage Route. They paid one hundred and fifty dollars each for their passage, and about the end of July, 1861, set out on that long, delightful trip, behind sixteen galloping horses, never stopping except for meals or to change teams, heading steadily into the sunset over the billowy plains and snow-clad Rockies, covering the seventeen hundred miles between St. Jo and Carson City in nineteen glorious days.

But one must read Mark Twain's *Roughing It* for the story of that long-ago trip—the joy and wonder of it, and the inspiration. "Even at this day," he writes, "it thrills me through and through to think of the life, the gladness, and the wild sense of freedom that used to make the blood dance in my face on those fine overland mornings."

It was a hot August day when they arrived, dusty, unshaven, and weather-beaten, and Samuel Clemens's life as a frontiersman began. Carson City, the capital of Nevada, was a wooden town with an assorted population of two thousand souls. The mining excitement was at its height and had brought together the drift of every race.

The Clemens brothers took up lodgings with a genial Irishwoman, the Mrs. O'Flannigan of *Roughing It*, and Orion established himself in a modest office, for there was no capitol building as yet, no government headquarters. Orion could do all the work, and Samuel Clemens, finding neither duties nor salary attached to his position, gave himself up to the study of the life about him, and to the enjoyment of the freedom of the frontier. Presently he had a following of friends who loved his quaint manner of speech and his yarns. On cool nights they would collect about Orion's office-stove, and he would tell stories in the wonderful way that one day would delight the world. Within a brief time Sam Clemens (he was always "Sam" to the pioneers) was the most notable figure on the Carson streets. His great, bushy head of auburn hair, his piercing, twinkling eyes, his loose, lounging walk, his careless disorder of dress invited a second look, even from strangers. From a river dandy he had become the roughest-clad of pioneers—rusty slouch hat, flannel shirt, coarse trousers slopping half in and half out of heavy cowhide boots, this was his make-up. Energetic citizens did not prophesy success for him. Often they saw him leaning against an awning support, staring drowsily at the motley human procession, for as much as an hour at a time. Certainly that could not be profitable.

But they did like to hear him talk.

He did not catch the mining fever at once. He was interested first in the riches that he could see. Among these was the timber-land around Lake Bigler (now Tahoe)—splendid acres, to be had for the asking. The lake itself was beautifully situated.

With an Ohio boy, John Kinney, he made an excursion afoot to Tahoe, a trip described in one of the best chapters of *Roughing It*. They staked out a timber claim and pretended to fence it and to build a house, but their chief employment was loafing in the quiet luxury of the great woods or drifting in a boat on the transparent water. They did not sleep in the house. In *Roughing It* he says:

It never occurred to us, for one thing; and, besides, it was built to hold the ground, and that was enough. We did not wish to strain it.

They made their camp-fires on the borders of the lake, and one evening it got away from them, fired the forest, and destroyed their fences and habitation. In a letter home he describes this fire in a fine, vivid way. At one place he says:

The level ranks of flame were relieved at intervals by the standard-bearers, as we called the tall dead trees, wrapped in fire, and waving their blazing banners a hundred feet in the air. Then we could turn from the scene to the lake, and see every branch and leaf and cataract of flame upon its banks perfectly reflected, as in a gleaming, fiery mirror.

He was acquiring the literary vision and touch. The description of this same fire in *Roughing It*, written ten years later, is scarcely more vivid.

Most of his letters home at this time tell of glowing prospects—the certainty of fortune ahead. The fever of the frontier is in them. Once, to Pamela Moffett, he wrote:

Orion and I have enough confidence in this country to think that, if the war lets us alone, we can make Mr. Moffett rich without its ever costing him a cent or a particle of trouble.

From the same letter we gather that the brothers are now somewhat interested in mining claims:

We have about 1,650 feet of mining-ground, and, if it proves good, Mr. Moffett's name will go in; and if not, I can get "feet" for him in the spring.

This was written about the end of October. Two months later, in midwinter, the mining fever came upon him with full force.

XX

THE MINER

THE wonder is that Samuel Clemens, always spec-
ulative and visionary, had not fallen an earlier
victim. Everywhere one heard stories of sudden
fortune—of men who had gone to bed paupers and
awakened millionaires. New and fabulous finds were
reported daily. Cart-loads of bricks—silver and
gold bricks—drove through the Carson streets.

Then suddenly from the newly opened Humboldt
region came the wildest reports. The mountains
there were said to be stuffed with gold. A correspondent of the *Territorial Enterprise* was unable to
find words to picture the riches of the Humboldt
mines.

The air for Samuel Clemens began to shimmer.
Fortune was waiting to be gathered in a basket. He
joined the first expedition for Humboldt—in fact,
helped to organize it. In *Roughing It* he says:

Hurry was the word! We wasted no time. Our party
consisted of four persons—a blacksmith sixty years of
age, two young lawyers, and myself. We bought a wagon
and two miserable old horses. We put eighteen hundred
pounds of provisions and mining-tools in the wagon and
drcve out of Carson on a chilly December afternoon.

THE MINER

The two young lawyers were W. H. Clagget, whom Clemens had known in Keokuk, and A. W. Oliver, called Oliphant in *Roughing It*. The blacksmith was named Tillou (Ballou in *Roughing It*), a sturdy, honest man with a knowledge of mining and the repair of tools. There were also two dogs in the party—a curly-tailed mongrel and a young hound.

The horses were the weak feature of the expedition. It was two hundred miles to Humboldt, mostly across sand. The miners rode only a little way, then got out to lighten the load. Later they pushed. Then it began to snow, also to blow, and the air became filled with whirling clouds of snow and sand. On and on they pushed and groaned, sustained by the knowledge that they must arrive some time, when right away they would be millionaires and all their troubles would be over.

The nights were better. The wind went down and they made a camp-fire in the shelter of the wagon, cooked their bacon, crept under blankets with the dogs to warm them, and Sam Clemens spun yarns till they fell asleep.

There had been an Indian war, and occasionally they passed the charred ruin of a cabin and new graves. By and by they came to that deadly waste known as the Alkali Desert, strewn with the carcasses of dead beasts and with the heavy articles discarded by emigrants in their eagerness to reach water. All day and night they pushed through that choking, waterless plain to reach camp on the other side. When they arrived at three in the morning, they dropped down exhausted. Judge

Oliver, the last survivor of the party, in a letter to the writer of these chapters, said:

The sun was high in the heavens when we were aroused from our sleep by a yelling band of Piute warriors. We were upon our feet in an instant. The picture of burning cabins and the lonely graves we had passed was in our minds. Our scalps were still our own, and not dangling from the belts of our visitors. Sam pulled himself together, put his hand on his head, as if to make sure he had not been scalped, and, with his inimitable drawl, said: "Boys, they have left us our scalps. Let us give them all the flour and sugar they ask for." And we did give them a good supply, for we were grateful.

The Indians left them unharmed, and the prospective millionaires moved on. Across that two hundred miles to the Humboldt country they pushed, arriving at the little camp of Unionville at the end of eleven weary days.

In *Roughing It* Mark Twain has told us of Unionville and the mining experience there. Their cabin was a three-sided affair with a cotton roof. Stones rolled down the mountainside on them; also, the author says, a mule and a cow.

The author could not gather fortune in a basket, as he had dreamed. Masses of gold and silver were not lying about. He gathered a back-load of yellow, glittering specimens, but they proved worthless. Gold in the rough did not glitter, and was not yellow. Tillou instructed the others in prospecting, and they went to work with pick and shovel—then with drill and blasting-powder. The prospect of immediately becoming millionaires vanished.

THE MINER

"One week of this satisfied me. I resigned," is Mark Twain's brief comment.

The Humboldt reports had been exaggerated. The Clemens-Clagget-Oliver-Tillou millionaire combination soon surrendered its claims. Clemens and Tillou set out for Carson City with a Prussian named Pfersdorff, who nearly got them drowned and got them completely lost in the snow before they arrived there. Oliver and Clagget remained in Unionville, began law practice, and were elected to office. It is not known what became of the wagon and horses and the two dogs.

It was the end of January when our miner returned to Carson. He was not discouraged—far from it. He believed he had learned something that would be useful to him in a camp where mines were a reality. Within a few weeks from his return we find him at Aurora, in the Esmeralda region, on the edge of California. It was here that the Clemens brothers owned the 1,650 feet formerly mentioned. He had come down to work it.

It was the dead of winter, but he was full of enthusiasm, confident of a fortune by early summer. To Pamela he wrote:

I expect to return to St. Louis in July—p r steamer. I don't say that I *will* return then, or that I shall *be able* to do it—but I *expect* to—you bet. . . . If nothing goes wrong, we'll strike the ledge in June.

He was trying to be conservative, and further along he cautions his sister not to get excited.

Don't you know I have only *talked* as yet, but proved nothing? Don't you know I have never held in my hands a gold or silver bar that belonged to me? Don't you know that people who always feel jolly, no matter where they are or what happens to them—who have the organ of hope preposterously developed—who are endowed with an uncongealable, sanguine temperament—who never feel concerned about the price of corn—and who cannot, by any possibility, discover any but the *bright* side of a picture—are very apt to go to extremes and exaggerate with a 40-horse microscopic power?

> But—but—
> In the bright lexicon of youth,
> There is no such word as fail,

and I'll prove it.

Whereupon he soars again, adding page after page full of glowing expectations and plans such as belong only with speculation in treasures buried in the ground—a very difficult place, indeed, to find them.

His money was about exhausted by this time, and funds to work the mining claims must come out of Orion's rather modest salary. The brothers owned all claims in partnership, and it was now the part of "Brother Sam" to do the active work. He hated the hard picking and prying and blasting into the flinty ledges, but the fever drove him on. He camped with a young man named Phillips at first, and, later on, with an experienced miner, Calvin H. Higbie, to whom *Roughing It* would one day be dedicated. They lived in a tiny cabin with a cotton roof, and around their rusty stove they would paw over their specimens and figure the fortune that their mines would be worth in the spring.

Food ran low, money gave out almost entirely, but they did not give up. When it was stormy and they could not dig, and the ex-pilot was in a talkative vein, he would sit astride the bunk and distribute to his hearers riches more valuable than any they would dig from the Esmeralda hills. At other times he did not talk at all, but sat in a corner and wrote. They thought he was writing home; they did not know that he was "literary." Some of his home letters had found their way into a Keokuk paper and had come back to Orion, who had shown them to an assistant on the *Territorial Enterprise*, of Virginia City. The *Enterprise* man had caused one of them to be reprinted, and this had encouraged its author to send something to the paper direct. He signed these contributions "Josh," and one told of

> An old, old horse whose name was Methusalem,
> Took him down and sold him in Jerusalem,
>   A long time ago.

He received no pay for these offerings and expected none. He considered them of no value. If any one had told him that he was knocking at the door of the house of fame, however feebly, he would have doubted that person's judgment or sincerity.

His letters to Orion, in Carson City, were hasty compositions, reporting progress and progress, or calling for remittances to keep the work going. On April 13, he wrote:

Work not begun on the Horatio and Derby—haven't seen it yet. It is still in the snow. Shall begin on it within three or four weeks—strike the ledge in July.

Again, later in the month:

I have been at work all day, blasting and digging in one of our new claims, "Dashaway," which I don't think a great deal of, but which I am willing to try. We are down now ten or twelve feet.

It must have been disheartening work, picking away at the flinty ledges. There is no further mention of the "Dashaway," but we hear of the "Flyaway," the "Annipolitan," the "Live Yankee," and of many another, each of which holds out a beacon of hope for a brief moment, then passes from notice forever. Still, he was not discouraged. Once he wrote:

I am a citizen here and I am satisfied, though 'Ratio and I are "strapped" and we haven't three days' rations in the house. I shall work the "Monitor" and the other claims with my own hands.

"The pick and shovel are the only claims I have confidence in now," he wrote, later; "my back is sore and my hands are blistered with handling them to-day."

His letters began to take on a weary tone. Once in midsummer he wrote that it was still snowing up there in the hills, and added, "It *always* snows here I expect. If we strike it rich, I've lost my guess, that's all." And the final heartsick line, "Don't you suppose they have pretty much quit writing at home?"

In time he went to work in a quartz-mill at ten dollars a week, though it was not entirely for the money, as in *Roughing It* he would have us believe. Samuel Clemens learned thoroughly what he undertook, and he proposed to master the science of mining. From Phillips and Higbie he had learned what there was to know about prospecting. He went to the mill to learn refining, so that, when his claims developed, he could establish a mill and personally superintend the work. His stay was brief. He contracted a severe cold and came near getting poisoned by the chemicals. Recovering, he went with Higbie for an outing to Mono Lake, a ghastly, lifeless alkali sea among the hills, vividly described in *Roughing It*.

At another time he went with Higbie on a walking trip to the Yosemite, where they camped and fished undisturbed, for in those days few human beings came to that far isolation. Discouragement did not reach them there—amid that vast grandeur and quiet the quest for gold hardly seemed worth while. Now and again that summer he went alone into the wilderness to find his balance and to get entirely away from humankind.

In *Roughing It* Mark Twain tells the story of how he and Higbie finally located a "blind lead," which made them really millionaires, until they forfeited their claim through the sharp practice of some rival miners and their own neglect. It is true that the "Wide West" claim was forfeited in some such manner, but the size of the loss was magnified in *Roughing It*, to make a good story. There was never a fortune in "Wide West," except the one sunk in it by its final owners. The story as told in *Roughing It* is a tale of what *might* have happened, and ends the author's days in the mines with a good story-book touch.

The mining career of Samuel Clemens really came to a close gradually, and with no showy climax. He fought hard and surrendered little by little, without owning, even to the end, that he was surrendering at all. It was the gift of resolution that all his life would make his defeats long and costly—his victories supreme.

By the end of July the money situation in the Aurora camp was getting desperate. Orion's depleted salary would no longer pay for food, tools, and blasting-powder, and the miner began to cast about for means to earn an additional sum, however small. The "Josh" letters to the *Enterprise* had awakened interest as to their author, and Orion had not failed to let "Josh's" identity be known. The result had been that here and there a coast paper had invited contributions and even suggested payment. A letter written by the Aurora miner at the end of July tells this part of the story:

My debts are greater than I thought for. . . . The fact is, I must have something to do, and that *shortly*, too. . . . Now write to the *Sacramento Union* folks, or to Marsh, and tell them that I will write as many letters a week as they want, for $10 a week. My board must be **paid**.

THE MINER

Tell them I have corresponded with the *New Orleans Crescent* and other papers—and the *Enterprise*.

If they want letters from here—who'll run from morning till night collecting material cheaper? I'll write a short letter twice a week, for the present, for the *Age*, for $5 per week. Now it has been a long time since I couldn't make my own living, and it shall be a long time before I loaf another year.

This all led to nothing, but about the same time the *Enterprise* assistant already mentioned spoke to Joseph T. Goodman, owner and editor of the paper, about adding "Josh" to their regular staff. "Joe" Goodman, a man of keen humor and literary perception, agreed that the author of the "Josh" letters might be useful to them. One of the sketches particularly appealed to him—a burlesque report of a Fourth of July oration.

"That is the kind of thing we want," he said. "Write to him, Barstow, and ask him if he wants to come up here."

Barstow wrote, offering twenty-five dollars a week —a tempting sum. This was at the end of July, 1862.

Yet the hard-pressed miner made no haste to accept the offer. To leave Aurora meant the surrender of all hope in the mines. the confession of another failure. He wrote Barstow, asking when he thought he might be needed. And at the same time, in a letter to Orion, he said:

I shall leave at midnight to-night, alone and on foot, for a walk of sixty or seventy miles through a totally uninhabited country. But do *you* write Barstow that I have left here for a week or so, and, in case he should want me, he must write me here, or let me know through you.

He had gone into the wilderness to fight out his battle alone, postponing the final moment of surrender—surrender that, had he known, only meant the beginning of victory. He was still undecided when he returned eight days later and wrote to his sister Pamela a letter in which there is no mention of newspaper prospects.

Just how and when the end came at last cannot be known; but one hot, dusty August afternoon, in Virginia City, a worn, travel-stained pilgrim dragged himself into the office of the *Territorial Enterprise*, then in its new building on C Street, and, loosening a heavy roll of blankets from his shoulder, dropped wearily into a chair. He wore a rusty slouch hat, no coat, a faded blue-flannel shirt, a navy revolver; his trousers were tucked into his boot-tops; a tangle of reddish-brown hair fell on his shoulders; a mass of tawny beard, dingy with alkali dust, dropped half-way to his waist.

Aurora lay one hundred and thirty miles from Virginia City. He had walked that distance, carrying his heavy load. Editor Goodman was absent at the moment, but the other proprietor, Dennis E. McCarthy, asked the caller to state his errand. The wanderer regarded him with a far-away look and said, absently, and with deliberation:

"My starboard leg seems to be unshipped. I'd

THE MINER

like about one hundred yards of line; I think I'm
falling to pieces." Then he added: "I want to see
Mr. Barstow or Mr. Goodman. My name is Clemens, and I've come to write for the paper."

It was the master of the world's widest estate
come to claim his kingdom.

XXI

THE TERRITORIAL ENTERPRISE

IN 1862 Virginia City, Nevada, was the most flourishing of mining towns. A half-crazy miner, named Comstock, had discovered there a vein of such richness that the "Comstock Lode" was presently glutting the mineral markets of the world. Comstock himself got very little out of it, but those who followed him made millions. Miners, speculators, adventurers swarmed in. Every one seemed to have money. The streets seethed with an eager, affluent, boisterous throng whose chief business seemed to be to spend the wealth that the earth was yielding in such a mighty stream.

Business of every kind boomed. Less than two years earlier, J. T. Goodman, a miner who was also a printer and a man of literary taste, had joined with another printer, Dennis McCarthy, and the two had managed to buy a struggling Virginia City paper, the *Territorial Enterprise*. But then came the high-tide of fortune. A year later the *Enterprise*, from a starving sheet in a leaky shanty, had become a large, handsome paper in a new building, and of such brilliant editorial management that it was the most widely considered journal on the Pacific coast.

Goodman was a fine, forceful writer, and he surrounded himself with able men. He was a young man, full of health and vigor, overflowing with the fresh spirit and humor of the West. Comstockers would always laugh at a joke, and Goodman was always willing to give it to them. The *Enterprise* was a newspaper, but it was willing to furnish entertainment even at the cost of news. William Wright, editorially next to Goodman, was a humorist of ability. His articles, signed Dan de Quille, were widely copied. R. M. Daggett (afterward United States Minister to Hawaii) was also an *Enterprise* man, and there were others of their sort.

Samuel Clemens fitted precisely into this group. He brought with him a new turn of thought and expression; he saw things with open eyes, and wrote of them in a fresh, wild way that Comstockers loved. He was allowed full freedom. Goodman suppressed nothing; his men could write as they chose. They were all young together—if they pleased themselves, they were pretty sure to please their readers. Often they wrote of one another—squibs and burlesques, which gratified the Comstock far more than mere news. It was just the school to produce Mark Twain.

The new arrival found acquaintance easy. The whole *Enterprise* force was like one family; proprietors, editor, and printers were social equals. Samuel Clemens immediately became "Sam" to his associates, just as De Quille was "Dan," and Goodman "Joe." Clemens was supposed to report city items, and did, in fact, do such work, which he found easy, for his pilot-memory made notes unnecessary.

He could gather items all day, and at night put down the day's budget well enough, at least, to delight his readers. When he was tired of facts, he would write amusing paragraphs, as often as not something about Dan, or a reporter on a rival paper. Dan and the others would reply, and the Comstock would laugh. Those were good old days.

Sometimes he wrote hoaxes. Once he told with great circumstance and detail of a petrified prehistoric man that had been found embedded in a rock in the desert, and how the coroner from Humboldt had traveled more than a hundred miles to hold an inquest over a man dead for centuries, and had refused to allow miners to blast the discovery from its position.

The sketch was really intended as a joke on the Humboldt coroner, but it was so convincingly written that most of the Coast papers took it seriously and reprinted it as the story of a genuine discovery. In time they awoke, and began to inquire as to who was the smart writer on the *Enterprise*.

Mark Twain did a number of such things, some of which are famous on the Coast to this day.

Clemens himself did not escape. Lamps were used in the *Enterprise* office, but he hated the care of a lamp, and worked evenings by the light of a candle. It was considered a great joke in the office to "hide Sam's candle" and hear him fume and rage, walking in a circle meantime—a habit acquired in the pilot-house—and scathingly denouncing the culprits. Eventually the office-boy, supposedly innocent, would bring another candle, and quiet would follow. Once the office force, including De Quille, McCarthy, and a printer named Stephen Gillis, of whom Clemens was very fond, bought a large imitation meerschaum pipe, had a German-silver plate set on it, properly engraved, and presented it to Samuel Clemens as genuine, in testimony of their great esteem. His reply to the presentation speech was so fine and full of feeling that the jokers felt ashamed of their trick. A few days later, when he discovered the deception, he was ready to destroy the lot of them. Then, in atonement, they gave him a real meerschaum. Such things kept the Comstock entertained.

There was a side to Samuel Clemens that, in those days, few of his associates saw. This was the poetic, the reflective side. Joseph Goodman, like Macfarlane in Cincinnati several years earlier, recognized this phase of his character and developed it. Often these two, dining or walking together, discussed the books and history they had read, quoted from poems that gave them pleasure. Clemens sometimes recited with great power the "Burial of Moses," whose noble phrasing and majestic imagery seemed to move him deeply. With eyes half closed and chin lifted, a lighted cigar between his fingers, he would lose himself in the music of the stately lines:

> By Nebo's lonely mountain,
>   On this side Jordan's wave,
> In a vale in the land of Moab
>   There lies a lonely grave.
> And no man knows that sepulcher,
>   And no man saw it e'er,
> For the angels of God upturned the sod,
>   And laid the dead man there.

That his own writing would be influenced by the simple grandeur of this poem we can hardly doubt. Indeed, it may have been to him a sort of literary touchstone, that in time would lead him to produce, as has been said, some of the purest English written by any modern author.

XXII

"MARK TWAIN"

IT was once when Goodman and Clemens were dining together that the latter asked to be allowed to report the proceedings of the coming legislature at Carson City. He knew nothing of such work, and Goodman hesitated. Then, remembering that Clemens would, at least, make his reports readable, whether they were parliamentary or not, he consented.

So, at the beginning of the year (1863), Samuel Clemens undertook a new and interesting course in the study of human nature—the political human nature of the frontier. There could have been no better school for him. His wit, his satire, his phrasing had full swing—his letters, almost from the beginning, were copied as choice reading up and down the Coast. He made curious blunders, at first, as to the proceedings, but his open confession of ignorance in the early letters made these blunders their chief charm. A young man named Gillespie, clerk of the House, coached him, and in return was christened "Young Jefferson's Manual," a title which he bore for many years.

A reporter named Rice, on a rival Virginia City

paper, the *Union*, also earned for himself a title through those early letters.

Rice concluded to poke fun at the *Enterprise* reports, pointing out their mistakes. But this was not wise. Clemens, in his next contribution, admitted that Rice's reports might be parliamentary enough, but declared his glittering technicalities were only to cover misstatements of fact. He vowed they were wholly untrustworthy, dubbed the author of them "The Unreliable," and never thereafter referred to him by any other term. Carson and the Comstock papers delighted in this foolery, and Rice became "The Unreliable" for life. There was no real feeling between Rice and Clemens. They were always the best of friends.

But now we arrive at the story of still another name, one of vastly greater importance than either of those mentioned, for it is the name chosen by Samuel Clemens for himself. In those days it was the fashion for a writer to have a pen-name, especially for his journalistic and humorous work. Clemens felt that his *Enterprise* letters, copied up and down the Coast, needed a mark of identity.

He gave the matter a good deal of thought. He wanted something brief and strong—something that would stick in the mind. It was just at this time that news came of the death of Capt. Isaiah Sellers, the old pilot who had signed himself "Mark Twain." Mark Twain! That was the name he wanted. It was not trivial. It had all the desired qualities. Captain Sellers would never need it again. It would do no harm to keep it alive—to give it a new meaning in a new land. Clemens took a trip from Carson up to Virginia City.

"Joe," he said to Goodman, "I want to sign my articles. I want to be identified to a wider audience."

"All right, Sam. What name do you want to use—Josh?"

"No, I want to sign them Mark Twain. It is an old river term, a leadsman's call, signifying two fathoms—twelve feet. It has a richness about it; it was always a pleasant sound for a pilot to hear on a dark night; it meant safe waters."

He did not mention that Captain Sellers had used and dropped the name. He was not proud of his part in that episode, and it was too recent for confession.

Goodman considered a moment. "Very well, Sam," he said, "that sounds like a good name."

A good name, indeed! Probably, if he had considered every combination of words in the language, he could not have found a better one. To-day we recognize it as the greatest *nom de plume* ever chosen, and, somehow, we cannot believe that the writer of *Tom Sawyer* and *Huck Finn* and *Roughing It* could have selected any other had he tried.

The name Mark Twain was first signed to a Carson letter, February 2, 1863, and after that to all of Samuel Clemens's work. The letters that had amused so many readers had taken on a new interest—the interest that goes with a name. It became immediately more than a pen-name. Clemens found he had attached a name to himself as well as to his letters. Everybody began to address him as Mark.

Within a few weeks he was no longer "Sam" or "Clemens," but Mark—Mark Twain. The Coast papers liked the sound of it. It began to mean something to their readers. By the end of that legislative session Samuel Clemens, as Mark Twain, had acquired out there on that breezy Western slope something resembling fame.

Curiously, he fails to mention any of this success in his letters home of that period. Indeed, he seldom refers to his work, but more often speaks of mining shares which he has accumulated, and their possible values. His letters are airy, full of the joy of life and of the wild doings of the frontier. Closing one of them, he says: "I have just heard five pistol-shots down the street. As such things are in my line, I will go and see about it."

And in a postscript, later, he adds:

5 A.M.—The pistol-shots did their work well. One man, a Jackson County Missourian, shot two of my friends (police officers) through the heart—both died within three minutes. The murderer's name is John Campbell.

The Comstock was a great school for Mark Twain, and in *Roughing It* he has left us a faithful picture of its long-vanished glory.

More than one national character came out of the Comstock school. Senator James G. Fair was one of them, and John Mackay, both miners with pick and shovel at first, though Mackay presently became a superintendent. Mark Twain one day laughingly offered to trade jobs with Mackay.

"No," Mackay said, "I can't trade. My business

is not worth as much as yours.   I have never swindled anybody, and I don't intend to begin now."

For both these men the future held splendid gifts: for Mackay vast wealth, for Mark Twain the world's applause, and neither would have long to wait.

XXIII

ARTEMUS WARD AND LITERARY SAN FRANCISCO

IT was about the end of 1863 that a new literary impulse came into Mark Twain's life. The gentle and lovable humorist Artemus Ward (Charles F. Browne) was that year lecturing in the West, and came to Virginia City. Ward had intended to stay only a few days, but the whirl of the Comstock fascinated him. He made the *Enterprise* office his headquarters and remained three weeks. He and Mark Twain became boon companions. Their humor was not unlike; they were kindred spirits, together almost constantly. Ward was then at the summit of his fame, and gave the younger man the highest encouragement, prophesying great things for his work. Clemens, on his side, was stirred, perhaps for the first time, with a real literary ambition, and the thought that he, too, might win a place of honor. He promised Ward that he would send work to the Eastern papers.

On Christmas Eve, Ward gave a dinner to the *Enterprise* staff, at Chaumond's, a fine French restaurant of that day. When refreshments came, Artemus lifted his glass, and said:

"I give you Upper Canada."

The company rose and drank the toast in serious silence. Then Mr. Goodman said:

"Of course, Artemus, it's all right, but why did you give us Upper Canada?"

"Because I don't want it myself," said Ward, gravely.

What would one not give to have listened to the talk of that evening! Mark Twain's power had awakened; Artemus Ward was in his prime. They were giants of a race that became extinct when Mark Twain died.

Goodman remained rather quiet during the evening. Ward had appointed him to order the dinner, and he had attended to this duty without mingling much in the conversation. When Ward asked him why he did not join the banter, he said:

"I am preparing a joke, Artemus, but I am keeping it for the present."

At a late hour Ward finally called for the bill. It was two hundred and thirty-seven dollars.

"What!" exclaimed Artemus.

"That's my joke," said Goodman.

"But I was only exclaiming because it was not twice as much," laughed Ward, laying the money on the table.

Ward remained through the holidays, and later wrote back an affectionate letter to Mark Twain.

"I shall always remember Virginia as a bright spot in my existence," he said, "as all others must, or rather, cannot be, as it were."

With Artemus Ward's encouragement, Mark Twain now began sending work eastward. The New

York *Sunday Mercury* published one, possibly more, of his sketches, but they were not in his best vein, and made little impression. He may have been too busy for outside work, for the legislative session of 1864 was just beginning. Furthermore, he had been chosen governor of the "Third House," a mock legislature, organized for one session, to be held as a church benefit. The "governor" was to deliver a message, which meant that he was to burlesque from the platform all public officials and personages, from the real governor down.

With the exception of a short talk he had once given at a printer's dinner in Keokuk, it was Mark Twain's first appearance as a speaker, and the beginning of a lifelong series of triumphs on the platform. The building was packed—the aisles full. The audience was ready for fun, and he gave it to them. Nobody escaped ridicule; from beginning to end the house was a storm of laughter and applause.

Not a word of this first address of Mark Twain's has been preserved, but those who heard it always spoke of it as the greatest effort of his life, as to them it seemed, no doubt.

For his Third House address, Clemens was presented with a gold watch, inscribed "To Governor Mark Twain." Everywhere, now, he was pointed out as a distinguished figure, and his quaint remarks were quoted. Few of these sayings are remembered to-day, though occasionally one is still unforgotten. At a party one night, being urged to make a conundrum, he said:

"Well, why am I like the Pacific Ocean?"

Several guesses were made, but he shook his head. Some one said:

"We give it up. Tell us, Mark, why *are* you like the Pacific Ocean?"

"I—don't—know," he drawled. "I was just—asking—for information."

The governor of Nevada was generally absent, and Orion Clemens was executive head of the territory. His wife, who had joined him in Carson City, was social head of the little capital, and Brother Sam, with his new distinction and now once more something of a dandy in dress, was society's chief ornament—a great change, certainly, from the early months of his arrival less than three years before.

It was near the end of May, 1864, when Mark Twain left Nevada for San Francisco. The immediate cause of his going was a duel—a duel elaborately arranged between Mark Twain and the editor of a rival paper, but never fought. In fact, it was mainly a burlesque affair throughout, chiefly concocted by that inveterate joker, Steve Gillis, already mentioned in connection with the pipe incident. The new dueling law, however, did not distinguish between real and mock affrays, and the prospect of being served with a summons made a good excuse for Clemens and Gillis to go to San Francisco, which had long attracted them. They were great friends, these two, and presently were living together and working on the same paper, the *Morning Call*, Clemens as a reporter and Gillis as a compositor.

Gillis, with his tendency to mischief, was a constant exasperation to his room-mate, who, goaded by some new torture, would sometimes denounce him in feverish terms. Yet they were never anything but the closest friends.

Mark Twain did not find happiness in his new position on the *Call*. There was less freedom and more drudgery than he had known on the *Enterprise*. His day was spent around the police court, attending fires, weddings, and funerals, with brief glimpses of the theaters at night.

Once he wrote: "It was fearful drudgery—soulless drudgery—and almost destitute of interest. It was an awful slavery for a lazy man."

It must have been so. There was little chance for original work. He had become just a part of a news machine. He saw many public abuses that he wished to expose, but the policy of the paper opposed him. Once, however, he found a policeman asleep on his beat. Going to a near-by vegetable stall, he borrowed a large cabbage-leaf, came back, and stood over the sleeper, gently fanning him. He knew the paper would not publish the policeman's negligence, but he could advertise it in his own way. A large crowd soon collected, much amused. When he thought the audience large enough, he went away. Next day the joke was all over the city.

He grew indifferent to the *Call* work, and, when an assistant was allowed him to do part of the running for items, it was clear to everybody that presently the assistant would be able to do it all.

But there was a pleasant and profitable side to the

San Francisco life. There were real literary people there—among them a young man, with rooms upstairs in the *Call* office, Francis Bret Harte, editor of the *Californian*, a new literary weekly which Charles Henry Webb had recently founded. Bret Harte was not yet famous, but his gifts were recognized on the Pacific slope, especially by the *Era* group of writers, the *Golden Era* being a literary monthly of considerable distinction. Joaquin Miller recalls, from his diary of that period, having seen Prentice Mulford, Bret Harte, Charles Warren Stoddard, Mark Twain, Artemus Ward, and others, all assembled there at one time—a remarkable group, certainly, to be dropped down behind the Sierras so long ago. They were a hopeful, happy lot, and sometimes received five dollars for an article, which, of course, seemed a good deal more precious than a much larger sum earned in another way.

Mark Twain had contributed to the *Era* while still in Virginia City, and now, with Bret Harte, was ranked as a leader of the group. The two were much together, and when Harte became editor of the *Californian* he engaged Clemens as a regular contributor at the very fancy rate of twelve dollars an article. Some of the brief chapters included to-day in *Sketches New and Old* were done at this time. They have humor, but are not equal to his later work, and beyond the Pacific slope they seem to have attracted little attention.

In *Roughing It* the author tells us how he finally was dismissed from the *Call* for general incompetency, and presently found himself in the depths of hard luck, debt, and poverty. But this is only his old habit of making a story on himself sound as uncomplimentary as possible. The true version is that the *Call* publisher and Mark Twain had a friendly talk and decided that it was better for both to break off the connection. Almost immediately he arranged to write a daily San Francisco letter for the *Enterprise*, for which he received thirty dollars a week. This, with his earnings from the *Californian*, made his total return larger than before. Very likely he was hard up from time to time—literary men are often that—but that he was ever in abject poverty, as he would have us believe, is just a good story and not history.

XXIV

THE DISCOVERY OF "THE JUMPING FROG"

MARK TWAIN'S daily letters to the *Enterprise* stirred up trouble for him in San Francisco. He was free, now, to write what he chose, and he attacked the corrupt police management with such fierceness that, when copies of the *Enterprise* got back to San Francisco, they started a commotion at the city hall. Then Mark Twain let himself go more vigorously than ever. He sent letters to the *Enterprise* that made even the printers afraid. Goodman, however, was fearless, and let them go in, word for word. The libel suit which the San Francisco chief of police brought against the *Enterprise* advertised the paper amazingly.

But now came what at the time seemed an unfortunate circumstance. Steve Gillis, always a fearless defender of the weak, one night rushed to the assistance of two young fellows who had been set upon by three roughs. Gillis, though small of stature, was a terrific combatant, and he presently put two of the assailants to flight and had the other ready for the hospital. Next day it turned out that the roughs were henchmen of the police, and Gillis was arrested.

Clemens went his bail, and advised Steve to go down to Virginia City until the storm blew over.

But it did not blow over for Mark Twain. The police department was only too glad to have a chance at the author of the fierce *Enterprise* letters, and promptly issued a summons for him, with an execution against his personal effects. If James N. Gillis, brother of Steve, had not happened along just then and spirited Mark Twain away to his mining-camp in the Tuolumne Hills, the beautiful gold watch given to the governor of the Third House might have been sacrificed in the cause of friendship.

As it was, he found himself presently in the far and peaceful seclusion of that land which Bret Harte would one day make famous with his tales of *Roaring Camp* and *Sandy Bar*. Jim Gillis was, in fact, the Truthful James of Bret Harte, and his cabin on Jackass Hill had been the retreat of Harte and many another literary wayfarer who had wandered there for rest and refreshment and peace. It was said the sick were made well, and the well made better, in Jim Gillis's cabin. There were plenty of books and a variety of out-of-door recreation. One could mine there if he chose. Jim would furnish the visiting author with a promising claim, and teach him to follow the little fan-like drift of gold specks to the pocket of treasure somewhere up the hillside.

Gillis himself had literary ability, though he never wrote. He told his stories, and with his back to the open fire would weave the most amazing tales, invented as he went along. His stories were generally wonderful adventures that had happened to his

faithful companion, Stoker; and Stoker never de-
nied them, but would smoke and look into the fire,
smiling a little sometimes, but never saying a word.
A number of the tales later used by Mark Twain
were first told by Jim Gillis in the cabin on Jackass
Hill. "Dick Baker's Cat" was one of these, the
jay-bird and acorn story in *A Tramp Abroad* was
another. Mark Twain had little to add to these
stories.

"They are not mine, they are Jim's," he said,
once; "but I never could get them to sound like
Jim—they were never as good as his."

It was early in December, 1864, when Mark Twain
arrived at the humble retreat, built of logs under a
great live-oak tree, and surrounded by a stretch of
blue-grass. A younger Gillis boy was there at the
time, and also, of course, Dick Stoker and his cat, Tom
Quartz, which every reader of *Roughing It* knows.

It was the rainy season, but on pleasant days
they all went pocket-mining, and, in January, Mark
Twain, Gillis, and Stoker crossed over into Calaveras County and began work near Angel's Camp, a
place well known to readers of Bret Harte. They
put up at a poor hotel in Angel's, and on good days
worked pretty faithfully. But it was generally raining, and the food was poor.

In his note-book, still preserved, Mark Twain
wrote: "January 27 (1865).—Same old diet—same
old weather—went out to the pocket-claim—had to
rush back."

So they spent a good deal of their time around the
rusty stove in the dilapidated tavern at Angel's

Camp. It seemed a profitless thing to do, but few experiences were profitless to Mark Twain, and certainly this one was not.

At this barren mining hotel there happened to be a former Illinois River pilot named Ben Coon, a solemn, sleepy person, who dozed by the stove or told slow, pointless stories to any one who would listen. Not many would stay to hear him, but Jim Gillis and Mark Twain found him a delight. They would let him wander on in his dull way for hours, and saw a vast humor in a man to whom all tales, however trivial or absurd, were serious history.

At last, one dreary afternoon, he told them about a frog—a frog that had belonged to a man named Coleman, who had trained it to jump, and how the trained frog had failed to win a wager because the owner of the rival frog had slyly loaded the trained jumper with shot. It was not a new story in the camps, but Ben Coon made a long tale of it, and it happened that neither Clemens nor Gillis had heard it before. They thought it amusing, and his solemn way of telling it still more so.

"I don't see no p'ints about that frog that's better than any other frog," became a catch phrase among the mining partners; and, "I 'ain't got no frog, but if I had a frog, I'd bet you."

Out on the claim, Clemens, watching Gillis and Stoker anxiously washing, would say, "I don't see no p'ints about that pan o' dirt that's any better than any other pan o' dirt." And so they kept the tale going. In his note-book Mark Twain made a brief memorandum of the story for possible use.

The mining was rather hopeless work. The constant and heavy rains were disheartening. Clemens hated it, and even when, one afternoon, traces of a pocket began to appear, he rebelled as the usual chill downpour set in.

"Jim," he said, "let's go home; we'll *freeze* here."

Gillis, as usual, was washing, and Clemens carrying the water. Gillis, seeing the gold "color" improving with every pan, wanted to go on washing and climbing toward the precious pocket, regardless of wet and cold. Clemens, shivering and disgusted, vowed that each pail of water would be his last. His teeth were chattering, and he was wet through. Finally he said:

"Jim, I won't carry any more water. This work is too disagreeable."

Gillis had just taken out a panful of dirt.

"Bring one more pail, Sam," he begged.

"Jim, I won't do it. I'm—freezing."

"Just one more pail, Sam!" Jim pleaded.

"No, sir; not a drop—not if I knew there was a million dollars in that pan."

Gillis tore out a page of his note-book and hastily posted a thirty-day-claim notice by the pan of dirt. Then they set out for Angel's Camp, never to return. It kept on raining, and a letter came from Steve Gillis, saying he had settled all the trouble in San Francisco. Clemens decided to return, and the miners left Angel's without visiting their claim again.

Meantime the rain had washed away the top of the pan of dirt they had left standing on the hillside, exposing a handful of nuggets, pure gold. Two strangers, Austrians, happening along, gathered it up and, seeing the claim notice posted by Jim Gillis, sat down to wait until it expired. They did not mind the rain—not under the circumstances—and the moment the thirty days were up they followed the lead a few pans farther and took out, some say ten, some say twenty, thousand dollars. In either case it was a good pocket that Mark Twain missed by one pail of water. Still, without knowing it, he had carried away in his note-book a single nugget of far greater value—the story of "The Jumping Frog."

He did not write it, however, immediately upon his return to San Francisco. He went back to his *Enterprise* letters and contributed some sketches to the *Californian*. Perhaps he thought the frog story too mild in humor for the slope. By and by he wrote it, and by request sent it to Artemus Ward to be used in a book that Ward was about to issue. It arrived too late, and the publisher handed it to the editor of the *Saturday Press*, Henry Clapp, saying:

"Here, Clapp, is something you can use in your paper."

The *Press* was struggling, and was glad to get a story so easily. "Jim Smiley and his Jumping Frog" appeared in the issue of November 18, 1865, and was at once copied and quoted far and near. It carried the name of Mark Twain across the mountains and the prairies of the Middle West; it bore it up and down the Atlantic slope. Some one said, then or later, that Mark Twain leaped into fame on the back of a jumping frog.

"THE JUMPING FROG"

Curiously, this did not at first please the author. He thought the tale poor. To his mother he wrote:

I do not know what to write; my life is so uneventful. I wish I was back there piloting up and down the river again. Verily, all is vanity and little worth—save piloting.

To think that, after writing many an article a man might be excused for thinking tolerably good, those New York people should single out a villainous backwoods sketch to compliment me on!—"Jim Smiley and his Jumping Frog"—a squib which would never have been written but to please Artemus Ward.

However, somewhat later he changed his mind considerably, especially when he heard that James Russell Lowell had pronounced the story the finest piece of humorous writing yet produced in America.

XXV

HAWAII AND ANSON BURLINGAME

MARK TWAIN remained about a year in San Francisco after his return from the Gillis cabin and Angel's Camp, adding to his prestige along the Coast rather than to his national reputation. Then, in the spring of 1866 he was commissioned by the *Sacramento Union* to write a series of letters that would report the life, trade, agriculture, and general aspects of the Hawaiian group. He sailed in March, and his four months in those delectable islands remained always to him a golden memory—an experience which he hoped some day to repeat. He was young and eager for adventure then, and he went everywhere—horseback and afoot—saw everything, did everything, and wrote of it all for his paper. His letters to the *Union* were widely read and quoted, and, though not especially literary, added much to his journalistic standing. He was a great sight-seer in those days, and a persevering one. No discomfort or risk discouraged him. Once, with a single daring companion, he crossed the burning floor of the mighty crater of Kilauea, racing across the burning lava, leaping wide and bottomless crevices where a misstep would have meant death. His open-air life on the river and in the mining-camps had nerved and hardened him for adventure. He was thirty years old and in his physical prime. His mental growth had been slower, but it was sure, and it would seem always to have had the right guidance at the right time.

Clemens had been in the islands three months when one day Anson Burlingame arrived there, *en route* to his post as minister to China. With him was his son Edward, a boy of eighteen, and General Van Valkenburg, minister to Japan. Young Burlingame had read about Jim Smiley's jumping frog and, learning that the author was in Honolulu, but ill after a long trip inland, sent word that the party would call on him next morning. But Mark Twain felt that he could not accept this honor, and, crawling out of bed, shaved himself and drove to the home of the American minister, where the party was staying. He made a great impression with the diplomats. It was an occasion of good stories and much laughter. On leaving, General Van Valkenburg said to him:

"California is proud of Mark Twain, and some day the American people will be, too, no doubt." Which was certainly a good prophecy.

It was only a few days later that the diplomats rendered him a great service. Report had come of the arrival at Sanpahoe of an open boat containing fifteen starving men, who had been buffeting a stormy sea for forty-three days—sailors from the missing ship *Hornet* of New York, which, it appeared, had been burned at sea. Presently eleven of the rescued men were brought to Honolulu and placed in the hospital.

Mark Twain recognized the great importance as news of this event. It would be a splendid beat if he could interview the castaways and be the first to get their story in his paper. There was no cable, but a vessel was sailing for San Francisco next morning. It seemed the opportunity of a lifetime, but he was now bedridden and could scarcely move.

Then suddenly appeared in his room Anson Burlingame and his party, and, almost before Mark Twain realized what was happening, he was on a cot and, escorted by the heads of two legations, was on his way to the hospital to get the precious interview. Once there, Anson Burlingame, with his gentle manner and courtly presence, drew from those enfeebled castaways all the story of the burning of the vessel, followed by the long privation and struggle that had lasted through forty-three fearful days and across four thousand miles of stormy sea. All that Mark Twain had to do was to listen and make notes. That night he wrote against time, and next morning, just as the vessel was drifting from the dock, a strong hand flung his bulky manuscript aboard and his great beat was sure. The three-column story, published in the *Sacramento Union* of July 9, gave the public the first detailed history of the great disaster. The telegraph carried it everywhere, and it was featured as a sensation.

Mark Twain and the Burlingame party were much together during the rest of their stay in Hawaii, and Samuel Clemens never ceased to love and honor the memory of Anson Burlingame. It was proper that he should do so, for he owed him much—far more than has already been told.

Anson Burlingame one day said to him: "You have great ability; I believe you have genius. What you need now is the refinement of association. Seek companionship among men of superior intellect and character. Refine yourself and your work. Never affiliate with inferiors; always climb."

This, coming to him from a man of Burlingame's character and position, was like a gospel from some divine source. Clemens never forgot the advice. It gave him courage, new hope, new resolve, new ideals.

Burlingame came often to the hotel, and they discussed plans for Mark Twain's future. The diplomat invited the journalist to visit him in China:

"Come to Pekin," he said, "and make my house your home."

Young Burlingame also came, when the patient became convalescent, and suggested walks. Once, when Clemens hesitated, the young man said:

"But there is a scriptural command for you to go."

"If you can quote one, I'll obey," said Clemens.

"Very well; the Bible says: 'If any man require thee to walk a mile, go with him Twain.'"

The walk was taken.

Mark Twain returned to California at the end of July, and went down to Sacramento. It was agreed that a special bill should be made for the *Hornet* report.

"How much do you think it ought to be, Mark?" asked one of the proprietors.

Clemens said: "Oh, I'm a modest man; I don't want the whole *Union* office; call it a hundred dollars a column."

There was a general laugh. The bill was made out at that figure, and he took it to the office for payment.

"The cashier didn't faint," he wrote many years later, "but he came rather near it. He sent for the proprietors, and they only laughed in their jolly fashion, and said it was robbery, but 'no matter, pay it. It's all right.' The best men that ever owned a paper." [1]

[1] "My Début as a Literary Person."

XXVI

MARK TWAIN, LECTURER

IN spite of the success of his Sandwich Island letters, Samuel Clemens felt, on his return to San Francisco, that his future was not bright. He was not a good, all-round newspaper man—he was special correspondent and sketch-writer, out of a job.

He had a number of plans, but they did not promise much. One idea was to make a book from his Hawaiian material. Another was to write magazine articles, beginning with one on the *Hornet* disaster. He did, in fact, write the *Hornet* article, and its prompt acceptance by *Harper's Magazine* delighted him, for it seemed a start in the right direction. A third plan was to lecture on the islands.

This prospect frightened him. He had succeeded in his "Third House" address of two years before, but then he had lectured without charge and for a church benefit. This would be a different matter.

One of the proprietors of a San Francisco paper, Col. John McComb, of the *Alta California*, was strong in his approval of the lecture idea.

"Do it, by all means," he said. "Take the largest house in the city, and charge a dollar a ticket."

Without waiting until his fright came back. Mark

153

Twain hurried to the manager of the Academy of Music, and engaged it for a lecture to be given October 2d (1866), and sat down and wrote his announcement. He began by stating what he would speak upon, and ended with a few absurdities, such as:

A SPLENDID ORCHESTRA

is in town, but has not been engaged.

Also

A DEN OF FEROCIOUS WILD BEASTS

will be on exhibition in the next block.

A GRAND TORCHLIGHT PROCESSION

may be expected; in fact, the public are privileged to expect whatever they please.

Doors open at 7 o'clock. The trouble to begin at 8 o'clock.

Mark Twain was well known in San Francisco, and was pretty sure to have a good house. But he did not realize this, and, as the evening approached, his dread of failure increased. Arriving at the theater, he entered by the stage door, half expecting to find the place empty. Then, suddenly, he became more frightened than ever; peering from the wings, he saw that the house was jammed—packed from the footlights to the walls! Terrified, his knees shaking, his tongue dry, he managed to emerge, and was greeted with a roar, a crash of applause that nearly finished him. Only for an instant—reaction followed; these people were his friends, and he was talking to them. He forgot to be afraid, and, as the applause came in great billows that rose ever higher, he felt himself borne with it as on a tide of happiness and success. His evening, from beginning to end, was a complete triumph. Friends declared that for descriptive eloquence, humor, and real entertainment nothing like his address had ever been delivered. The morning papers were enthusiastic.

Mark Twain no longer hesitated as to what he should do now. He would lecture. The book idea no longer attracted him; the appearance of the *Hornet* article, signed, through a printer's error, "Mark Swain," cooled his desire to be a magazine contributor. No matter—lecturing was the thing. Dennis McCarthy, who had sold his interest in the *Enterprise*, was in San Francisco. Clemens engaged this honest, happy-hearted Irishman as manager, and the two toured California and Nevada with continuous success.

Those who remember Mark Twain as a lecturer in that early day say that on entering he would lounge loosely across the platform, his manuscript—written on wrapping-paper and carried under his arm—looking like a ruffled hen. His delivery they recall as being even more quaint and drawling than in later life. Once, when his lecture was over, an old man came up to him and said:

"Be them your natural tones of eloquence?"

In those days it was thought proper that a lecturer should be introduced, and Clemens himself used to tell of being presented by an old miner, who said:

"Ladies and gentlemen, I know only two things

about this man: the first is that he's never been in jail, and the second is, I don't know why."

When he reached Virginia, his old friend Goodman said, "Sam, you don't need anybody to introduce you," and he suggested a novel plan. That night, when the curtain rose, it showed Mark Twain seated at a piano, playing and singing, as if still cub pilot on the *John J. Roe:*

> "Had an old horse whose name was Methusalem,
> Took him down and sold him in Jerusalem,
>   A long time ago."

Pretending to be surprised and startled at the burst of applause, he sprang up and began to talk. How the audience enjoyed it!

Mark Twain continued his lecture tour into December, and then, on the 15th of that month, sailed by way of the Isthmus of Panama for New York. He had made some money, and was going home to see his people. He had planned to make a trip around the world later, contributing a series of letters to the *Alta California*, lecturing where opportunity afforded. He had been on the Coast five and a half years, and to his professions of printing and piloting had added three others— mining, journalism, and lecturing. Also, he had acquired a measure of fame. He could come back to his people with a good account of his absence and a good heart for the future.

But it seems now only a chance that he arrived at all. Crossing the Isthmus, he embarked for New York on what proved to be a cholera ship. For a time there were one or more funerals daily. An entry in his diary says:

Since the last two hours all laughter, all levity, has ceased on the ship—a settled gloom is upon the faces of the passengers.

But the winter air of the North checked the contagion, and there were no new cases when New York City was reached.

Clemens remained but a short time in New York, and was presently in St. Louis with his mother and sister. They thought he looked old, but he had not changed in manner, and the gay banter between mother and son was soon as lively as ever. He was thirty-one now, and she sixty-four, but the years had made little difference. She petted him, joked with him, and scolded him. In turn, he petted and comforted and teased her. She decided he was the same Sam and always would be—a true prophecy.

He visited Hannibal and lectured there, receiving an ovation that would have satisfied even Tom Sawyer. In Keokuk he lectured again, then returned to St. Louis to plan his trip around the world.

He was not to make a trip around the world, however—not then. In St. Louis he saw the notice of the great *Quaker City* Holy Land excursion—the first excursion of the kind ever planned—and was greatly taken with the idea. Impulsive as always, he wrote at once to the *Alta California*, proposing that they send him as their correspondent on this grand ocean picnic. The cost of passage was $1,200, and the *Alta* hesitated, but Colonel McComb, already mentioned, assured his associates that the investment would be sound. The *Alta* wrote, accepting Mark Twain's proposal, and agreed to pay twenty dollars each for letters. Clemens hurried to New York to secure a berth, fearing the passenger-list might be full. Furthermore, with no one of distinction to vouch for him, according to advertised requirements, he was not sure of being accepted. Arriving in New York, he learned from an *Alta* representative that passage had already been reserved for him, but he still doubted his acceptance as one of the distinguished advertised company. His mind was presently relieved on this point. Waiting his turn at the booking-desk, he heard a newspaper man inquire:

"What notables are going?"

A clerk, with evident pride, rattled off the names: "Lieutenant - General Sherman, Henry Ward Beecher, and Mark Twain; also, probably, General Banks."

It was very pleasant to hear the clerk say that. Not only was he accepted, but billed as an attraction.

The *Quaker City* would not sail for two months yet, and during the period of waiting Mark Twain was far from idle. He wrote New York letters to the *Alta*, and he embarked in two rather important ventures—he published his first book and he delivered a lecture in New York City.

Both these undertakings were planned and carried out by friends from the Coast. Charles Henry Webb, who had given up his magazine to come East, had collected *The Celebrated Jumping Frog of Calaveras County, and Other Sketches*, and, after trying in vain to find a publisher for them, brought them out himself, on the 1st of May, 1867.[1] It seems curious now that any publisher should have declined the little volume, for the sketches, especially the frog story, had been successful, and there was little enough good American humor in print. However, publishing was a matter not lightly undertaken in those days.

Mark Twain seems to have been rather pleased with the appearance of his first book. To Bret Harte he wrote:

The book is out and is handsome. It is full of . . . errors, . . . but be a friend and say nothing about those things. When my hurry is over, I will send you a copy to pizen the children with.

The little cloth-and-gold volume, so valued by book-collectors to-day, contained the frog story and twenty-six other sketches, some of which are still preserved in Mark Twain's collected works. Most of them were not Mark Twain's best literature, but they were fresh and readable and suited the taste of that period. The book sold very well, and, while it did not bring either great fame or fortune to its author, it was by no means a failure.

The "hurry" mentioned in Mark Twain's letter to Bret Harte related to his second venture—that is to say, his New York lecture, an enterprise managed by an old Comstock friend, Frank Fuller, ex-Governor of Utah. Fuller, always a sanguine and

[1] The printing was done by John A. Gray & Green, the firm for which the boy Sam Clemens had set type thirteen years before.

energetic person, had proposed the lecture idea as soon as Mark Twain arrived in New York. Clemens shook his head.

"I have no reputation with the general public here," he said. "We couldn't get a baker's dozen to hear me."

But Fuller insisted, and eventually engaged the largest hall in New York, the Cooper Union. Full of enthusiasm and excitement, he plunged into the business of announcing and advertising his attraction, and inventing schemes for the sale of seats. Clemens caught Fuller's enthusiasm by spells, but between times he was deeply depressed. Fuller had got up a lot of tiny hand-bills, and had arranged to hang bunches of these in the horse-cars. The little dangling clusters fascinated Clemens, and he rode about to see if anybody else noticed them. Finally, after a long time, a passenger pulled off one of the bills and glanced at it. A man with him asked:

"Who's Mark Twain?"

"Goodness knows! I don't."

The lecturer could not ride any farther. He hunted up his patron.

"Fuller," he groaned, "there isn't a sign—a ripple of interest."

Fuller assured him that things were "working underneath," and would be all right. But Clemens wrote home: "Everything looks shady, at least, if not dark." And he added that, after hiring the largest house in New York, he must play against Schuyler Colfax, Ristori, and a double troupe of Japanese jugglers, at other places of amusement.

MARK TWAIN, LECTURER

When the evening of the lecture approached and only a few tickets had been sold, the lecturer was desperate.

"Fuller," he said, "there'll be nobody in Cooper Union that night but you and me. I am on the verge of suicide. I would commit suicide if I had the pluck and the outfit. You must paper the house, Fuller. You must send out a flood of complimentaries!"

"Very well," said Fuller. "What we want this time is reputation, anyway—money is secondary. I'll put you before the choicest and most intelligent audience that was ever gathered in New York City."

Fuller immediately sent out complimentary tickets to the school-teachers of New York and Brooklyn —a general invitation to come and hear Mark Twain's great lecture on the Sandwich Islands. There was nothing to do after that but wait results.

Mark Twain had lost faith—he did not believe anybody in New York would come to hear him even on a free ticket. When the night arrived, he drove with Fuller to the Cooper Union half an hour before the lecture was to begin. Forty years later he said:

"I couldn't keep away. I wanted to see that vast Mammoth Cave, and die. But when we got near the building, I saw all the streets were blocked with people and that traffic had stopped. I couldn't believe that these people were trying to get to the Cooper Institute—but they were; and when I got to the stage, at last, the house was jammed full— packed; there wasn't room enough left for a child.

"I was happy and I was excited beyond expression. I poured the Sandwich Islands out on those people, and they laughed and shouted to my entire content. For an hour and fifteen minutes I was in paradise."

So in its way this venture was a success. It brought Mark Twain a good deal of a reputation in New York, even if no financial profit, though, in spite of the flood of complimentaries, there was a cash return of something like three hundred dollars. This went a good way toward paying the expenses, while Fuller, in his royal way, insisted on making up the deficit, declaring he had been paid for everything in the fun and joy of the game.

"Mark," he said, "it's all right. The fortune didn't come, but it will. The fame has arrived; with this lecture and your book just out, you are going to be the most-talked-of man in the country. Your letters to the *Alta* and the *Tribune* will get the widest reception of any letters of travel ever written."

XXVII

AN INNOCENT ABROAD, AND HOME AGAIN

IT was early in May—the 6th—that Mark Twain
had delivered his Cooper Union lecture, and a
month later, June 8, 1867, he sailed on the *Quaker
City*, with some sixty-six other "pilgrims," on the
great Holy Land excursion, the story of which has
been so fully and faithfully told in *The Innocents
Abroad*.

What a wonderful thing it must have seemed in
that time for a party of excursionists to have a ship
all to themselves to go a-gipsying in from port to port
of antiquity and romance! The advertised celeb-
rities did not go, none of them but Mark Twain, but
no one minded, presently, for Mark Twain's sayings
and stories kept the company sufficiently entertained, and sometimes he would read aloud to his
fellow-passengers from the newspaper letters he was
writing, and invite comment and criticism. That
was entertainment for them, and it was good for
him, for it gave him an immediate audience, always
inspiring to an author. Furthermore, the comments
offered were often of the greatest value, especially
suggestions from one Mrs. Fairbanks, of Cleveland,
a middle-aged, cultured woman, herself a corre-

spondent for her husband's paper, the *Herald*. It requires not many days for acquaintances to form on shipboard, and in due time a little group gathered regularly each afternoon to hear Mark Twain read what he had written of their day's doings, though some of it he destroyed later because Mrs. Fairbanks thought it not his best.

All of the "pilgrims" mentioned in *The Innocents Abroad* were real persons. "Dan" was Dan Slote, Mark Twain's room-mate; the Doctor who confused the guides was Dr. A. Reeves Jackson, of Chicago; the poet Lariat was Bloodgood H. Cutter, an eccentric from Long Island; "Jack" was Jack Van Nostrand, of New Jersey; and "Moult" and "Blücher" and "Charlie" were likewise real, the last named being Charles J. Langdon, of Elmira, N. Y., a boy of eighteen, whose sister would one day become Mark Twain's wife.

It has been said that Mark Twain first met Olivia Langdon on the *Quaker City*, but this is not quite true; he met only her picture—the original was not on that ship. Charlie Langdon, boy fashion, made a sort of hero of the brilliant man called Mark Twain, and one day in the Bay of Smyrna invited him to his cabin and exhibited his treasures, among them a dainty miniature of a sister at home, Olivia, a sweet, delicate creature whom the boy worshiped.

Samuel Clemens gazed long at the exquisite portrait and spoke of it reverently, for in the sweet face he seemed to find something spiritual. Often after that he came to young Langdon's cabin to look at the pictured countenance, in his heart dreaming of a day when he might learn to know its owner.

We need not follow in detail here the travels of the "pilgrims" and their adventures. Most of them have been fully set down in *The Innocents Abroad*, and with not much elaboration, for plenty of amusing things were happening on a trip of that kind, and Mark Twain's old note-books are full of the real incidents that we find changed but little in the book. If the adventures of Jack, Dan, and the Doctor are embroidered here and there, the truth is always there, too.

Yet the old note-books have a very intimate interest of their own. It is curious to be looking through them to-day, trying to realize that those penciled memoranda were the fresh first impressions that would presently grow into the world's most delightful book of travel; that they were set down in the very midst of that historic little company that frolicked through Italy and climbed wearily the arid Syrian hills.

It required five months for the *Quaker City* to make the circuit of the Mediterranean and return to New York. Mark Twain in that time contributed fifty two or three letters to the *Alta California* and six to the New York *Tribune*, or an average of nearly three a week—a vast amount of labor to be done in the midst of sight-seeing. And what letters of travel they were! The most remarkable that had been written up to that time. Vivid, fearless, full of fresh color, humor, poetry, they came as a revelation to a public weary of the tiresome descriptive drivel of that day. They preached a new gospel in travel literature—the gospel of seeing honestly and speaking frankly—a gospel that Mark Twain would continue to preach during the rest of his career.

Furthermore, the letters showed a great literary growth in their author. No doubt the cultivated associations of the ship, the afternoon reading aloud of his work, and Mrs. Fairbanks's advice had much to do with this. But we may believe, also, that the author's close study of the King James version of the Old Testament during the weeks of travel through Palestine exerted a powerful influence upon his style. The man who had recited "The Burial of Moses" to Joe Goodman, with so much feeling, could not fail to be mastered by the simple yet stately Bible phrase and imagery. Many of the fine descriptive passages in *The Innocents Abroad* have something almost Biblical in their phrasing. The writer of this memoir heard in childhood *The Innocents Abroad* read aloud, and has never forgotten the poetic spell that fell upon him as he listened to a paragraph written of Tangier:

Here is a crumbled wall that was old when Columbus discovered America; old when Peter the Hermit roused the knightly men of the Middle Ages to arm for the first Crusade; old when Charlemagne and his paladins beleaguered enchanted castles and battled with giants and genii in the fabled days of the olden time; old when Christ and His disciples walked the earth; stood where it stands to-day when the lips of Memnon were vocal and men bought and sold in the streets of ancient Thebes.

AN INNOCENT ABROAD

Mark Twain returned to America to find himself, if not famous, at least in very high repute. The *Alta* and *Tribune* letters had carried his name to every corner of his native land. He was in demand now. To his mother he wrote:

I have eighteen offers to lecture, at $100 each, in various parts of the Union—have declined them all. . . . Belong on the *Tribune* staff and shall write occasionally. Am offered the same berth to-day on the *Herald*, by letter.

He was in Washington at this time, having remained in New York but one day. He had accepted a secretaryship from Senator Stewart of Nevada, but this arrangement was a brief one. He required fuller freedom for his Washington correspondence and general literary undertakings.

He had been in Washington but a few days when he received a letter that meant more to him than he could possibly have dreamed at the moment. It was from Elisha Bliss, Jr., manager of the American Publishing Company, of Hartford, Connecticut, and it suggested gathering the Mediterranean travel-letters into a book. Bliss was a capable, energetic man, with a taste for humor, and believed there was money for author and publisher in the travel-book.

The proposition pleased Mark Twain, who replied at once, asking for further details as to Bliss's plan. Somewhat later he made a trip to Hartford, and the terms for the publication of *The Innocents Abroad* were agreed upon. It was to be a large illustrated book for subscription sale, and the author was to receive five per cent. of the selling price. Bliss had offered him the choice between this royalty and ten thousand dollars cash. Though much tempted by the large sum to be paid in hand, Mark Twain decided in favor of the royalty plan—"the best business judgment I ever displayed," he used to say afterward. He agreed to arrange the letters for book publication, revising and rewriting where necessary, and went back to Washington well pleased. He did not realize that his agreement with Bliss marked the beginning of one of the most notable publishing connections in American literary history.

XXVIII

CERTAINLY this was a momentous period in Mark Twain's life. It was a time of great events, and among them was one which presently would come to mean more to him than all the rest— the beginning of his acquaintance with Olivia Langdon.

One evening in late December when Samuel Clemens had come to New York to visit his old *Quaker City* room-mate, Dan Slote, he found there other ship comrades, including Jack Van Nostrand and Charlie Langdon. It was a joyful occasion, but one still happier followed it. Young Langdon's father and sister Olivia were in New York, and an evening or two later the boy invited his distinguished *Quaker City* shipmate to dine with them at the old St. Nicholas Hotel. We may believe that Samuel Clemens went willingly enough. He had never forgotten the September day in the Bay of Smyrna when he had first seen the sweet-faced miniature— now, at last he looked upon the reality.

Long afterward he said: "It was forty years ago. From that day to this she has never been out of my mind."

Charles Dickens gave a reading that night at Steinway Hall. The Langdons attended, and Samuel Clemens with them. He recalled long after that Dickens wore a black velvet coat with a fiery-red flower in his buttonhole, and that he read the storm scene from *David Copperfield*—the death of James Steerforth; but he remembered still more clearly the face and dress and the slender, girlish figure of Olivia Langdon at his side.

Olivia Langdon was twenty-two years old at this time, delicate as the miniature he had seen, though no longer in the fragile health of her girlhood. Gentle, winning, lovable, she was the family idol, and Samuel Clemens was no less her worshiper from the first moment of their meeting.

Miss Langdon, on her part, was at first rather dazed by the strange, brilliant, handsome man, so unlike anything she had known before. When he had gone, she had the feeling that something like a great meteor had crossed her sky. To her brother, who was eager for her good opinion of his celebrity, she admitted her admiration, if not her entire approval. Her father had no doubts. With a keen sense of humor and a deep knowledge of men, Jervis Langdon was from that first evening the devoted champion of Mark Twain. Clemens saw Miss Langdon again during the holidays, and by the week's end he had planned to visit Elmira—soon. But fate managed differently. He was not to see Elmira for the better part of a year.

He returned to his work in Washington—the preparation of the book and his newspaper correspondence. It was in connection with the latter that he first met General Grant, then not yet President. The incident, characteristic of both men, is worth remembering. Mark Twain had called by permission, elated with the prospect of an interview. But when he looked into the square, smileless face of the soldier he found himself, for the first time in his life, without anything particular to say. Grant nodded slightly and waited. His caller wished something would happen. It did. His inspiration returned.

"General," he said, "I seem to be slightly embarrassed. Are you?"

Grant's severity broke up in laughter. There were no further difficulties.

Work on the book did not go so well. There were many distractions in Washington, and Clemens did not like the climate there. Then he found the *Alta* had copyrighted his letters and were reluctant to allow him to use them. He decided to sail at once for San Francisco. If he could arrange the *Alta* matter, he would finish his work there. He did, in fact, carry out this plan, and all difficulties vanished on his arrival. His old friend Colonel McComb obtained for him free use of the *Alta* letters. The way was now clear for his book. His immediate need of funds, however, induced him to lecture. In May he wrote Bliss:

I lectured here on the trip (the *Quaker City* excursion) the other night; $1,600 in gold in the house; every seat taken and paid for before night.

He settled down to work now with his usual

energy, editing and rewriting, and in two months had the big manuscript ready for delivery.

Mark Twain's friends urged him to delay his return to "the States" long enough to make a lecture tour through California and Nevada. He must give his new lecture, they told him, to his old friends. He agreed, and was received at Virginia City, Carson, and elsewhere like a returning conqueror. He lectured again in San Francisco just before sailing.

The announcement of his lecture was highly original. It was a hand-bill supposed to have been issued by the foremost citizens of San Francisco, a mock protest against his lecture, urging him to return to New York without inflicting himself on them again. On the same bill was printed his reply. In it he said:

I will torment the people if I want to. It only costs them $1 apiece, and, if they can't stand it, what do they stay here for?

He promised positively to sail on July 6th if they would let him talk just this once.

There was a good deal more of this drollery on the bill, which ended with the announcement that he would appear at the Mercantile Library on July 2d. It is unnecessary to say that the place was jammed on that evening. It was probably the greatest lecture event San Francisco has ever known. Four days later, July 6, 1868, Mark Twain sailed, *via* Aspinwall, for New York, and on the 28th delivered the manuscript of *The Innocents Abroad, or the New Pilgrim's Progress,* to his Hartford publisher.

XXIX

THE VISIT TO ELMIRA AND ITS CONSEQUENCES

SAMUEL CLEMENS now decided to pay his long-deferred visit to the Langdon home in Elmira. Through Charlie Langdon he got the invitation renewed, and for a glorious week enjoyed the generous hospitality of the beautiful Langdon home and the society of fair Olivia Langdon—Livy, as they called her—realizing more and more that for him there could never be any other woman in the world. He spoke no word of this to her, but on the morning of the day when his visit would end he relieved himself to Charlie Langdon, much to the young man's alarm. Greatly as he admired Mark Twain himself, he did not think him, or, indeed, any man, good enough for "Livy," whom he considered little short of a saint. Clemens was to take a train that evening, but young Langdon said, when he recovered:

"Look here, Clemens, there's a train in half an hour. I'll help you catch it. Don't wait until to-night; go now!"

Mark Twain shook his head.

"No, Charlie," he said, in his gentle drawl. "I

want to enjoy your hospitality a little longer. I promise to be circumspect, and I'll go to-night."

That night after dinner, when it was time to take the train, a light two-seated wagon was at the gate. Young Langdon and his guest took the back seat, which, for some reason, had not been locked in its place. The horse started with a quick forward spring, and the seat with its two occupants described a circle and landed with force on the cobbled street.

Neither passenger was seriously hurt—only dazed a little for the moment. But to Mark Twain there came a sudden inspiration. Here was a chance to prolong his visit. When the Langdon household gathered with restoratives, he did not recover at once, and allowed himself to be supported to an arm-chair for further remedies. Livy Langdon showed especial anxiety.

He was not allowed to go, *now*, of course; he must stay until it was certain that his recovery was complete. Perhaps he had been internally injured. His visit was prolonged two weeks, two weeks of pure happiness, and when he went away he had fully resolved to win Livy Langdon for his wife.

Mark Twain now went to Hartford to look after his book proofs, and there for the first time met the Rev. Joseph H. Twichell, who would become his closest friend. The two men, so different in many ways, always had the fondest admiration for each other; each recognized in the other great courage, humanity, and sympathy. Clemens would gladly have remained in Hartford that winter. Twichell presented him to many congenial people, including Charles Dudley Warner, Harriet Beecher Stowe, and other writing folk. But flattering lecture offers were made him, and he could no longer refuse.

He called his new lecture "The Vandal Abroad," it being chapters from the forthcoming book, and it was a great success everywhere. His houses were crowded; the newspapers were enthusiastic. His delivery was described as a "long, monotonous drawl, with fun invariably coming in at the end of a sentence—after a pause." He began to be recognized everywhere—to have great popularity. People came out on the street to see him pass.

Many of his lecture engagements were in central New York, no great distance from Elmira. He had a standing invitation to visit the Langdon home, and went when he could. His courtship, however, was not entirely smooth. Much as Mr. Langdon honored his gifts and admired him personally, he feared that his daughter, who had known so little of life and the outside world, and the brilliant traveler, lecturer, author, might not find happiness in marriage. Many absurd stories have been told of Mark Twain's first interview with Jervis Langdon on this subject, but these are without foundation. It was an earnest discussion on both sides, and left Samuel Clemens rather crestfallen, though not without hope. More than once the subject was discussed between the two men that winter as the lecturer came and went, his fame always growing. In time the Langdon household had grown to feel that he belonged to them. It would be going only a step further to make him really one of the family.

There was no positive engagement at first, for it was agreed between Clemens and Jervis Langdon that letters should be sent by Mr. Langdon to those who had known his would-be son-in-law earlier, with inquiries as to his past conduct and general character. It was a good while till answers to these came, and when they arrived Samuel Clemens was on hand to learn the result. Mr. Langdon had a rather solemn look when they were alone together.

Clemens asked, "You've heard from those gentlemen out there?"

"Yes, and from another gentleman I wrote to concerning you."

"They don't appear to have been very enthusiastic, from your manner."

"Well, yes, some of them were."

"I suppose I may ask what particular form their emotion took."

"Oh, yes, yes; they agree unanimously that you are a brilliant, able man—a man with a future, and that you would make about the worst husband on record."

The applicant had a forlorn look. "There is nothing very evasive about that," he said.

Langdon reflected.

"Haven't you any other friend that you could suggest?"

"Apparently none whose testimony would be valuable."

Jervis Langdon held out his hand.

"You have at least one," he said. "*I* believe in you. I know you better than they do."

The engagement of Samuel Langhorne Clemens and Olivia Lewis Langdon was ratified next day, February 4, 1869. To Jane Clemens her son wrote: "She is a little body, but she hasn't her peer in Christendom."

XXX

THE NEW BOOK AND A WEDDING

CLEMENS closed his lecture tour in March with a profit of something more than eight thousand dollars. He had intended to make a spring tour of California, but went to Elmira instead. The revised proofs of his book were coming now, and he and gentle Livy Langdon read them together. Samuel Clemens realized presently that the girl he had chosen had a delicate literary judgment. She became all at once his editor, a position she held until her death. Her refining influence had much to do with Mark Twain's success, then and later, and the world owes her a debt of gratitude. Through that first pleasant summer these two worked at the proofs and planned for their future, and were very happy indeed.

It was about the end of July when the big book appeared at last, and its success was startling. Nothing like it had ever been known before. Mark Twain's name seemed suddenly to be on every tongue—his book in everybody's hands. From one end of the country to the other, readers were hailing him as the greatest humorist and descriptive writer of modern times. By the first of the year more than thirty thousand volumes had been sold. It was a book of travel; its lowest price was three and a half dollars; the record has not been equaled since. In England also large editions had been issued, and translations into foreign languages were under way. It was and is a great book, because it is a human book—a book written straight from the heart.

If Mark Twain had not been famous before, he was so now. Indeed, it is doubtful if any other American author was so widely known and read as the author of *The Innocents Abroad* during that first half-year after its publication.

Yet for some reason he still did not regard himself as a literary man. He was a journalist, and began to look about for a paper which he could buy —his idea being to establish a business and a home. Through Mr. Langdon's assistance, he finally obtained an interest in the Buffalo *Express*, and the end of the year 1869 found him established as its associate editor, though still lecturing here and there, because his wedding-day was near at hand and there must be no lack of funds.

It was the 2d of February, 1870, that Samuel Clemens and Olivia Langdon were married. A few days before, he sat down one night and wrote to Jim Gillis, away out in the Tuolumne Hills, and told him of all his good fortune, recalling their days at Angel's Camp, and the absurd frog story, which he said had been the beginning of his happiness. In the five years since then he had traveled a long way, but he had not forgotten.

On the morning of his wedding-day Mark Twain

received from his publisher a check for four thousand dollars, his profit from three months' sales of the book, a handsome sum.

The wedding was mainly a family affair. Twichell and his wife came over from Hartford—Twichell to assist Thomas K. Beecher in performing the ceremony. Jane Clemens could not come, nor Orion and his wife; but Pamela, a widow now, and her daughter Annie, grown to a young lady, arrived from St. Louis. Not more than one hundred guests gathered in the stately Langdon parlors that in future would hold so much history for Samuel Clemens and Olivia Langdon—so much of the story of life and death that thus made its beginning there. Then, at seven in the evening, they were married, and the bride danced with her father, and the Rev. Thomas Beecher declared she wore the longest gloves he had ever seen.

It was the next afternoon that the wedding-party set out for Buffalo. Through a Mr. Slee, an agent of Mr. Langdon's, Clemens had engaged, as he supposed, a boarding-house, quiet and unpretentious, for he meant to start his married life modestly. Jervis Langdon had a plan of his own for his daughter, but Clemens had received no inkling of it, and had full faith in the letter which Slee had written, saying that a choice and inexpensive boarding-house had been secured. When, about nine o'clock that night, the party reached Buffalo, they found Mr. Slee waiting at the station. There was snow, and sleighs had been ordered. Soon after starting, the sleigh of the bride and groom fell behind and drove about rather aimlessly, apparently going nowhere in particular.

This disturbed the groom, who thought they should arrive first and receive their guests. He criticized Slee for selecting a house that was so hard to find, and when they turned at last into Delaware Avenue, Buffalo's finest street, and stopped before a handsome house, he was troubled concerning the richness of the locality.

They were on the steps when the door opened and a perfect fairyland of lights and decoration was revealed within. The friends who had gone ahead came out with greetings to lead in the bride and groom. Servants hurried forward to take bags and wraps. They were ushered inside; they were led through beautiful rooms, all newly appointed and garnished. The bridegroom was dazed, unable to understand the meaning of it all—the completeness of their possession. At last his young wife put her hand upon his arm.

"Don't you understand, Youth?" she said—that was always her name for him. "Don't you understand? It is ours, all ours—everything—a gift from father."

But still he could not quite grasp it, and Mr. Langdon brought a little box and, opening it, handed them the deeds.

Nobody quite remembers what was the first remark that Samuel Clemens made, but either then or a little later he said:

"Mr. Langdon, whenever you are in Buffalo, if it's twice a year, come right here. Bring your bag and stay overnight if you want to. It sha'n't cost you a cent."

XXXI

MARK TWAIN remained less than two years in Buffalo—a period of much affliction.

In the beginning, prospects could hardly have been brighter. His beautiful home seemed perfect. At the office he found work to his hand, and enjoyed it. His co-editor, J. W. Larned, who sat across the table from him, used to tell later how Mark enjoyed his work as he went along—the humor of it—frequently laughing as some new absurdity came into his mind. He was not very regular in his arrivals, but he worked long hours and turned in a vast amount of "copy"—skits, sketches, editorials, and comments of a varied sort. Not all of it was humorous; he would stop work any time on an amusing sketch to attack some abuse or denounce an injustice, and he did it in scorching words that made offenders pause. Once, when two practical jokers had sent in a marriage notice of persons not even contemplating matrimony, he wrote:

This deceit has been practised maliciously by a couple of men whose small souls will escape through their pores some day if they do not varnish their hides.

MARK TWAIN IN BUFFALO

In May he considerably increased his income by undertaking a department called "Memoranda" for the new *Galaxy* magazine. The outlook was now so promising that to his lecture agent, James Redpath, he wrote:

DEAR RED: I'm not going to lecture any more forever. I've got things ciphered down to a fraction now. I know just about what it will cost to live, and I can make the money without lecturing. Therefore, old man, count me out.

And in a second letter:

I guess I'm out of the field permanently. Have got a lovely wife, a lovely house bewitchingly furnished, a lovely carriage, and a coachman whose style and dignity are simply awe-inspiring, nothing less; and I'm making more money than necessary, by considerable, and therefore why crucify myself nightly on the platform! The subscriber will have to be excused, for the present season, at least.

The little household on Delaware Avenue was indeed a happy place during those early months. Neither Clemens nor his wife in those days cared much for society, preferring the comfort of their own home. Once when a new family moved into a house across the way they postponed calling until they felt ashamed. Clemens himself called first. One Sunday morning he noticed smoke pouring from an upper window of their neighbor's house. The occupants, seated on the veranda, evidently did not suspect their danger. Clemens stepped across to the gate and, bowing politely, said:

"My name is Clemens; we ought to have called on you before, and I beg your pardon for intruding now in this informal way, but your house is on fire."

It was at the moment when life seemed at its best that shadows gathered. Jervis Langdon had never accepted his son-in-law's playful invitation to "bring his bag and stay overnight," and now the time for it was past. In the spring his health gave way. Mrs. Clemens, who adored him, went to Elmira to be at his bedside. Three months of lingering illness brought the end. His death was a great blow to Mrs. Clemens, and the strain of watching had been very hard. Her own health, never robust, became poor. A girlhood friend, who came to cheer her with a visit, was taken down with typhoid fever. Another long period of anxiety and nursing ended with the young woman's death in the Clemens home.

To Mark Twain and his wife it seemed that their bright days were over. The arrival of little Langdon Clemens, in November, brought happiness, but his delicate hold on life was so uncertain that the burden of anxiety grew.

Amid so many distractions Clemens found his work hard. His "Memoranda" department in the *Galaxy* must be filled and be bright and readable. His work at the office could not be neglected. Then, too, he had made a contract with Bliss for another book—*Roughing It*—and he was trying to get started on that.

He began to chafe under the relentless demands of the magazine and newspaper. Finally he could stand it no longer. He sold his interest in the

Express, at a loss, and gave up the " Memoranda."
In the closing number (April, 1871) he said:

For the last eight months, with hardly an interval, I
have had for my fellows and comrades, night and day,
doctors and watchers of the sick! During these eight
months death has taken two members of my home circle
and malignantly threatened two others. All this I have
experienced, yet all the time have been under contract to
furnish humorous matter, once a month, for this magazine. . . . To be a pirate on a low salary and with no
share of the profits in the business used to be my idea of
an uncomfortable occupation, but I have other views
now. To be a monthly humorist in a cheerless time is
drearier.

XXXII

AT WORK ON "ROUGHING IT"

THE Clemens family now went to Elmira, to Quarry Farm—a beautiful hilltop place, over-looking the river and the town—the home of Mrs. Clemens's sister, Mrs. Theodore Crane. They did not expect to return to Buffalo, and the house there was offered for sale. For them the sunlight had gone out of it.

Matters went better at Quarry Farm. The invalids gained strength; work on the book progressed. The Clemenses that year fell in love with the place that was to mean so much to them in the many summers to come.

Mark Twain was not altogether satisfied, however, with his writing. He was afraid it was not up to his literary standard. His spirits were at low ebb when his old first editor, Joe Goodman, came East and stopped off at Elmira. Clemens hurried him out to the farm, and, eagerly putting the chapters of *Roughing It* into his hands, asked him to read them. Goodman seated himself comfortably by a window, while the author went over to a table and pretended to write, but was really watching Goodman, who read page after page solemnly and with great deliberation. Presently Mark Twain could stand it no longer. He threw down his pen, exclaiming:

"I knew it! I knew it! I've been writing nothing but rot. You have sat there all this time reading without a smile—but I am not wholly to blame. I have been trying to write a funny book with dead people and sickness everywhere. Oh, Joe, I wish I could die myself!"

"Mark," said Goodman, "I was reading critically, not for amusement, and so far as I have read, and can judge, this is one of the best things you have ever written. I have found it perfectly absorbing. You are doing a *great book!*"

That was enough. Clemens knew that Goodman never spoke idly of such matters. The author of *Roughing It* was a changed man—full of enthusiasm, eager to go on. He offered to pay Goodman a salary to stay and furnish inspiration. Goodman declined the salary, but remained for several weeks, and during long walks which the two friends took over the hills gave advice, recalled good material, and was a great help and comfort. In May, Clemens wrote to Bliss that he had twelve hundred manuscript pages of the new book written and was turning out from thirty to sixty-five per day. He was in high spirits. The family health had improved—once more prospects were bright. He even allowed Redpath to persuade him to lecture again during the coming season. Selling his share of the *Express* at a loss had left Mark Twain considerably in debt, and lecture profits would furnish the quickest means of payment.

When the summer ended the Clemens family took up residence in Hartford, Connecticut, in the fine old Hooker house, on Forest Street. Hartford held many attractions for Mark Twain. His publishers were located there, also it was the home of a distinguished group of writers, and of the Rev. "Joe" Twichell. Neither Clemens nor his wife had felt that they could return to Buffalo. The home there was sold —its contents packed and shipped. They did not see it again.

His book finished, Mark Twain lectured pretty steadily that winter, often in the neighborhood of Boston, which was lecture headquarters. Mark Twain enjoyed Boston. In Redpath's office one could often meet and "swap stories" with Josh Billings (Henry W. Shaw) and Petroleum V. Nasby (David R. Locke)—well-known humorists of that day—while in the strictly literary circle there were William Dean Howells, Thomas Bailey Aldrich, Bret Harte (who by this time had become famous and journeyed eastward), and others of their sort. They were all young and eager and merry, then, and they gathered at luncheons in snug corners and talked gaily far into the dimness of winter afternoons. Harte had been immediately accorded a high place in the Boston group. Mark Twain as a strictly literary man was still regarded rather doubtfully by members of the older set—the Brahmins, as they were called—but the young men already hailed him joyfully, reveling in the fine, fearless humor of his writing, his wonderful talk, his boundless humanity.

XXXIII

IN ENGLAND

MARK TWAIN closed his lecture season in February (1872), and during the same month his new book, *Roughing It*, came from the press. He disliked the lecture platform, and he felt that he could now abandon it. He had made up his loss in Buffalo and something besides. Furthermore, the advance sales on his book had been large.

Roughing It, in fact, proved a very successful book. Like *The Innocents Abroad*, it was the first of its kind, fresh in its humor and description, true in its picture of the frontier life he had known. In three months forty thousand copies had been sold, and now, after more than forty years, it is still a popular book. The life it describes is all gone—the scenes are changed. It is a record of a vanished time—a delightful history—as delightful to-day as ever.

Eighteen hundred and seventy-two was an eventful year for Mark Twain. In March his second child, a little girl whom they named Susy, was born, and three months later the boy, Langdon, died. He had never been really strong, and a heavy cold and diphtheria brought the end.

Clemens did little work that summer. He took

his family to Saybrook, Connecticut, for the sea air, and near the end of August, when Mrs. Clemens had regained strength and courage, he sailed for England to gather material for a book on English life and customs. He felt very friendly toward the English, who had been highly appreciative of his writings, and he wished their better acquaintance. He gave out no word of the book idea, and it seems unlikely that any one in England ever suspected it. He was there three months, and beyond some note-book memoranda made during the early weeks of his stay he wrote not a line. He was too delighted with everything to write a book—a book of his kind. In letters home he declared the country to be as beautiful as fairyland. By all classes attentions were showered upon him—honors such as he had never received even in America. W. D. Howells writes: [1]

In England rank, fashion, and culture rejoiced in him. Lord mayors, lord chief justices, and magnates of many kinds were his hosts; he was desired in country houses, and his bold genius captivated the favor of periodicals that spurned the rest of our nation.

He could not make a book—a humorous book—out of these people and their country; he was too fond of them.

England fairly reveled in Mark Twain. At one of the great banquets, a roll of the distinguished guests was called, and the names properly applauded. Mark Twain, busily engaged in low conversation with his neighbor, applauded without listening, vigorously or mildly, as the others led. Finally a name was followed by a great burst of long and vehement clapping. This must be some very great person indeed, and Mark Twain, not to be outdone in his approval, stoutly kept his hands going when all others had finished.

"Whose name was that we were just applauding?" he asked of his neighbor.

"Mark Twain's."

But it was no matter; they took it all as one of his jokes. He was a wonder and a delight to them. Whatever he did or said was to them supremely amusing. When, on one occasion, a speaker humorously referred to his American habit of carrying a cotton umbrella, his reply that he did so "because it was the only kind of an umbrella that an Englishman wouldn't steal," was repeated all over England next day as one of the finest examples of wit since the days of Swift.

He returned to America at the end of November, promising to come back and lecture to them the following year.

XXXIV

A NEW BOOK AND NEW ENGLISH TRIUMPHS

BUT if Mark Twain could find nothing to write of in England, he found no lack of material in America. That winter in Hartford, with Charles Dudley Warner, he wrote *The Gilded Age*. The Warners were neighbors, and the families visited back and forth. One night at dinner, when the two husbands were criticizing the novels their wives were reading, the wives suggested that their author husbands write a better one. The challenge was accepted. On the spur of the moment Warner and Clemens agreed that they would write a book together, and began it immediately.

Clemens had an idea already in mind. It was to build a romance around that lovable dreamer, his mother's cousin, James Lampton, whom the reader will recall from an earlier chapter. Without delay he set to work and soon completed the first three hundred and ninety-nine pages of the new story. Warner came over and, after listening to its reading, went home and took up the story. In two months the novel was complete, Warner doing most of the romance, Mark Twain the character parts. War-

If he dreamed at all, that night, no gossiping spirit disturbed his visions to whisper in his ear of certain events transpiring in the East, more than a thousand miles away, that were destined to develop influences which would at no very distant day profoundly affect the fate & fortunes of the Hawkins family.

Now comes in Warner's first Chapter.

A PAGE FROM THE MANUSCRIPT OF "THE GILDED AGE." THE END OF MARK TWAIN'S FIRST INSTALMENT ner's portion was probably pure fiction, but Mark Twain's chapters were full of history.

Judge Hawkins and wife were Mark Twain's father and mother; Washington Hawkins, his brother Orion. Their doings, with those of James Lampton as Colonel Sellers, were, of course, elaborated, but the story of the Tennessee land, as told in that book, is very good history indeed. Laura Hawkins, however, was only real in the fact that she bore the name of Samuel Clemens's old playmate. *The Gilded Age*, published later in the year, was well received and sold largely. The character of Colonel Sellers at once took a place among the great fiction characters of the world, and is probably the best known of any American creation. His watchword, "There's millions in it!" became a byword.

The Clemenses decided to build in Hartford. They bought a plot of land on Farmington Avenue, in the literary neighborhood, and engaged an architect and builder. By spring, the new house was well under way, and, matters progressing so favorably, the owners decided to take a holiday while the work was going on. Clemens had been eager to show England to his wife; so, taking little Susy, now a year old, they sailed in May, to be gone half a year.

They remained for a time in London—a period of honors and entertainment. If Mark Twain had been a lion on his first visit, he was hardly less than royalty now. His rooms at the Langham Hotel were like a court. The nation's most distinguished men— among them Robert Browning, Sir John Millais,

Lord Houghton, and Sir Charles Dilke—came to pay their respects. Authors were calling constantly. Charles Reade and Wilkie Collins could not get enough of Mark Twain. Reade proposed to join with him in writing a novel, as Warner had done. Lewis Carroll did not call, being too timid, but they met the author of *Alice in Wonderland* one night at a dinner, "the shyest full-grown man, except Uncle Remus, I ever saw," Mark Twain once declared.

Little Susy and her father thrived on London life, but it wore on Mrs. Clemens. At the end of July they went quietly to Edinburgh, and settled at Veitch's Hotel, on George Street. The strain of London life had been too much for Mrs. Clemens, and her health became poor. Unacquainted in Edinburgh, Clemens only remembered that Dr. John Brown, author of *Rab and His Friends*, lived there. Learning the address, he walked around to 23 Rutland Street, and made himself known. Doctor Brown came forthwith, and Mrs. Clemens seemed better from the moment of his arrival.

The acquaintance did not end there. For a month the author of *Rab* and the little Clemens family were together daily. Often they went with him to make his round of visits. He was always leaning out of the carriage to look at dogs. It was told of him that once when he suddenly put his head from a carriage window he dropped back with a disappointed look.

"Who was it?" asked his companion. "Some one you know?"

"No, a dog I *don't* know."

Dr. John was beloved by everybody in Scotland,

and his story of *Rab* had won him a world-wide following. Children adored him. Little Susy and he were playmates, and he named her "Megalopis," a Greek term, suggested by her great, dark eyes.

Mark Twain kept his promise to lecture to a London audience. On the 13th of October, in the Queen's Concert Rooms, Hanover Square, he gave "Our Fellow Savages of the Sandwich Islands." The house was packed. Clemens was not introduced. He appeared on the platform in evening dress, assuming the character of a manager, announcing a disappointment. Mr. Clemens, he said, had fully expected to be present. He paused, and loud murmurs arose from the audience. He lifted his hand and the noise subsided. Then he added, "I am happy to say that Mark Twain is present and will now give his lecture." The audience roared its approval.

He continued his lectures at Hanover Square through the week, and at no time in his own country had he won such a complete triumph. He was the talk of the streets. The papers were full of him. The *London Times* declared his lectures had only whetted the public appetite for more. His manager, George Dolby (formerly manager for Charles Dickens), urged him to remain and continue the course through the winter. Clemens finally agreed that he would take his family back to America and come back himself within the month. This plan he carried out. Returning to London, he lectured steadily for two months in the big Hanover Square rooms, giving his *Roughing It* address, and it was only toward the end that his audience showed any sign of diminishing. There is probably no other such a lecture triumph on record.

Mark Twain was at the pinnacle of his first glory: thirty-six, in full health, prosperous, sought by the world's greatest, hailed in the highest places almost as a king. Tom Sawyer's dreams of greatness had been all too modest. In its most dazzling moments his imagination had never led him so far.

14

XXXV

BEGINNING "TOM SAWYER"

IT was at the end of January, 1874, when Mark Twain returned to America. His reception abroad had increased his prestige at home. Howells and Aldrich came over from Boston to tell him what a great man he had become—to renew those Boston days of three years before—to talk and talk of all the things between the earth and sky. And Twichell came in, of course, and Warner, and no one took account of time, or hurried, or worried about anything at all.

"We had two such days as the aging sun no longer shines on in his round," wrote Howells, long after, and he tells how he and Aldrich were so carried away with Clemens's success in subscription publication that on the way back to Boston they planned a book to sell in that way. It was to be called *Twelve Memorable Murders*, and they had made two or three fortunes from it by the time they reached Boston.

"But the project ended there. We never killed a single soul," Howells once confessed to the writer of this memoir.

Act. 1.

=

Scene 1.

=

A village cottage, with back
door looking into garden.
A closet & the ordinary
furniture. Old lady of
50, cheaply & neatly dressed.
Wears spectacles — knitting.

=

Aunt Winny. (the old lady) — Tom!

[to answer.] Tom! [to
answer.] What's gone with
that bag, I wonder ? You

FIRST MANUSCRIPT PAGE OF "TOM SAWYER." BEGUN AS A PLAY
ABOUT 1872. "AUNT WINNY" LATER BECAME "AUNT POLLY"

At Quarry Farm that summer Mark Twain began the writing of *The Adventures of Tom Sawyer*. He had been planning for some time to set down the story of those far-off days along the river-front at Hannibal, with John Briggs, Tom Blankenship, and the rest of that graceless band, and now in the cool luxury of a little study which Mrs. Crane had built for him on the hillside he set himself to spin the fabric of his youth. The study was a delightful place to work. It was octagonal in shape, with windows on all sides, something like a pilot-house. From any direction the breeze could come, and there were fine views. To Twichell he wrote:

It is a cozy nest, and just room in it for a sofa, table, and three or four chairs, and when the storm sweeps down the remote valley and the lightning flashes behind the hills beyond, and the rain beats on the roof over my head, imagine the luxury of it!

He worked steadily there that summer. He would begin mornings, soon after breakfast, keeping at it until nearly dinner-time, say until five or after, for it was not his habit to eat the midday meal. Other members of the family did not venture near the place; if he was wanted urgently, a horn was blown. His work finished, he would light a cigar and, stepping lightly down the stone flight that led to the house-level, he would find where the family had assembled and read to them his day's work. Certainly those were golden days, and the tale of Tom and Huck and Joe Harper progressed. To Dr. John Brown, in Scotland, he wrote:

BEGINNING "TOM SAWYER"

I have been writing fifty pages of manuscript a day, on an average, for some time now, . . . and consequently have been so wrapped up in it and dead to everything else that I have fallen mighty short in letter-writing.

But the inspiration of Tom and Huck gave out when the tale was half finished, or perhaps it gave way to a new interest. News came one day that a writer in San Francisco, without permission, had dramatized *The Gilded Age*, and that it was being played by John T. Raymond, an actor of much power. Mark Twain had himself planned to dramatize the character of Colonel Sellers and had taken out dramatic copyright. He promptly stopped the California production, then wrote the dramatist a friendly letter, and presently bought the play of him, and set in to rewrite it. It proved a great success. Raymond played it for several years. Colonel Sellers on the stage became fully as popular as in the book, and very profitable indeed.

XXXVI

THE NEW HOME

THE new home in Hartford was ready that autumn—the beautiful house finished, or nearly finished, the handsome furnishings in place. It was a lovely spot. There were trees and grass—a green, shady slope that fell away to a quiet stream. The house itself, quite different from the most of the houses of that day, had many wings and balconies, and toward the back a great veranda that looked down the shaded slope. The kitchen was not at the back. As Mark Twain was unlike any other man that ever lived, so his house was not like other houses. When asked why he built the kitchen toward the street, he said:

"So the servants can see the circus go by without running into the front yard."

But this was probably his afterthought. The kitchen wing extended toward Farmington Avenue, but it was a harmonious detail of the general plan.

Many frequenters have tried to express the charm of Mark Twain's household. Few have succeeded, for it lay not in the house itself, nor in its furnishings, beautiful as these things were, but in the personality of its occupants—the daily round of their

lives—the atmosphere which they unconsciously created. From its wide entrance-hall and tiny, jewell-
like conservatory below to the billiard-room at the
top of the house, it seemed perfectly appointed,
serenely ordered, and full of welcome. The home of
one of the most unusual and unaccountable person-
alities in the world was filled with gentleness and
peace. It was Mrs. Clemens who was chiefly responsible. She was no longer the half-timid, inexperi-
enced girl he had married. Association, study, and
travel had brought her knowledge and confidence.
When the great ones of the world came to visit
America's most picturesque literary figure, she gave
welcome to them, and filled her place at his side
with such sweet grace that those who came to pay
their dues to him often returned to pay still greater
devotion to his companion. William Dean Howells,
so often a visitor there, once said to the writer:

"Words cannot express Mrs. Clemens—her fine-
ness, her delicate, wonderful tact." And again, "She
was not only a beautiful soul, but a woman of sin-
gular intellectual power."

There were always visitors in the Clemens home.
Above the mantel in the library was written: "*The
ornament of a house is the friends that frequent it,*" and
the Clemens home never lacked of those ornaments,
and they were of the world's best. No distinguished
person came to America that did not pay a visit to
Hartford and Mark Twain. Generally it was not
merely a call, but a stay of days. The welcome was
always genuine, the entertainment unstinted. George
Warner, a close neighbor, once said:

"The Clemens house was the only one I have ever known where there was never any preoccupation in the evenings and where visitors were always welcome. Clemens was the best kind of a host; his evenings after dinner were an unending flow of stories."

As for friends living near, they usually came and went at will, often without the ceremony of knocking or formal leave-taking. The two Warner families were among these, the home of Charles Dudley Warner being only a step away. Dr. and Mrs. Harriet Beecher Stowe were also close neighbors, while the Twichell parsonage was not far. They were all like one great family, of which Mark Twain's home was the central gathering-place.

XXXVII

"OLD TIMES," "SKETCHES," AND "TOM SAWYER"

THE Rev. Joseph H. Twichell and Mark Twain used to take many long walks together, and once they decided to walk from Hartford to Boston—about one hundred miles. They decided to allow three days for the trip, and really started one morning, with some luncheon in a basket, and a little bag of useful articles. It was a bright, brisk November day, and they succeeded in getting to Westford, a distance of twenty-eight miles, that evening. But they were lame and foot-sore, and next morning, when they had limped six miles or so farther, Clemens telegraphed to Redpath:

We have made thirty-five miles in less than five days. This shows the thing can be done. Shall finish now by rail. Did you have any bets on us?

He also telegraphed Howells that they were about to arrive in Boston, and they did, in fact, reach the Howells home about nine o'clock, and found excellent company—the Cambridge set—and a most welcome supper waiting. Clemens and Twichell were ravenous. Clemens demanded food immediately. Howells writes:

I can see him now as he stood up in the midst of our friends, with his head thrown back, and in his hands a dish of those scalloped oysters without which no party in Cambridge was really a party, exulting in the tale of his adventure, which had abounded in the most original characters and amusing incidents at every mile of their progress.

The pedestrians returned to Hartford a day or two later—by train. It was during another, though less extended, tour which Twichell and Clemens made that fall, that the latter got his idea for a Mississippi book. Howells had been pleading for something for the January *Atlantic*, of which he was now chief editor, but thus far Mark Twain's inspiration had failed. He wrote at last, "My head won't go," but later, the same day, he sent another hasty line.

I take back the remark that I can't write for the January number, for Twichell and I have had a long walk in the woods, and I got to telling him about old Mississippi days of steamboating glory and grandeur as I saw them (during four years) *from the pilot-house.* He said, "What a virgin subject to hurl into a magazine!" I hadn't thought of that before. Would you like a series of papers to run through three months, or six, or nine— or about four months, say?

Howells wrote at once, welcoming the idea. Clemens forthwith sent the first instalment of that marvelous series of river chapters which rank to-day among the very best of his work. As pictures of the vanished Mississippi life they are so real, so convincing, so full of charm that they can never grow old. As long as any one reads of the Mississippi they will look up those chapters of Mark Twain's piloting days. When the first number appeared, John Hay wrote:

It is perfect; no more, no less. I don't see how you do it."

The "Old Times" chapter ran through seven numbers of the *Atlantic*, and show Mark Twain at his very best. They form now most of the early chapters of *Life on the Mississippi*. The remainder of that book was added about seven years later.

Those were busy literary days for Mark Twain. Writing the river chapters carried him back, and hardly had he finished them when he took up the neglected story of Tom and Huck, and finished that under full steam. He at first thought of publishing it in the *Atlantic*, but decided against this plan. He sent Howells the manuscript to read, and received the fullest praise. Howells wrote:

It is altogether the best boy's story I ever read. It will be an immense success.

Clemens, however, delayed publication. He had another volume in press—a collection of his sketches —among them the "Jumping Frog," and others of his California days. The "Jumping Frog" had been translated into French, and in this book Mark Twain published the French version and then a literal re-translation of his own, which is one of the most amusing features in the volume. As an example, the stranger's remark, "I don't see no p'ints about that frog that's any better than any other frog," in the literal retranslation becomes, "I no saw not that that frog had nothing of better than each frog," and Mark Twain parenthetically adds, "If that isn't grammar gone to seed, then I count myself no judge."

Sketches New and Old went very well, but the book had no such sale as *The Adventures of Tom Sawyer*, which appeared a year later, December, 1876. From the date of its issue it took its place as foremost of American stories of boy life, a place that to this day it shares only with *Huck Finn*. Mark Twain's own boy life in the little drowsy town of Hannibal, with John Briggs and Tom Blankenship—their adventures in and about the cave and river—made perfect material. The story is full of pure delight. The camp on the island is a picture of boy heaven. No boy that reads it but longs for the woods and a camp-fire and some bacon strips in the frying-pan. It is all so thrillingly told and so vivid. We know certainly that it must all have happened. *The Adventures of Tom Sawyer* has taken a place side by side with *Treasure Island*.

XXXVIII

HOME PICTURES

MARK TWAIN was now regarded by many as the foremost American author. Certainly he was the most widely known. As a national feature he rivaled Niagara Falls. No civilized spot on earth that his name had not reached. Letters merely addressed "Mark Twain" found their way to him. "Mark Twain, United States," was a common superscription. "Mark Twain, The World," also reached him without delay, while "Mark Twain, Somewhere," and "Mark Twain, Anywhere," in due time came to Hartford. "Mark Twain, God Knows Where," likewise arrived promptly, and in his reply he said, "He did." Then a letter addressed "The Devil Knows Where" also reached him, and he answered, "*He* did, too." Surely these were the farthermost limits of fame.

Countless anecdotes went the rounds of the press. Among them was one which happened to be true:

Their near neighbor, Mrs. Harriet Beecher Stowe, was leaving for Florida one morning, and Clemens ran over early to say good-by. On his return Mrs. Clemens looked at him severely.

"Why, Youth," she said, "you haven't on any collar and tie."

He said nothing, but went to his room, wrapped up those items in a neat package, which he sent over by a servant to Mrs. Stowe, with the line:

Herewith receive a call from the rest of me.

Mrs. Stowe returned a witty note, in which she said he had discovered a new principle—that of making calls by instalments, and asked whether in extreme cases a man might not send his clothes and be himself excused.

Most of his work Mark Twain did at Quarry Farm. Each summer the family—there were two little girls now, Susy and Clara—went to that lovely place on the hilltop above Elmira, where there were plenty of green fields and cows and horses and apple-trees, a spot as wonderful to them as John Quarles's farm had been to their father, so long ago. All the family loved Quarry Farm, and Mark Twain's work went more easily there. His winters were not suited to literary creation—there were too many social events, though once—it was the winter of '76—he wrote a play with Bret Harte, who came to Hartford and stayed at the Clemens home while the work was in progress. It was a Chinese play, "Ah Sin," and the two had a hilarious time writing it, though the result did not prove much of a success with the public. Mark Twain often tried plays—one with Howells, among others—but the Colonel Sellers play was his only success.

Grand dinners, trips to Boston and New York, guests in his own home, occupied much of Mark Twain's winter season. His leisure he gave to his children and to billiards. He had a passion for the game, and at any hour of the day or night was likely to be found in the room at the top of the house, knocking the balls about alone or with any visitor that he had enticed to that den. He mostly received his callers there, and impressed them into the game. If they could play, well and good. If not, so much the better; he could beat them extravagantly, and he took huge delight in such contests. Every Friday evening a party of billiard lovers—Hartford men —gathered and played, and told stories, and smoked until the room was blue. Clemens never tired of the game. He could play all night. He would stay until the last man dropped from sheer weariness, and then go on knocking the balls about alone.

But many evenings at home—early evenings—he gave to Susy and Clara. They had learned his gift as a romancer and demanded the most startling inventions. They would bring him a picture requiring him to fit a story to it without a moment's delay. Once he was suddenly ordered by Clara to make a story out of a plumber and a "bawgunstictor," which, on the whole, was easier than some of their requirements. Along the book-shelves were ornaments and pictures. A picture of a girl whom they called "Emeline" was at one end, and at the other a cat. Every little while they compelled him to make a story beginning with the cat and ending with Emeline. Always a new story, and never the other way about. The literary path from the cat to Emeline was a perilous one, but in time he could have traveled it in his dreams.

XXXIX

TRAMPING ABROAD

IT was now going on ten years since the publication of *The Innocents Abroad*, and there was a demand for another Mark Twain book of travel. Clemens considered the matter, and decided that a walking-tour in Europe might furnish the material he wanted. He spoke to his good friend, the Rev. "Joe" Twichell, and invited him to become his guest on such an excursion, because, as he explained, he thought he could "dig material enough out of Joe to make it a sound investment." As a matter of fact, he loved Twichell's companionship, and was always inviting him to share his journeys—to Boston, to Bermuda, to Washington—wherever interest or fancy led him. His plan now was to take the family to Germany in the spring, and let Twichell join them later for a summer tramp down through the Black Forest and Switzerland. Meantime the Clemens household took up the study of German. The children had a German nurse—others a German teacher. The household atmosphere became Teutonic. Of course it all amused Mark Twain, as everything amused him, but he was a good student. In a brief time he had a fair knowledge of every-day German and a

really surprising vocabulary. The little family sailed
in April (1878), and a few weeks later were settled in
the Schloss Hotel, on a hill above Heidelberg, over-
looking the beautiful old castle, the ancient town,
with the Neckar winding down the hazy valley—as
fair a view as there is in all Germany.

Clemens found a room for his work in a small
house not far from the hotel. On the day of his
arrival he had pointed out this house and said he
had decided to work there—that his room would be
the middle one on the third floor. Mrs. Clemens
laughed, and thought the occupants of the house
might be surprised when he came over to take possession. They amused themselves by watching "his
people" and trying to make out what they were
like. One day he went over that way, and, sure
enough, there was a sign, "Furnished Rooms," and
the one he had pointed out from the hotel was vacant.
It became his study forthwith.

The travelers were delighted with their location.
To Howells, Clemens wrote:

Our bedroom has two great glass bird-cages (inclosed
balconies), one looking toward the Rhine Valley and sunset, the other looking up the Neckar *cul de sac*, and,
naturally, we spent nearly all our time in these. We
have tables and chairs in them. . . . It must have been
a noble genius who devised this hotel. Lord! how blessed
is the repose, the tranquillity of this place! Only two
sounds: the happy clamor of the birds in the groves and
the muffled music of the Neckar tumbling over the op-
posing dikes. It is no hardship to lie awake awhile
nights, for this subdued roar has exactly the sound of a

steady rain beating upon a roof. It is so healing to the spirit; and it bears up the thread of one's imaginings as the accompaniment bears up a song.

Twichell was summoned for August, and wrote back eagerly at the prospect:

Oh, my! Do you realize, Mark, what a symposium it is to be? I do. To begin with, I am thoroughly tired, and the rest will be worth everything. To walk with you and talk with you for weeks together—why, it's my dream of luxury!

Meantime the struggle with the "awful German language" went on. Rosa, the maid, was required to speak to the children only in German, though little Clara at first would have none of it. Susy, two years older, tried, and really made progress, but one day she said, pathetically:

"Mama, I wish Rosa was made in English."

But presently she was writing to "Aunt Sue" (Mrs. Crane) at Quarry Farm:

I know a lot of German; everybody says I know a lot. I give you a million dollars to see you, and you would give two hundred dollars to see the lovely woods we see.

Twichell arrived August 1st. Clemens met him at Baden-Baden, and they immediately set forth on a tramp through the Black Forest, excursioning as they pleased and having a blissful time. They did not always walk. They were likely to take a carriage or a donkey-cart, or even a train, when one conveniently happened along. They did not hurry, but idled and talked and gathered flowers, or gossiped with wayside natives—picturesque peasants in the Black Forest costume. In due time they crossed into Switzerland and prepared to conquer the Alps.

The name Mark Twain had become about as well known in Europe as it was in America. His face, however, was less familiar. He was not often recognized in these wanderings, and his pen-name was carefully concealed. It was a relief to him not to be an object of curiosity and lavish attention. Twichell's conscience now and then prompted him to reveal the truth. In one of his letters home he wrote how a young man at a hotel had especially delighted in Mark's table conversation, and how he (Twichell) had later taken the young man aside and divulged the speaker's identity.

I could not forbear telling him who Mark was, and the mingled surprise and pleasure his face exhibited made me glad I had done so.

They did not climb many of the Alps on foot. They did scale the Rigi, after which Mark Twain was not in the best walking trim; though later they conquered Gemmi Pass—no small undertaking—that trail that winds up and up until the traveler has only the glaciers and white peaks and the little high-blooming flowers for company.

All day long the friends would tramp and walk together, and when they did not walk they would hire a diligence or any vehicle that came handy, but, whatever their means of travel the joy of comradeship amid those superb surroundings was the same.

In Twichell's letters home we get pleasant pictures of the Mark Twain of that day:

Mark, to-day, was immensely absorbed in flowers. He scrambled around and gathered a great variety, and manifested the intensest pleasure in them. . . . Mark is splendid to walk with amid such grand scenery, for he talks so well about it, has such a power of strong, picturesque expression. I wish you might have heard him to-day. His vigorous speech nearly did justice to the things we saw.

And in another place:

He can't bear to see the whip used, or to see a horse pull hard. To-day when the driver clucked up his horse and quickened his pace a little, Mark said, "The fellow's got the notion that we were in a hurry."

Another extract refers to an incident which Mark Twain also mentions in *A Tramp Abroad:* [1]

Mark is a queer fellow. There is nothing so delights him as a swift, strong stream. You can hardly get him to leave one when once he is in the influence of its fascinations. To throw in stones and sticks seems to afford him rapture.

Twichell goes on to tell how he threw some driftwood into a racing torrent and how Mark went running down-stream after it, waving and shouting in a sort of mad ecstasy.

When a piece went over a fall and emerged to view in the foam below, he would jump up and down and yell. He acted just like a boy.

[1] Chapter XXXIII.

Boy he was, then and always. Like Peter Pan, he never really grew up—that is, if growing up means to grow solemn and uninterested in play.

Climbing the Gorner Grat with Twichell, they sat down to rest, and a lamb from a near-by flock ventured toward them. Clemens held out his hand and called softly. The lamb ventured nearer, curious but timid.

It was a scene for a painter: the great American humorist on one side of the game, and the silly little creature on the other, with the Matterhorn for a background. Mark was reminded that the time he was consuming was valuable, but to no purpose. The Gorner Grat could wait. He held on with undiscouraged perseverance till he carried his point; the lamb finally put its nose in Mark's hand, and he was happy all the rest of the day.

In *A Tramp Abroad* Mark Twain burlesques most of the walking-tour with Harris (Twichell), feeling, perhaps, that he must make humor at whatever cost. But to-day the other side of the picture seems more worth while. That it seemed so to him, also, even at the time, we may gather from a letter he sent after Twichell when it was all over and Twichell was on his way home:

DEAR OLD JOE,—It is actually all over! I was so low-spirited at the station yesterday, and this morning, when I woke, I couldn't seem to accept the dismal truth that you were really gone and the pleasant tramping and talking at an end. Ah, my boy! It has been such a rich holiday for me, and I feel under such deep and honest obligations to you for coming. I am putting out of my mind all memory of the time when I misbehaved toward you and hurt you; I am resolved to consider it forgiven, and to store up and remember only the charming hours of the journey and the times when I was not unworthy to be with you and share a companionship which to me stands first after Livy's.

Clemens had joined his family at Lausanne, and presently they journeyed down into Italy, returning later to Germany—to Munich, where they lived quietly with Fräulein Dahlweiner at No. 1a Karlstrasse, while he worked on his new book of travel. When spring came they went to Paris, and later to London, where the usual round of entertainment briefly claimed them. It was the 3d of September, 1879, when they finally reached New York. The papers said that Mark Twain had changed in his year and a half of absence. He had, somehow, taken on a traveled look. One paper remarked that he looked older than when he went to Germany, and that his hair had turned quite gray.

XL

"THE PRINCE AND THE PAUPER"

THEY went directly to Quarry Farm, where Clemens again took up work on his book, which he hoped to have ready for early publication. But his writing did not go as well as he had hoped, and it was long after they had returned to Hartford that the book was finally in the printer's hands.

Meantime he had renewed work on a story begun two years before at Quarry Farm. Browsing among the books there one summer day, he happened to pick up *The Prince and the Page*, by Charlotte M. Yonge. It was a story of a prince disguised as a blind beggar, and, as Mark Twain read, an idea came to him for an altogether different story, or play, of his own. He would have a prince and a pauper change places, and through a series of adventures learn each the trials and burdens of the other life. He presently gave up the play idea, and began it as a story. His first intention had been to make the story quite modern, using the late King Edward VII. (then Prince of Wales) as his prince, but it seemed to him that it would not do to lose a prince among the slums of modern London — he could not make it seem real; so he followed back through history until he came to the little son of Henry VIII., Edward Tudor, and decided that he would do.

It was the kind of a story that Mark Twain loved to read and to write. By the end of that first summer he had finished a good portion of the exciting adventures of *The Prince and the Pauper*, and then, as was likely to happen, the inspiration waned and the manuscript was laid aside.

But with the completion of *A Tramp Abroad*—a task which had grown wearisome—he turned to the luxury of romance with a glad heart. To Howells he wrote that he was taking so much pleasure in the writing that he wanted to make it last.

Did I ever tell you the plot of it? It begins at 9 A.M., January 27, 1547. . . . My idea is to afford a realizing sense of the exceeding severity of the laws of that day by inflicting some of their penalties upon the king himself, and allowing him a chance to see the rest of them applied to others.

Susy and Clara Clemens were old enough now to understand the story, and as he finished the chapters he read them aloud to his small home audience—a most valuable audience, indeed, for he could judge from its eager interest, or lack of attention, just the measure of his success.

These little creatures knew all about the writing of books. Susy's earliest recollection was *Tom Sawyer* read aloud from the manuscript. Also they knew about plays. They could not remember a time when they did not take part in evening charades—a favorite amusement in the Clemens home.

"THE PRINCE AND THE PAUPER"

Mark Twain, who always loved his home and played with his children, invented the charades and their parts for them, at first, but as they grew older they did not need much help. With the Twichell and Warner children they organized a little company for their productions, and entertained the assembled households. They did not make any preparation for their parts. A word was selected and the syllables of it whispered to the little actors. Then they withdrew to the hall, where all sorts of costumes had been laid out for the evening, dressed their parts, and each group marched into the library, performed its syllable, and retired, leaving the audience of parents to guess the answer. Now and then, even at this early day, they gave little plays, and of course Mark Twain could not resist joining them. In time the plays took the place of the charades and became quite elaborate, with a stage and scenery, but we shall hear of this later on.

The Prince and the Pauper came to an end in due season, in spite of the wish of both author and audience for it to go on forever. It was not published at once, for several reasons, the main one being that *A Tramp Abroad* had just been issued from the press, and a second book might interfere with its sale.

As it was, the *Tramp* proved a successful book— never as successful as the *Innocents*, for neither its humor nor its description had quite the fresh quality of the earlier work. In the beginning, however, the sales were large, the advance orders amounting to twenty-five thousand copies, and the return to the author forty thousand dollars for the first year.

XLI

GENERAL GRANT AT HARTFORD

A THIRD little girl came to the Clemens household during the summer of 1880. They were then at Quarry Farm, and Clemens wrote to his friend Twichell:

DEAR OLD JOE,—Concerning Jean Clemens, if anybody said he "didn't see no p'ints about that frog that's any better than any other frog," I should think he was convicting himself of being a pretty poor sort of an observer. . . . It is curious to note the change in the stock-quotations of the Affection Board. Four weeks ago the children put Mama at the head of the list right along, where she has always been, but now:

> Jean
> Mama
> Motley ⎫
> Fräulein ⎬ cats
> Papa

That is the way it stands now. Mama is become No. 2; I have dropped from 4 and become No. 5. Some time ago it used to be nip and tuck between me and the cats, but after the cats "developed" I didn't stand any more show.

Those were happy days at Quarry Farm. The little new baby thrived on that summer hilltop.

Also, it may be said, the cats. Mark Twain's children had inherited his love for cats, and at the farm were always cats of all ages and varieties. Many of the bed-time stories were about these pets —stories invented by Mark Twain as he went along —stories that began anywhere and ended nowhere, and continued indefinitely from evening to evening, trailing off into dreamland.

The great humorist cared less for dogs, though he was never unkind to them, and once at the farm a gentle hound named Bones won his affection. When the end of the summer came and Clemens, as was his habit, started down the drive ahead of the carriage, Bones, half-way to the entrance, was waiting for him. Clemens stooped down, put his arms about him, and bade him an affectionate good-by.

Eighteen hundred and eighty was a Presidential year. Mark Twain was for General Garfield, and made a number of remarkable speeches in his favor. General Grant came to Hartford during the campaign, and Mark Twain was chosen to make the address of welcome. Perhaps no such address of welcome was ever made before. He began:

I am among those deputed to welcome you to the sincere and cordial hospitalities of Hartford, the city of the historic and revered Charter Oak, of which most of the town is built.

He seemed to be at a loss what to say next, and, leaning over, pretended to whisper to Grant. Then, as if he had been prompted by the great soldier, he straightened up and poured out a fervid eulogy on

Grant's victories, adding, in an aside, as he finished, "I nearly forgot that part of my speech," to the roaring delight of his hearers, while Grant himself grimly smiled.

He then spoke of the General being now out of public employment, and how grateful his country was to him, and how it stood ready to reward him in every conceivable—*inexpensive*—way.

Grant had smiled more than once during the speech, and when this sentence came out at the end his composure broke up altogether, while the throng shouted approval. Clemens made another speech that night at the opera-house—a speech long remembered in Hartford as one of the great efforts of his life.

A very warm friendship had grown up between Mark Twain and General Grant. A year earlier, on the famous soldier's return from his trip around the world, a great birthday banquet had been given him in Chicago, at which Mark Twain's speech had been the event of the evening. The colonel who long before had chased the young pilot-soldier through the Mississippi bottoms had become his conquering hero, and Grant's admiration for America's foremost humorist was most hearty. Now and again Clemens urged General Grant to write his memoirs for publication, but the hero of many battles was afraid to venture into the field of letters. He had no confidence in his ability to write. He did not realize that the man who had written "I will fight it out on this line if it takes all summer," and, later, "Let us have peace," was capable of English as terse and forceful as the Latin of Cæsar's *Commentaries*

XLII

MANY INVESTMENTS

*T*HE *Prince and the Pauper*, delayed for one reason and another, did not make its public appearance until the end of 1881. It was issued by Osgood, of Boston, and was a different book in every way from any that Mark Twain had published before. Mrs. Clemens, who loved the story, had insisted that no expense should be spared in its making, and it was, indeed, a handsome volume. It was filled with beautiful pen-and-ink drawings, and the binding was rich. The dedication to its two earliest critics read:

> To those good-mannered and agreeable
> children, Susy and Clara Clemens.

The story itself was unlike anything in Mark Twain's former work. It was pure romance, a beautiful, idyllic tale, though not without his touch of humor and humanity on every page. And how breathlessly interesting it is! We may imagine that first little audience—the "two good-mannered and agreeable children," drawing up in their little chairs by the fireside, hanging on every paragraph of the adventures of the wandering prince and Tom Canty, the pauper king, eager always for more.

The story, at first, was not entirely understood by the reviewers. They did not believe it could be serious. They expected a joke in it somewhere. Some even thought they had found it. But it was not a joke, it was just a simple tale—a beautiful picture of a long-vanished time. One critic, wiser than the rest, said:

The characters of those two boys, twin in spirit, will rank with the purest and loveliest creations of child-life in the realm of fiction.

Mark Twain was now approaching the fullness of his fame and prosperity. The income from his writing was large; Mrs. Clemens possessed a considerable fortune of her own; they had no debts. Their home was as perfectly appointed as a home could well be, their family life was ideal. They lived in the large, hospitable way which Mrs. Clemens had known in her youth, and which her husband, with his Southern temperament, loved. Their friends were of the world's chosen, and they were legion in number. There were always guests in the Clemens home—so many, indeed, were constantly coming and going that Mark Twain said he was going to set up a private 'bus to save carriage hire. Yet he loved it all dearly, and for the most part realized his happiness.

Unfortunately, there were moments when he forgot that his lot was satisfactory, and tried to improve it. His Colonel Sellers imagination, inherited from both sides of his family, led him into financial adventures which were generally unprofitable. There

were no silver-mines in the East into which to empty
money and effort, as in the old Nevada days, but
there were plenty of other things—inventions, stock
companies, and the like.

When a man came along with a patent steam-generator which would save ninety per cent. of the usual
coal-supply, Mark Twain invested whatever bank
surplus he had at the moment, and saw that money
no more forever.

After the steam-generator came a steam-pulley, a
small affair, but powerful enough to relieve him of
thirty-two thousand dollars in a brief time.

A new method of marine telegraphy was offered
him by the time his balance had grown again, a
promising contrivance, but it failed to return the
twenty-five thousand dollars invested in it by Mark
Twain. The list of such adventures is too long to
set down here. They differ somewhat, but there is
one feature common to all—none of them paid. At
last came a chance in which there was really a fortune. A certain Alexander Graham Bell, an inventor, one day appeared, offering stock in an invention
for carrying the human voice on an electric wire.
But Mark Twain had grown wise, he thought. Long
after he wrote:

I declined. I said I did not want any more to do
with wildcat speculation. . . . I said I didn't want it at
any price. He (Bell) became eager; and insisted I take
five hundred dollars' worth. He said he would sell me
as much as I wanted for five hundred dollars; offered to
let me gather it up in my hands and measure it in a plug-
hat; said I could have a whole hatful for five hundred

dollars. But I was a burnt child, and resisted all these temptations—resisted them easily; went off with my money, and next day lent five thousand of it to a friend who was going to go bankrupt three days later.

It was the chance of fortune thus thrown away which, perhaps, led him to take up later with an engraving process—an adventure which lasted through several years and ate up a heavy sum. Altogether, these experiences in finance cost Mark Twain a fair-sized fortune, though, after all, they were as nothing compared with the great type-machine calamity which we shall hear of in a later chapter.

XLIII

BACK TO THE RIVER, WITH BIXBY

FORTUNATELY, Mark Twain was not greatly upset by his losses. They exasperated him for the moment, perhaps, but his violence waned presently, and the whole matter was put aside forever. His work went on with slight interference. Looking over his *Mississippi* chapters one day, he was taken with a new interest in the river, and decided to make the steamboat trip between St. Louis and New Orleans, to report the changes that had taken place in his twenty-one years of absence. His Boston publisher, Osgood, agreed to accompany him, and a stenographer was engaged to take down conversations and comments.

At St. Louis they took passage on the steamer *Gold Dust* — Clemens under an assumed name, though he was promptly identified. In his book he tells how the pilot recognized him and how they became friends. Once, in later years, he said:

"I spent most of my time up there with him. When we got down below Cairo, where there was a big, full river—for it was high-water season and there was no danger of the boat hitting anything so long as she kept in the river—I had her most of the time on his watch. He would lie down and sleep and leave me there to dream that the years had not slipped away; that there had been no war, no mining days, no literary adventures; that I was still a pilot, happy and care-free as I had been twenty years before."

To heighten the illusion he had himself called regularly with the four-o'clock watch, in order not to miss the mornings. The points along the river were nearly all new to him, everything had changed, but during high-water this mattered little. He was a pilot again—a young fellow in his twenties, speculating on the problems of existence and reading his fortunes in the stars. The river had lost none of its charm for him. To Bixby he wrote:

I'd rather be a pilot than anything else I've ever been in my life. How do you run Plum Point?

He met Bixby at New Orleans. Bixby was a captain now, on the splendid new Anchor Line steamer *City of Baton Rouge*, one of the last of the fine river boats. Clemens made the return trip to St. Louis with Bixby on the *Baton Rouge*—almost exactly twenty-five years from their first trip together. To Bixby it seemed wonderfully like those old days back in the fifties.

"Sam was making notes in his memorandum-book, just as he always did," said Bixby, long after, to the writer of this history.

Mark Twain decided to see the river above St. Louis. He went to Hannibal to spend a few days with old friends. "Delightful days," he wrote home, "loitering around all day long, and talking with grayheads who were boys and girls with me thirty or forty years ago." He took boat for St. Paul and saw the upper river, which he had never seen before. He thought the scenery beautiful, but he found a sadness everywhere because of the decay of the river trade. In a note-book entry he said: "The romance of boating is gone now. In Hannibal the steamboat-man is no longer a god."

He worked at the *Mississippi* book that summer at the farm, but did not get on very well, and it was not until the following year (1883) that it came from the press. Osgood published it, and Charles L. Webster, who had married Mark Twain's niece, Annie (daughter of his sister Pamela), looked after the agency sales. Mark Twain, in fact, was preparing to become his own publisher, and this was the beginning. Webster was a man of ability, and the book sold well.

Life on the Mississippi is one of Mark Twain's best books—one of those which will live longest. The first twenty chapters are not excelled in quality anywhere in his writings. The remainder of the book has an interest of its own, but it lacks the charm of those memories of his youth—the mellow light of other days which enhances all of his better work.

XLIV

A READING-TOUR WITH CABLE

EVERY little while Mark Twain had a fever of play-writing, and it was about this time that he collaborated with W. D. Howells on a second Colonel Sellers play. It was a lively combination.

Once to the writer Howells said: "Clemens took one scene and I another. We had loads of fun about it. We cracked our sides laughing over it as we went along. We thought it mighty good, and I think to this day it was mighty good."

But actors and managers did not agree with them. Raymond, who had played the original Sellers, declared that in this play the Colonel had not become merely a visionary, but a lunatic. The play was offered elsewhere, and finally Mark Twain produced it at his own expense. But perhaps the public agreed with Raymond, for the venture did not pay.

It was about a year after this (the winter of 1884–5) that Mark Twain went back to the lecture platform—or rather, he joined with George W. Cable in a reading-tour. Cable had been giving readings on his own account from his wonderful Creole stories, and had visited Mark Twain in Hartford. While there he had been taken down with the mumps, and it was during his convalescence that the plan for a combined reading-tour had been made. This was early in the year, and the tour was to begin in the autumn.

Cable, meantime, having quite recovered, conceived a plan to repay Mark Twain's hospitality. It was to be an April-fool—a great complimentary joke. A few days before the first of the month he had a "private and confidential" circular letter printed, and mailed it to one hundred and fifty of Mark Twain's friends and admirers in Boston, New York, and elsewhere, asking that they send the humorist a letter to arrive April 1, requesting his autograph. It would seem that each one receiving this letter must have responded to it, for on the morning of April 1st an immense pile of letters was unloaded on Mark Twain's table. He did not know what to make of it, and Mrs. Clemens, who was party to the joke, slyly watched results. They were the most absurd requests for autographs ever written. He was fooled and mystified at first, then realizing the nature and magnitude of the joke, he entered into it fully—delighted, of course, for it was really a fine compliment. Some of the letters asked for autographs by the yard, some by the pound. Some commanded him to sit down and copy a few chapters from *The Innocents Abroad.*. Others asked that his autograph be attached to a check. John Hay requested that he copy a hymn, a few hundred lines of Young's *Night Thoughts*, etc., and added:

I want my boy to form a taste for serious and elevated poetry, and it will add considerable commercial value to have it in your handwriting.

Altogether, the reading of the letters gave Mark Twain a delightful day.

The platform tour of Clemens and Cable that fall was a success. They had good houses, and the work of these two favorites read by the authors of it made a fascinating program.

They continued their tour westward as far as Chicago and gave readings in Hannibal and Keokuk. Orion Clemens and his wife once more lived in Keokuk, and with them Jane Clemens, brisk and active for her eighty-one years. She had visited Hartford more than once and enjoyed "Sam's fine house," but she chose the West for home. Orion Clemens, honest, earnest, and industrious, had somehow missed success in life. The more prosperous brother, however, made an allowance ample for all. Mark Twain's mother attended the Keokuk reading. Later, at home, when her children asked her if she could still dance (she had been a great dancer in her youth), she rose, and in spite of her fourscore, tripped as lightly as a girl. It was the last time that Mark Twain would see her in full health.

At Christmas-time Cable and Clemens took a fortnight's holiday, and Clemens went home to Hartford. There a grand surprise awaited him. Mrs. Clemens had made an adaptation of *The Prince and the Pauper* for the stage, and his children, with those of the neighborhood, had learned the parts. A good stage had been set up in George Warner's home, with a pretty drop-curtain and very good scenery indeed. Clemens arrived in the late afternoon, and felt an air of mystery in the house, but did not guess what it meant. By and by he was led across the grounds to George Warner's home, into a large room, and placed in a seat directly fronting the stage. Then presently the curtain went up, the play began, and he knew. As he watched the little performers playing so eagerly the parts of his story, he was deeply moved and gratified.

It was only the beginning of *The Prince and the Pauper* production. The play was soon repeated, Clemens himself taking the part of Miles Hendon. In a "biography" of her father which Susy began a little later, she wrote:

Papa had only three days to learn the part in, but still we were all sure he could do it. . . . I was the prince, and Papa and I rehearsed two or three times a day for the three days before the appointed evening. Papa acted his part beautifully, and he added to the scene, making it a good deal longer. He was inexpressibly funny, with his great slouch hat and gait—oh, such a gait!

Susy's sister, Clara, took the part of Lady Jane Gray, while little Jean, aged four, in the part of a court official, sat at a small table and constantly signed state papers and death-warrants.

XLV

"THE ADVENTURES OF HUCKLEBERRY FINN"

MEANTIME, Mark Twain had really become a publisher. His nephew by marriage, Charles L. Webster, who, with Osgood, had handled the *Mississippi* book, was now established under the firm name of Charles L. Webster & Co., Samuel L. Clemens being the company. Clemens had another book ready, and the new firm were to handle it throughout.

The new book was a story which Mark Twain had begun one day at Quarry Farm, nearly eight years before. It was to be a continuation of the adventures of Tom Sawyer and Huck Finn, especially of the latter as told by himself. But the author had no great opinion of the tale and presently laid it aside. Then some seven years later, after his trip down the river, he felt again the inspiration of the old days, and the story of Huck's adventures had been continued and brought to a close. The author believed in it by this time, and the firm of Webster & Co. was really formed for the purpose of publishing it.

Mark Twain took an active interest in the process. From the pages of *Life* he selected an artist—a

young man named E. W. Kemble, who would later
become one of our foremost illustrators of Southern
character. He also gave attention to the selection
of the paper and the binding—even to the method
of canvassing for the sales. In a note to Webster,
he wrote:

Get at your canvassing early and drive it with all your
might. . . . If we haven't 40,000 subscriptions we simply
postpone publication till we've got them.

Mark Twain was making himself believe that he
was a business man, and in this instance, at least,
he seems to have made no mistake. Some advanced
chapters of *Huck* appeared serially in the *Century
Magazine*, and the public was eager for more. By
the time the *Century* chapters were finished the
forty thousand advance subscriptions for the book
had been taken, and Huck Finn's own story, so long
pushed aside and delayed, came grandly into its
own. Many grown-up readers and most critics declared that it was greater than the *Tom Sawyer*
book, though the younger readers generally like the
first book the best, it being rather more in the ju-
venile vein. Huck's story, in fact, was soon causing
quite grown-up discussions—discussions as to its
psychology and moral phases, matters which do not
interest small people, who are always on Huck's side
in everything, and quite willing that he should take
any risk of body or soul for the sake of Nigger Jim.
Poor, vagrant Ben Blankenship, hiding his runaway
negro in an Illinois swamp, could not dream that his

humanity would one day supply the moral episode
for an immortal book!

As literature, the story of *Huck Finn* holds a
higher place than that of *Tom Sawyer*. As stories,
they stand side by side, neither complete without
the other, and both certain to live as long as there
are real boys and girls to read them.

XLVI

MARK TWAIN was now a successful publisher, but his success thus far was nothing to what lay just ahead. One evening he learned that General Grant, after heavy financial disaster, had begun writing the memoirs which he (Clemens) had urged him to undertake some years before. Next morning he called on the General to learn the particulars. Grant had contributed some articles to the *Century* war series, and felt in a mood to continue the work. He had discussed with the *Century* publishers the matter of a book. Clemens suggested that such a book should be sold only by subscription and prophesied its enormous success. General Grant was less sure. His need of money was very great and he was anxious to get as much return as possible, but his faith was not large. He was inclined to make no special efforts in the matter of publication. But Mark Twain prevailed. Like his own Colonel Sellers, he talked glowingly and eloquently of millions. He first offered to direct the general to his own former subscription publisher, at Hartford, then finally proposed to publish it himself, offering Grant seventy per cent. of the net returns, and to pay all office expenses out of his own share.

Of course there could be nothing for any publisher in such an arrangement unless the sales were enormous. General Grant realized this, and at first refused to consent. Here was a friend offering to bankrupt himself out of pure philanthropy, a thing he could not permit. But Mark Twain came again and again, and finally persuaded him that purely as a business proposition the offer was warranted by the certainty of great sales.

So the firm of Charles L. Webster & Co. undertook the Grant book, and the old soldier, broken in health and fortune, was liberally provided with

FACSIMILE OF GENERAL GRANT'S LAST WRITING

means that would enable him to finish his task with his mind at peace. He devoted himself steadily to the work—at first writing by hand, then dictating to a stenographer that Webster & Co. provided. His disease, cancer, made fierce ravages, but he "fought it out on that line," and wrote the last pages of his memoirs by hand when he could no longer speak aloud. Mark Twain was much with him, and cheered him with anecdotes and news of the advance sale of his book. In one of his memoranda of that time Clemens wrote:

To-day (May 26) talked with General Grant about his and my first great Missouri campaign, in 1861. He surprised an empty camp near Florida, Missouri, on Salt River, which I had been occupying a day or two before. How near he came to playing the d—— with his future publisher.

At Mount McGregor, a few weeks before the end, General Grant asked if any estimate could now be made of the sum which his family would obtain from his work, and was deeply comforted by Clemens's prompt reply that more than one hundred thousand sets had already been sold, the author's share of which would exceed one hundred and fifty thousand dollars. Clemens added that the gross return would probably be twice as much more.

The last notes came from Grant's hands soon after that, and a few days later, July 23, 1885, his task completed, he died. To Henry Ward Beecher Clemens wrote:

One day he put his pencil aside and said there was nothing more to do. If I had been there I could have foretold the shock that struck the world three days later.

In a memorandum estimate made by Mark Twain soon after the canvass for the Grant memoirs had begun, he had prophesied that three hundred thousand sets of the book would be sold, and that he would pay General Grant in royalties $420,000. This prophecy was more than fulfilled. The first check paid to Mrs. Grant—the largest single royalty check in history — was for $200,000. Later payments brought her royalty return up to nearly $450,000. For once, at least, Mark Twain's business vision had been clear. A fortune had been realized for the Grant family. Even his own share was considerable, for out of that great sale more than a hundred thousand dollars' profit was realized by Webster & Co.

XLVII

THE HIGH-TIDE OF FORTUNE

THAT summer at Quarry Farm was one of the happiest they had ever known. Mark Twain, nearing fifty, was in the fullness of his manhood and in the brightest hour of his fortune. Susy, in her childish "biography," begun at this time, gives us a picture of him. She begins:

We are a happy family! We consist of Papa, Mama, Jean, Clara, and me. It is Papa I am writing about, and I shall have no trouble in not knowing what to say about him, as he is a very striking character. Papa's appearance has been described many times, but very incorrectly; he has beautiful, curly, gray hair, not any too thick or any too long, just right; a Roman nose, which greatly improves the beauty of his features, kind blue eyes, and a small mustache; he has a wonderfully shaped head and profile; he has a very good figure—in short, is an extraordinarily fine-looking man. . . .

He is a very good man, and a very funny one; he has got a temper, but we all have in this family. He is the loveliest man I ever saw, or ever hope to see, and oh, so absent-minded!

We may believe this is a true picture of Mark Twain at fifty. He did not look young for his years,

243

but he was still young in spirit and body. Susy tells how he blew bubbles for the children, filling them with tobacco smoke. Also, how he would play with the cats and come clear down from his study to see how a certain kitten was getting along.

Susy adds that "there are eleven cats at the farm now," and tells of the day's occupations, but the description is too long to quote. It reveals a beautiful, busy life.

Susy herself was a gentle, thoughtful, romantic child. One afternoon she discovered a wonderful tangle of vines and bushes, a still, shut-in corner not far from the study. She ran breathlessly to her aunt.

"Can I have it—can Clara and I have it all for our own?"

The petition was granted and the place was called Helen's Bower, for they were reading *Thaddeus of Warsaw*, and the name appealed to Susy's poetic fancy. Something happened to the "bower"—an unromantic workman mowed it down—but by this time there was a little house there which Mrs. Clemens had built, just for the children. It was a complete little cottage, when furnished. There was a porch in front, with comfortable chairs. Inside were also chairs, a table, dishes, shelves, a broom, even a stove—small, but practical. They called the little house "Ellerslie," out of Grace Aguilar's *Days of Robert Bruce*. There alone, or with their Langdon cousins, how many happy summers they played and dreamed away. Secluded by a hillside and happy trees, overlooking the hazy, distant town, it was a world apart—a corner of story-book land. When the end of the summer came its little owners went about bidding their treasures good-by, closing and kissing the gates of Ellerslie.

Looking back now, Mark Twain at fifty would seem to have been in his golden prime. His family was ideal—his surroundings idyllic. Favored by fortune, beloved by millions, honored now even in the highest places, what more had life to give? When November 30th brought his birthday, one of the great Brahmins, Dr. Oliver Wendell Holmes, wrote him a beautiful poem. Andrew Lang, England's foremost critic, also sent verses, while letters poured in from all sides.

And Mark Twain realized his fortune and was disturbed by it. To a friend he said: "I am frightened at the proportions of my prosperity. It seems to me that whatever I touch turns to gold."

XLVIII

BUSINESS DIFFICULTIES.   PLEASANTER THINGS

FOR the time it would seem that Mark Twain
had given up authorship for business. The success of the Grant book had filled his head with plans
for others of a like nature. The memoirs of General
McClellan and General Sheridan were arranged for.
Almost any war-book was considered a good venture. And there was another plan afoot. Pope Leo
XIII., in his old age, had given sanction to the preparation of his memoirs, and it was to be published,
with his blessing, by Webster & Co., of Hartford.
It was generally believed that such a book would
have a tremendous sale, and Colonel Sellers himself
could not have piled the figures higher than did his
creator in counting his prospective returns. Every
Catholic in the world must have a copy of the Pope's
book, and in America alone there were millions.
Webster went to Rome to consult with the Pope in
person, and was received in private audience. Mark
Twain's publishing firm seemed on the top wave of
success.

The McClellan and Sheridan books were issued,
and, in due time, the *Life of Pope Leo XIII.*—published simultaneously in six languages—issued from

the press. A large advance sale had been guaranteed
by the general canvassing agents—a fortunate thing,
as it proved. For, strange as it may seem, the book
did not prove a great success. It is hard to explain
just why. Perhaps Catholics felt that there had
been so many popes that the life of any particular
one was no great matter. The book paid, but not
largely. The McClellan and Sheridan books, likewise, were only partially successful. Perhaps the
public was getting tired of war memoirs. Webster
& Co. undertook books of a general sort—travel,
fiction, poetry. Many of them did not pay. Their
business from a march of triumph had become a
battle. They undertook a *Library of American Literature*, a work of many volumes, costly to make
and even more so to sell. To float this venture they
were obliged to borrow large sums.

It seems unfortunate that Mark Twain should
have been disturbed by these distracting things during what should have been his literary high-tide. As
it was, his business interests and cares absorbed the
energy that might otherwise have gone into books.
He was not entirely idle. He did an occasional
magazine article or story, and he began a book
which he worked at from time to time—the story
of a Connecticut Yankee who suddenly finds himself back in the days of King Arthur's reign. Webster was eager to publish another book by his great
literary partner, but the work on it went slowly.
Then Webster broke down from two years of overwork, and the business management fell into other
hands. Though still recognized as a great publish-

ing-house, those within the firm of Charles L. Webster & Co. knew that its prospects were not bright.

Furthermore, Mark Twain had finally invested in another patent, the type-setting machine mentioned in a former chapter, and the demands for cash to promote this venture were heavy. To his sister Pamela, about the end of 1887, he wrote: "The type-setter goes on forever at $3,000 a month. . . . We'll be through with it in three or four months, I reckon"—a false hope, for the three or four months would lengthen into as many years.

But if there were clouds gathering in the business sky, they were not often allowed to cast a shadow in Mark Twain's home. The beautiful house in Hartford was a place of welcome and merriment, of many guests and of happy children. Especially of happy children: during these years—the latter half of the 'eighties—when Mark Twain's fortunes were on the decline, his children were at the age to have a good time, and certainly they had it. The dramatic stage which had been first set up at George Warner's for the Christmas *Prince and Pauper* performance was brought over and set up in the Clemens school-room, and every Saturday there were plays or rehearsals, and every little while there would be a grand general performance in the great library downstairs, which would accommodate just eighty-four chairs, filled by parents of the performers and invited guests. In notes dictated many years later, Mark Twain said:

We dined as we could, probably with a neighbor, and by quarter to eight in the evening the hickory fire in the hall was pouring a sheet of flame up the chimney, the house was in a drench of gas-light from the ground floor up, the guests were arriving, and there was a babble of hearty greetings, with not a voice in it that was not old and familiar and affectionate; and when the curtain went up, we looked out from the stage upon none but faces dear to us, none but faces that were lit up with welcome for us.

He was one of the children himself, you see, and therefore on the stage with the others. Katy Leary, for thirty years in the family service, once said to the author: "The children were crazy about acting, and we all enjoyed it as much as they did, especially Mr. Clemens, who was the best actor of all. I have never known a happier household than theirs was during those years."

The plays were not all given by the children. Mark Twain had kept up his German study, and a class met regularly in his home to struggle with the problems of *der*, *die*, and *das*. By and by he wrote a play for the class, "Meisterschaft," a picturesque mixture of German and English, which they gave twice, with great success. It was unlike anything attempted before or since. No one but Mark Twain could have written it. Later (January, 1888), in modified form, it was published in the *Century Magazine*. It is his best work of this period.

Many pleasant and amusing things could be recalled from these days if one only had room. A visit with Robert Louis Stevenson was one of them. Stevenson was stopping at a small hotel near Washington Square, and he and Clemens sat on a bench in the sunshine and talked through at least one golden afternoon. What marvelous talk that must have been! *Huck Finn* was one of Stevenson's favorites, and once he told how he had insisted on reading the book aloud to an artist who was painting his portrait. The painter had protested at first, but presently had fallen a complete victim to Huck's story. Once, in a letter, Stevenson wrote:

My father, an old man, has been prevailed upon to read *Roughing It* (his usual amusement being found in theology), and after one evening spent with the book he declared: "I am frightened. It cannot be safe for a man at my time of life to laugh so much."

Mark Twain had been a "mugwump" during the Blaine-Cleveland campaign in 1880, which means that he had supported the independent Democratic candidate, Grover Cleveland. He was, therefore, in high favor at the White House during both Cleveland administrations, and called there informally whenever business took him to Washington. But on one occasion (it was his first visit after the President's marriage) there was to be a party, and Mrs. Clemens, who could not attend, slipped a little note into the pocket of his evening waistcoat, where he would be sure to find it when dressing, warning him as to his deportment. Being presented to young Mrs. Cleveland, he handed her a card on which he had written, "He didn't," and asked her to sign her name below those words. Mrs. Cleveland protested that she must know first what it was that he hadn't done, finally agreeing to sign if he would tell her immediately all about it, which he promised to do. She signed, and he handed her Mrs. Clemens's note. It was very brief. It said, "Don't wear your arctics in the White House."

Mrs. Cleveland summoned a messenger and had the card mailed immediately to Mrs. Clemens.

Absent-mindedness was characteristic of Mark Twain. He lived so much in the world within that to him the material outer world was often vague and shadowy. Once when he was knocking the balls about in the billiard-room, George, the colored butler, a favorite and privileged household character, brought up a card. So many canvassers came to sell him one thing and another that Clemens promptly assumed this to be one of them. George insisted mildly, but firmly, that, though a stranger, the caller was certainly a gentleman, and Clemens grumblingly descended the stairs. As he entered the parlor the caller arose and extended his hand. Clemens took it rather limply, for he had noticed some water-colors and engravings leaning against the furniture as if for exhibition, and he was instantly convinced that the caller was a picture-canvasser. Inquiries by the stranger as to Mrs. Clemens and the children did not change Mark Twain's conclusion. He was polite, but unresponsive, and gradually worked the visitor toward the front door. His inquiry as to the home of Charles Dudley Warner caused him to be shown eagerly in that direction.

Clemens, on his way back to the billiard-room, heard Mrs. Clemens call him—she was ill that day: "Youth!"

"Yes, Livy." He went in for a word.

"George brought me Mr. B.'s card. I hope you were nice to him; the B.s were so nice to us, once, in Europe, while you were gone."

"The B.s! Why, Livy!"

"Yes, of course; and I asked him to be sure to call when he came to Hartford."

"Well, he's been here."

"Oh Youth, have you done anything?"

"Yes, of course I have. He seemed to have some pictures to sell, so I sent him over to Warner's. I noticed he didn't take them with him. Land sakes! Livy, what can I do?"

"Go right after him—go quick! Tell him what you have done."

He went without further delay, bareheaded and in his slippers, as usual. Warner and B. were in cheerful conversation. They had met before. Clemens entered gaily.

"Oh, yes, I see! You found him all right. Charlie, we met Mr. B. and his wife in Europe, and they made things pleasant for us. I wanted to come over here *with* him, but I was a good deal occupied just then. Livy isn't very well, but she seems now a good deal better; so I just followed along to have a good talk, all together."

He stayed an hour, and whatever bad impression had formed in B.'s mind faded long before the hour ended. Returning home, Clemens noticed the pictures still on the parlor floor.

"George," he said, "what pictures are these that gentleman left?"

BUSINESS DIFFICULTIES

"Why, Mr. Clemens, those are our own pictures! Mrs. Clemens had me set them around to see how they would look in new places. The gentleman was only looking at them while he waited for you to come down."

It was in June, 1888, that Yale College conferred upon Mark Twain the degree of Master of Arts. He was proud of the honor, for it was recognition of a kind that had not come to him before—remarkable recognition, when we remember how as a child he had hated all schools and study, having ended his class-room days before he was twelve years old. He could not go to New Haven at the time, but later in the year made the students a delightful address. In his capacity of Master of Arts, he said, he had come down to New Haven to institute certain college reforms.

By advice, I turned my earliest attention to the Greek department. I told the Greek professor I had concluded to drop the use of the Greek-written character, because it is so hard to spell with and so impossible to read after you get it spelt. Let us draw the curtain there. I saw by what followed that nothing but early neglect saved him from being a very profane man.

He said he had given advice to the mathematical department with about the same result. The astronomy department he had found in a bad way. He had decided to transfer the professor to the law department and to put a law-student in his place.

A boy will be more biddable, more tractable—also cheaper. It is true he cannot be intrusted with important work at first, but he can comb the skies for nebulæ till he gets his hand in.

It was hardly the sort of an address that the holder of a college degree is expected to make, but doctors and students alike welcomed it hilariously from Mark Twain.

Not many great things happened to Mark Twain during this long period of semi-literary inaction, but many interesting ones. When Bill Nye, the humorist, and James Whitcomb Riley joined themselves in an entertainment combination, Mark Twain introduced them to their first Boston audience—a great event to them, and to Boston. Clemens himself gave a reading now and then, but not for money. Once, when Col. Richard Malcolm Johnston and Thomas Nelson Page were to give a reading in Baltimore, Page's wife fell ill, and Colonel Johnston wired to Charles Dudley Warner, asking him to come in Page's stead. Warner, unable to go, handed the telegram to Clemens, who promptly answered that he would come. They read to a packed house, and when the audience had gone and the returns were counted, an equal amount was handed to each of the authors. Clemens pushed his share over to Johnston, saying:

"That's yours, Colonel. I'm not reading for money these days."

Colonel Johnston, to whom the sum was important, tried to thank him, but Clemens only said:

"Never mind, Colonel; it only gives me pleasure to do you that little favor. You can pass it along some day."

BUSINESS DIFFICULTIES

As a matter of fact, Mark Twain himself was beginning to be hard pressed for funds at this time, but was strong in the faith that he would presently be a multi-millionaire. The type-setting machine was still costing a vast sum, but each week its inventor promised that a few more weeks or months would see it finished, and then a tide of wealth would come rolling in. Mark Twain felt that a man with shiploads of money almost in port could not properly entertain the public for pay. He read for institutions, schools, benefits, and the like, without charge.

XLIX

ONE day during the summer of 1889 a notable meeting took place in Elmira. On a blazing forenoon a rather small and very hot young man, in a slow, sizzling hack made his way up East Hill to Quarry Farm. He inquired for Mark Twain, only to be told that he was at the Langdon home, down in the town which the young man had just left. So he sat for a little time on the pleasant veranda, and Mrs. Crane and Susy Clemens, who were there, brought him some cool milk and listened to him talk in a way which seemed to them very entertaining and wonderful. When he went away he left his card with a name on it strange to them—strange to the world at that time. The name was Rudyard Kipling. Also on the card was the address Allahabad, and Susy kept it, because, to her, India was fairyland.

Kipling went down into Elmira and found Mark Twain. In his book *American Notes* he has left an account of that visit. He claimed that he had traveled around the world to see Mark Twain, and his article begins:

You are a contemptible lot over yonder. Scme of you are commissioners, and some are lieutenant-governors, and some have the V. C., and a few are privileged to walk about the Mall arm in arm with the viceroy; but I have seen Mark Twain this golden morning, have shaken his hand, and smoked a cigar—no, two cigars—with him, and talked with him for more than two hours!

But one should read the article entire—it is so worth while. Clemens also, long after, dictated an account of the meeting.

Kipling came down and spent a couple of hours with me, and at the end of that time I had surprised him as much as he had surprised me—and the honors were easy. I believed that he knew more than any person I had met before, and I knew that he knew that I knew less than any person *he* had met before. . . . When he had gone, Mrs. Langdon wanted to know about my visitor. I said:

"He is a stranger to me, but he is a most remarkable man—and I am the other one. Between us we cover all knowledge. He knows all that can be known, and I know the rest."

He *was* a stranger to me and all the world, and remained so for twelve months, but then he became suddenly known and universally known. . . . George Warner came into our library one morning, in Hartford, with a small book in his hand, and asked me if I had ever heard of Rudyard Kipling. I said "No."

He said I would hear of him very soon, and that the noise he made would be loud and continuous. . . . A day or two later he brought a copy of the London *World* which had a sketch of Kipling in it, and a mention of the fact that he had traveled in the United States. According to the sketch he had passed through Elmira. This remark, with the additional fact that he hailed from India, attracted my attention—also Susy's. She went to her room and brought his card from its place in the frame of her mirror, and the Quarry Farm visitor stood identified.

A theatrical production of *The Prince and the Pauper*, dramatized by Mrs. A. S. Richardson, was one of the events of this period. It was a charming performance, even if not a great financial success, and little Elsie Leslie, who played the double part of the Prince and Tom Canty, became a great favorite in the Clemens home. She was also a favorite of the actor and playwright, William Gillette,[1] and once when Clemens and Gillette were together they decided to give the little girl a surprise—a pair of slippers, in fact, embroidered by themselves. In his presentation letter to her, Mark Twain wrote:

Either of us could have thought of a single slipper, but it took both of us to think of two slippers. In fact, one of us did think of one slipper, and then, quick as a flash, the other thought of the other one.

He apologized for his delay:

You see, it was my first attempt at art, and I couldn't rightly get the hang of it, along at first. And then I was so busy I couldn't get a chance to work at home, and they wouldn't let me embroider on the cars; they said it made the other passengers afraid. . . . Take the slippers and wear them next your heart, Elsie dear, for every

[1] Gillette was originally a Hartford boy. Mark Twain had recognized his ability, advanced him funds with which to complete his dramatic education, and Gillette's first engagement seems to have been with the Colonel Sellers company. Mark Twain often advanced money in the interest of education. A young sculptor he sent to Paris for two years' study. Among others, he paid the way of two colored students through college.

stitch in them is a testimony of the affection which two of your loyalest friends bear you. Every single stitch cost us blood. I've got twice as many pores in me now as I used to have. . . . Do not wear these slippers in public, dear; it would only excite envy; and, as like as not, somebody would try to shoot you.

For five years Mark Twain had not published a book. Since the appearance of *Huck Finn* at the end of 1884 he had given the public only an occasional magazine story or article. His business struggle and the type-setter had consumed not only his fortune, but his time and energy. Now, at last, however, a book was ready. *A Connecticut Yankee in King Arthur's Court* came from the press of Webster & Co. at the end of 1889, a handsome book, elaborately and strikingly illustrated by Dan Beard—a pretentious volume which Mark Twain really considered his last. "It's my swan-song, my retirement from literature permanently," he wrote Howells, though certainly he was young, fifty-four, to have reached this conclusion.

The story of the *Yankee*—a fanciful narrative of a skilled Yankee mechanic swept backward through the centuries to the dim day of Arthur and his Round Table—is often grotesque enough in its humor, but under it all is Mark Twain's great humanity in fierce and noble protest against unjust laws, the tyranny of an individual or of a ruling class—oppression of any sort. As in *The Prince and the Pauper*, the wandering heir to the throne is brought in contact with cruel injustice and misery, so in the *Yankee* the king himself becomes one of a band of fettered slaves, and through degradation and horror of soul acquires mercy and humility.

The *Yankee in King Arthur's Court* is a splendidly imagined tale. Edmund Clarence Stedman and William Dean Howells have ranked it very high. Howells once wrote: "Of all the fanciful schemes in fiction, it pleases me most." The *Yankee* has not held its place in public favor with Mark Twain's earlier books, but it is a wonderful tale, and we cannot afford to leave it unread.

When the summer came again, Mark Twain and his family decided for once to forego Quarry Farm for a season in the Catskills, and presently found themselves located in a cottage at Onteora in the midst of a most delightful colony. Mrs. Mary Mapes Dodge, then editor of *St. Nicholas*, was there, and Mrs. Custer and Brander Matthews and Lawrence Hutton and a score of other congenial spirits. There was constant visiting from one cottage to another, with frequent gatherings at the Inn, which was general headquarters. Susy Clemens, now eighteen, was a central figure, brilliant, eager, intense, ambitious for achievement—lacking only in physical strength. She was so flower-like, it seemed always that her fragile body must be consumed by the flame of her spirit. It was a happy summer, but it closed sadly. Clemens was called to Keokuk in August, to his mother's bedside. A few weeks later came the end, and Jane Clemens had closed her long and useful life. She was in her eighty-eighth year. A little later, at Elmira, followed the death of Mrs. Clemens's mother, a sweet and gentle woman.

L

THE MACHINE. GOOD-BY TO HARTFORD. "JOAN" IS BEGUN

IT was hoped that the profits from the *Yankee* would provide for all needs until the great sums which were to come from the type-setter should come rolling in. The book did yield a large return, but, alas! the hope of the type-setter, deferred year after year and month after month, never reached fulfilment. Its inventor, James W. Paige, whom Mark Twain once called "a poet, a most great and genuine poet, whose sublime creations are written in steel," during ten years of persistent experiment had created one of the most marvelous machines ever constructed. It would set and distribute type, adjust the spaces, detect flaws—would perform, in fact, anything that a human being could do, with more exactness and far more swiftness. Mark Twain, himself a practical printer, seeing it in its earlier stages of development, and realizing what a fortune must come from a perfect type-setting machine, was willing to furnish his last dollar to complete the invention. But there the trouble lay. It could never be complete. It was too intricate, too much like a human being, too easy to get out of order, too hard to set right. Paige, fully confident, always believed he was just on the verge of perfecting some appliance that would overcome all difficulties, and the machine finally consisted of twenty thousand minutely exact parts, each of which required expert workmanship and had to be fitted by hand. Mark Twain once wrote:

All other wonderful inventions of the human brain sink pretty nearly into commonplaces contrasted with this awful, mechanical miracle.

This was true, and it conveys the secret of its failure. It was too much of a miracle to be reliable. Sometimes it would run steadily for hours, but then some part of its delicate mechanism would fail, and days, even weeks, were required to repair it. It is all too long a story to be given here. It has been fully told elsewhere.[1] By the end of 1890 Mark Twain had put in all his available capital, and was heavily in debt. He had spent one hundred and ninety thousand dollars on the machine, no penny of which would ever be returned. Outside capital to carry on the enterprise was promised, but it failed him. Still believing that there were "millions in it," he realized that for the present, at least, he could do no more.

Two things were clear: he must fall back on authorship for revenue, and he must retrench. In the present low stage of his fortunes he could no longer afford to live in the Hartford house. He decided to take the family abroad, where living was cheaper,

---

[1] In *Mark Twain—A Biography*, by the same author.

and where he might be able to work with fewer distractions.

He began writing at a great rate articles and stories for the magazines. He hunted out the old play he had written with Howells long before, and made a book of it, *The American Claimant*. Then, in June, 1891, they closed the beautiful Hartford house, where for seventeen years they had found an ideal home; where the children had grown through their sweet, early life; where the world's wisest had come and gone, pausing a little to laugh with the world's greatest merrymaker. The furniture was shrouded, the curtains drawn, the light shut away.

While the carriage was waiting, Mrs. Clemens went back and took a last look into each of the rooms, as if bidding a kind of good-by to the past. Then she entered the carriage, and Patrick McAleer, who had been with Mark Twain and his wife since their wedding-day, drove them to the station for the last time.

Mark Twain had a contract for six newspaper letters at one thousand dollars each. He was troubled with rheumatism in his arm, and wrote his first letter from Aix-les-Bains, a watering-place—a "health-factory," as he called it—and another from Marienbad. They were in Germany in August, and one day came to Heidelberg, where they occupied their old apartment of thirteen years before, room forty, in the Schloss Hotel, with its far prospect of wood and hill, the winding Neckar, and the blue, distant valley of the Rhine. Then, presently, they came to Switzerland, to Ouchy-Lausanne, by lovely

Lake Geneva, and here Clemens left the family and, with a guide and a boatman, went drifting down the Rhône in a curious, flat-bottomed craft, thinking to find material for one or more articles, possibly for a book. But drifting down that fair river through still

DOWN THE RHÔNE—SKETCH BY MARK TWAIN

September days, past ancient, drowsy villages, among sloping vineyards, where grapes were ripening in the tranquil sunlight, was too restful and soothing for work. In a letter home, he wrote:

It's too delicious, floating with the swift current under the awning these superb, sunshiny days, in peace and quietness. Some of the curious old historical towns strangely persuade me, but it's so lovely afloat that I don't stop, but view them from the outside and sail on. . . . I want to do all the rivers of Europe in an open boat in summer weather.

One afternoon, about fifteen miles below the city of Valence, he made a discovery. Dreamily observing the eastward horizon, he noticed that a distant blue mountain presented a striking profile outline of Napoleon Bonaparte. It seemed really a great

natural wonder, and he stopped that night at the
village just below, Beauchastel, a hoary huddle of
houses with the roofs all run together, and took a
room at the little hotel, with a window looking to
the eastward, from which, next morning, he saw the
profile of the great stone face, wonderfully outlined
against the sunrise. He was excited over his discovery, and made a descriptive note of it and an
outline sketch. Then, drifting farther down the
river, he characteristically forgot all about it and
did not remember it again for ten years, by which
time he had forgotten the point on the river where
the Napoleon could be seen, forgotten even that he
had made a note and sketch giving full details. He
wished the Napoleon to be found again, believing,
as he declared, that it would become one of the natural wonders of the world. To travelers going to

THE "LOST NAPOLEON"—SKETCH IN NOTE-BOOK

France he attempted to describe it, and some of these tried to find it; but, as he located it too far down the Rhône, no one reported success, and in time he spoke of his discovery as the "Lost Napoleon." It was not until after Mark Twain's death that it was rediscovered, and then by the writer of this memoir, who, having Mark Twain's note-book,[1] with its exact memoranda, on another September day, motoring up the Rhône, located the blue profile of the reclining Napoleon opposite the gray village of Beauchastel. It is a really remarkable effigy, and deserves to be visited.

Clemens finished his trip at Arles—a beautiful trip from beginning to end, but without literary result. When he undertook to write of it, he found that it lacked incident, and, what was worse, it lacked humor. To undertake to create both was too much. After a few chapters he put the manuscript aside, unfinished, and so it remains to this day.

The Clemens family spent the winter in Berlin, a gay winter, with Mark Twain as one of the distinguished figures of the German capital. He was received everywhere and made much of. Once a small, choice dinner was given him by Kaiser William II., and, later, a breakfast by the Empress. His books were great favorites in the German royal family. The Kaiser particularly enjoyed the *Mississippi* book, while the essay on "The Awful German Language," in the *Tramp Abroad*, he pronounced one of the finest pieces of humor ever written. Mark Twain's

---

[1] At Mark Twain's death his various literary effects passed into the hands of his biographer and literary executor, the present writer.

books were favorites, in fact, throughout Germany. The door-man in his hotel had them all in his little room, and, discovering one day that their guest, Samuel L. Clemens, and Mark Twain were one, he nearly exploded with excitement. Dragging the author to his small room, he pointed to the shelf:

"There," he said, "you wrote them! I've found it out. Ach! I did not know it before, and I ask a million pardons."

Affairs were not going well in America, and in June Clemens made a trip over to see what could be done. Probably he did very little, and he was back presently at Nauheim, a watering-place, where he was able to work rather quietly. He began two stories—one of them, "The Extraordinary Twins," which was the first form of *Pudd'nhead Wilson;* the other, "Tom Sawyer Abroad," for *St. Nicholas.* Twichell came to Nauheim during the summer, and one day he and Clemens ran over to Homburg, not far away. The Prince of Wales (later King Edward VII.) was there, and Clemens and Twichell, walking in the park, met the Prince with the British ambassador, and were presented. Twichell, in an account of the meeting, said:

The meeting between the Prince and Mark was a most cordial one on both sides, and presently the Prince took Mark Twain's arm and the two marched up and down, talking earnestly together, the Prince solid, erect, and soldier-like; Clemens weaving along in his curious, swinging gait, in full tide of talk, and brandishing a sun umbrella of the most scandalous description.

At Villa Viviani, an old, old mansion outside of Florence, on the hill toward Settignano, Mark Twain finished *Tom Sawyer Abroad*, also *Pudd'nhead Wilson*, and wrote the first half of a book that really had its beginning on the day when, an apprentice-boy in Hannibal, he had found a stray leaf from the pathetic story of Joan of Arc. All his life she had been his idol, and he had meant some day to write of her. Now, in this weather-stained old palace, looking down on Florence, medieval and hazy, and across to the villa-dotted hills, he began one of the most beautiful stories ever written, *The Personal Recollections of Joan of Arc*. He wrote in the first person, assuming the character of Joan's secretary, Sieur Louis de Conte, who in his old age is telling the great tale of the Maid of Orleans. It was Mark Twain's purpose, this time, to publish anonymously. Walking the floor one day at Viviani, and smoking vigorously, he said to Mrs. Clemens and Susy:

"I shall never be accepted seriously over my own signature. People always want to laugh over what I write, and are disappointed if they don't find a joke in it. This is to be a serious book. It means more to me than anything else I have ever undertaken. I shall write it anonymously."

So it was that the gentle Sieur de Conte took up the pen, and the tale of Joan was begun in the ancient garden of Viviani, a setting appropriate to its lovely form.

He wrote rapidly when once his plan was perfected and his material arranged. The reading of his

youth and manhood was now recalled, not merely as
reading, but as remembered reality. It was as if
he were truly the old Sieur de Conte, saturated with
memories, pouring out the tender, tragic tale. In six
weeks he had written one hundred thousand words—
remarkable progress at any time, the more so when
we consider that some of the authorities he consulted were in a foreign tongue. He had always
more or less kept up his study of French, begun so long
ago on the river, and it stood him now in good stead.
Still, it was never easy for him, and the multitude
of notes that still exist along the margin of his French
authorities show the magnitude of his work. Others
of the family went down into the city almost daily,
but he stayed in the still garden with Joan. Florence
and its suburbs were full of delightful people, some
of them old friends. There were luncheons, dinners,
teas, dances, and the like always in progress, but he
resisted most of these things, preferring to remain
the quaint old Sieur de Conte, following again the
banner of the Maid of Orleans marshaling her twi-
light armies across his illumined page.

But the next spring, March, 1893, he was obliged
to put aside the manuscript and hurry to America
again, fruitlessly, of course, for a financial stress was
on the land; the business of Webster & Co. was on
the down-grade—nothing could save it. There was
new hope in the old type-setting machine, but his
faith in the resurrection was not strong. The strain
of his affairs was telling on him. The business owed
a great sum, with no prospect of relief. Back in

Europe again, Mark Twain wrote F. D. Hall, his business manager in New York:

I am terribly tired of business. I am by nature and disposition unfit for it, and I want to get out of it. I am standing on a volcano. Get me out of business.

Tantalizing letters continued to come, holding out hope in the business—the machine—in any straw that promised a little support through the financial storm. Again he wrote Hall:

Great Scott, but it's a long year for you and me! I never knew the almanac to drag so. . . . I watch for your letters hungrily—just as I used to watch for the telegram saying the machine was finished—but when "next week *certainly*" suddenly swelled into "three weeks *sure*," I recognized the old familiar tune I used to hear so much. W—— don't know what sickheartedness is, but he is in a fair way to find out.

They closed Viviani in June and returned to Germany. By the end of August Clemens could stand no longer the strain of his American affairs, and, leaving the family at some German baths, he once more sailed for New York.

LI

THE FAILURE OF WEBSTER & CO.   AROUND THE WORLD.
SORROW

IN a room at the Players Club—"a cheap room,"
he wrote home, "at $1.50 per day"—Mark Twain
spent the winter, hoping against hope to weather the
financial storm.   His fortunes were at a lower ebb
than ever before;   lower even than during those
bleak mining days among the Esmeralda hills.   Then
there had been no one but himself, and he was young.
Now, at fifty-eight, he had precious lives dependent
upon him, and he was weighed down by debt.   The
liabilities of his firm were fully two hundred thousand
dollars—sixty thousand of which were owing to Mrs.
Clemens for money advanced—but the large remaining sum was due to banks, printers, binders,
and the manufacturers of paper.   A panic was on
the land and there was no business.   What he was
to do Clemens did not know.   He spent most of his
days in his room, trying to write, and succeeded in
finishing several magazine articles.   Outwardly cheerful, he hid the bitterness of his situation.

A few, however, knew the true state of his affairs.
One of these one night introduced him to Henry H.
Rogers, the Standard Oil millionaire.

"Mr. Clemens," said Mr. Rogers, "I was one of your early admirers. I heard you lecture a long time ago, on the Sandwich Islands."

They sat down at a table, and Mark Twain told amusing stories. Rogers was in a perpetual gale of laughter. They became friends from that evening, and in due time the author had confessed to the financier all his business worries.

"You had better let me look into things a little," Rogers said, and he advised Clemens to "stop walking the floor."

It was characteristic of Mark Twain to be willing to unload his affairs upon any one that he thought able to bear the burden. He became a new man overnight. With Henry Rogers in charge, life was once more worth while. He accepted invitations from the Rogers family and from many others, and was presently so gay, so widely sought, and seen in so many places that one of his acquaintances, "Jamie" Dodge, dubbed him the "Belle of New York."

Henry Rogers, meanwhile, was "looking into things." He had reasonable faith in the type-machine, and advanced a large sum on the chance of its proving a success. This, of course, lifted Mark Twain quite into the clouds. Daily he wrote and cabled all sorts of glowing hopes to his family, then in Paris. Once he wrote:

The ship is in sight now. . . . When the anchor is down, then I shall say: Farewell—a long farewell—to *business!* I will *never* touch it again! I will live in literature, I will wallow in it, revel in it; I will swim in ink!

Once he cabled, "Expect good news in ten days"; and a little later, "Look out for good news"; and in a few days, "Nearing success."

Those Sellers-like messages could not but appeal to Mrs. Clemens's sense of humor, even in those dark days. To her sister she wrote, "They make me laugh, for they are so like my beloved Colonel."

The affairs of Webster & Co. Mr. Rogers found in a bad way. When, at last, in April, 1894, the crisis came—a demand by the chief creditors for payment—he advised immediate assignment as the only course.

So the firm of Webster & Co. closed its doors. The business which less than ten years before had begun so prosperously had ended in failure. Mark Twain, nearing fifty-nine, was bankrupt. When all the firm's effects had been sold and applied on the accounts, he was still more than seventy thousand dollars in debt. Friends stepped in and offered to lend him money, but he declined these offers. Through Mr. Rogers a basis of settlement at fifty cents on the dollar was arranged, and Mark Twain said, "Give me time, and I will pay the other fifty."

No one but his wife and Mr. Rogers, however, believed that at his age he would be able to make good the promise. Many advised him not to attempt it, but to settle once and for all on the legal basis as arranged. Sometimes, in moments of despondency, he almost surrendered. Once he said:

"I need not dream of paying it. I never could manage it."

But these were only the hard moments. For the

most part he kept up good heart and confidence. It is true that he now believed again in the future of the type-setter, and that returns from it would pay him out of bankruptcy. But later in the year this final hope was taken away. Mr. Rogers wrote to him that in the final test the machine had failed to prove itself practical and that the whole project had been finally and permanently abandoned. The shock of disappointment was heavy for the moment, but then it was over—completely over—for that old mechanical demon, that vampire of invention that had sapped his fortune so long, was laid at last. The worst had happened; there was nothing more to dread. Within a week Mark Twain (he was now back in Paris with the family) had settled down to work once more on the *Recollections of Joan*, and all mention and memory of the type-setter was forever put away. The machine stands to-day in the Sibley College of Engineering, where it is exhibited as the costliest piece of mechanism for its size ever constructed. Mark Twain once received a letter from an author who had written a book to assist inventors and patentees, asking for his indorsement. He replied:

DEAR SIR,—I have, as you say, been interested in patents and patentees. If your book tells how to exterminate inventors, send me nine editions. Send them by express.

Very truly yours,

S. L. CLEMENS.

Those were economical days. There was no income except from the old books, and at the time this was not large. The Clemens family, however, was cheerful, and Mark Twain was once more in splendid working form. The story of Joan hurried to its tragic conclusion. Each night he read to the family what he had written that day, and Susy, who was easily moved, would say, "Wait—wait till I get my handkerchief," and one night when the last pages had been written and read, and the fearful scene at Rouen had been depicted, Susy wrote in her diary, "To-night Joan of Arc was burned at the stake!" Meaning that the book was finished.

Nov 30, 1908

I like the Joan of Arc best of all my books; & it is the best, I know it perfectly well. And besides, it furnished me seven times the pleasure afforded me by any of the others: 12 years of preparation & 2 years of writing. The others needed no preparation, & got none.

Mark Twain

Susy herself had fine literary taste, and might have written had not her greater purpose been to sing. There are fragments of her writing that show the true literary touch. Both Susy and her father cared more for *Joan* than for any of the former books. To Mr. Rogers Clemens wrote, "Possibly the book may not sell, but that is nothing—it was written for love." It was placed serially with *Harper's Magazine* and appeared anonymously, but the public soon identified the inimitable touch of Mark Twain.

It was now the spring of 1895, and Mark Twain had decided upon a new plan to restore his fortunes. Platform work had always paid him well, and though he disliked it now more than ever, he had resolved upon something unheard of in that line—nothing less, in fact, than a platform tour around the world. In May, with the family, he sailed for America, and after a month or two of rest at Quarry Farm he set out with Mrs. Clemens and Clara and with his American agent, J. B. Pond, for the Pacific coast. Susy and Jean remained behind with their aunt at the farm. The travelers left Elmira at night, and they always remembered the picture of Susy, standing under the electric light of the railway platform, waving them good-by.

Mark Twain's tour of the world was a success from the beginning. Everywhere he was received with splendid honors—in America, in Australia, in New Zealand, in India, in Ceylon, in South Africa— wherever he went his welcome was a grand ovation, his theaters and halls were never large enough to hold his audiences. With the possible exception of General Grant's long tour in 1878–9 there had hardly been a more gorgeous progress than Mark Twain's trip around the world. Everywhere they were overwhelmed with attention and gifts. We cannot begin to tell the story of that journey here. In *Following the Equator* the author himself tells it in his own delightful fashion.

From time to time along the way Mark Twain forwarded his accumulated profits to Mr. Rogers to apply against his debts, and by the time they sailed from South Africa the sum was large enough to encourage him to believe that, with the royalties to be derived from the book he would write of his travels, he might be able to pay in full and so face the world once more a free man. Their long trip—it had lasted a full year—was nearing its end. They would spend the winter in London—Susy and Jean were notified to join them there. They would all be reunited again. The outlook seemed bright once more.

They reached England the last of July. Susy and Jean, with Katy Leary, were to arrive on the 12th of August. But the 12th did not bring them—it brought, instead, a letter. Susy was not well, the letter said; the sailing had been postponed. The letter added that it was nothing serious, but her parents cabled at once for later news. Receiving no satisfactory answer, Mrs. Clemens, full of forebodings, prepared to sail with Clara for America. Clemens would remain in London to arrange for the winter residence. A cable came, saying Susy's recovery would be slow but certain. Mrs. Clemens and Clara sailed immediately. In some notes he once dictated, Mark Twain said:

That was the 15th of August, 1896. Three days later, when my wife and Clara were about half-way across the ocean, I was standing in our dining-room, thinking of nothing in particular, when a cablegram was put into my hand. It said, "Susy was peacefully released to-day."

Mark Twain's life had contained other tragedies, but no other that equaled this one. The dead girl had been his heart's pride; it was a year since they parted, and now he knew he would never see her again. The blow had found him alone and among strangers. In that day he could not even reach out to those upon the ocean, drawing daily nearer to the heartbreak.

Susy Clemens had died in the old Hartford home. She had been well for a time at the farm, but then her health had declined. She worked continuously at her singing lessons and overtried her strength. Then she went on a visit to Mrs. Charles Dudley Warner, in Hartford; but she did not rest, working harder than ever at her singing. Finally she was told that she must consult a physician. The doctor came and prescribed soothing remedies, and advised that she have the rest and quiet of her own home. Mrs. Crane came from Elmira, also her uncle Charles Langdon. But Susy became worse, and a few days later her malady was pronounced meningitis. This was the 15th of August, the day that her mother and Clara sailed from England. She was delirious

and burning with fever, but at last sank into uncon-
sciousness. She died three days later, and on the
night that Mrs. Clemens and Clara arrived was
taken to Elmira for burial.

They laid her beside the little brother that had
died so long before, and ordered a headstone with
some lines which they had found in Australia, written
by Robert Richardson:

> Warm summer sun, shine kindly here;
> Warm southern wind, blow softly here;
> Green sod above, lie light, lie light!—
> Good night, dear heart, good night, good night.

LII

EUROPEAN ECONOMIES

WITH Clara and Jean, Mrs. Clemens returned
to England, and in a modest house on Tedworth Square, a secluded corner of London, the
stricken family hid themselves away for the winter.
Few, even of their closest friends, knew of their
whereabouts. In time the report was circulated
that Mark Twain, old, sick, and deserted by his
family, was living in poverty, toiling to pay his
debts. Through the London publishers a distant
cousin, Dr. James Clemens, of St. Louis, located
the house on Tedworth Square, and wrote, offering
assistance. He was invited to call, and found a
quiet place—the life there simple—but not poverty.
By and by there was another report—this time that
Mark Twain was dead. A reporter found his way
to Tedworth Square, and, being received by Mark
Twain himself, asked what he should say.

Clemens regarded him gravely, then, in his slow,
nasal drawl, "Say—that the report of my death—
has been grossly—exaggerated," a remark that a day
later was amusing both hemispheres. He could not
help his humor; it was his natural form of utterance
—the medium for conveying fact, fiction, satire,

philosophy. Whatever his depth of despair, the quaint surprise of speech would come, and it would be so until his last day.

By November he was at work on his book of travel, which he first thought of calling "Around the World." He went out not at all that winter, and the work progressed steadily, and was complete by the following May (1897).

Meantime, during his trip around the world, Mark Twain's publishers had issued two volumes of his work — the *Joan of Arc* book, and another *Tom Sawyer* book, the latter volume combining two rather short stories, "Tom Sawyer Abroad," published serially in *St. Nicholas*, and "Tom Sawyer, Detective." The *Joan of Arc* book, the tenderest and most exquisite of all Mark Twain's work—a tale told with the deepest sympathy and the rarest delicacy—was dedicated by the author to his wife, as being the only piece of his writing which he considered worthy of this honor. He regarded it as his best book, and this was an opinion that did not change. Twelve years later—it was on his seventy-third birthday— he wrote as his final verdict, November 30, 1908:

I like the *Joan of Arc* best of all my books; and it *is* the best; I know it perfectly well, and, besides, it furnished me seven times the pleasure afforded me by any of the others; twelve years of preparation and two years of writing. The others needed no preparation and got none. MARK TWAIN.

The public at first did not agree with the author's estimate, and the demand for the book was not large. But the public amended its opinion. The demand for *Joan* increased with each year until its sales ranked with the most popular of Mark Twain's books.

The new stories of Tom and Huck have never been as popular as the earlier adventures of this pair of heroes. The shorter stories are less important and perhaps less alive, but they are certainly very readable tales, and nobody but Mark Twain could have written them.

Clemens began some new stories when his travel book was out of the way, but presently with the family was on the way to Switzerland for the summer. They lived at Weggis, on Lake Lucerne, in the Villa Buhlegg—a very modest five-franc-a-day *pension*, for they were economizing and putting away money for the debts. Mark Twain was not in a mood for work, and, besides, proofs of the new book —*Following the Equator*, as it is now called—were coming steadily. But on the anniversary of Susy's death (August 18th) he wrote a poem, "In Memoriam," in which he touched a literary height never before attained. It was published in *Harper's Magazine*, and now appears in his collected works.

Across from Villa Buhlegg on the lake-front there was a small shaded inclosure where he loved to sit and look out on the blue water and lofty mountains, one of which, Rigi, he and Twichell had climbed nineteen years before. The little retreat is still there, and to-day one of the trees bears a tablet (in German), "Mark Twain's Rest."

Autumn found the family in Vienna, located for

the winter at the Hôtel Métropole. Mrs. Clemens realized that her daughters must no longer be deprived of social and artistic advantages. For herself, she longed only for retirement.

Vienna is always a gay city, a center of art and culture and splendid social functions. From the moment of his arrival, Mark Twain and his family were in the midst of affairs. Their room at the Métropole became an assembling-place for distinguished members of the several circles that go to make up the dazzling Viennese life. Mrs. Clemens, to her sister in America, once wrote:

Such funny combinations are here sometimes: one duke, several counts, several writers, several barons, two princes, newspaper women, etc.

Mark Twain found himself the literary lion of the Austrian capital. Every club entertained him and roared with delight at his German speeches. Wherever he appeared on the streets he was recognized. "Let him pass! Don't you see it is Herr Mark Twain!" commanded an officer to a guard who, in the midst of a great assemblage, had presumed to bar the way.

LIII

MARK TWAIN PAYS HIS DEBTS

MARK TWAIN wrote much and well during this period, in spite of his social life. His article "Concerning the Jews" was written that first winter in Vienna—a fine piece of special pleading; also the greatest of his short stories—one of the greatest of *all* short stories—"The Man that Corrupted Hadleyburg."

But there were good reasons why he should write better now; his mind was free of a mighty load— he had paid his debts!

Soon after his arrival in Vienna he had written to Mr. Rogers:

Let us begin on those debts. I cannot bear the weight any longer. It totally unfits me for work.

He had accumulated a large sum for the purpose, and the royalties from the new book were beginning to roll in. Payment of the debts was begun. At the end of December he wrote again:

Land, we are glad to see those debts diminishing. For the first time in my life I am getting more pleasure from paying money out than from pulling it in.

MARK TWAIN PAYS HIS DEBTS

A few days later he wrote to Howells that he had "turned the corner"; and again:

We've lived close to the bone and saved every cent we could, and there's no undisputed claim now that we can't cash. . . . I hope you will never get the like of the load saddled on to you that was saddled on to me, three years ago. And yet there is such a solid pleasure in *paying* the things that I reckon it is worth while to get into that kind of a hobble, after all. Mrs. Clemens gets millions of delight out of it, and the children have never uttered one complaint about the scrimping from the beginning.

By the end of January, 1898, Clemens had accumulated enough money to make the final payments to his creditors. At the time of his failure he had given himself five years to achieve this result. But he had needed less than four. A report from Mr. Rogers showed that a balance of thirteen thousand dollars would remain to his credit after the last accounts were wiped away.

Clemens had tried to keep his money affairs out of the newspapers, but the payment of the final claims could not be concealed, and the press made the most of it. Head-lines shouted it. Editorials heralded Mark Twain as a second Walter Scott, because Scott, too, had labored to lift a great burden of debt. Never had Mark Twain been so beloved by his fellow-men.

One might suppose now that he had had enough of invention and commercial enterprises of every sort—that is, one who did not know Mark Twain might suppose this—but it would not be true. Within a month after his debts were paid he was negotiating with the Austrian inventor Szczepanik for the American rights in a wonderful carpet-pattern machine, and, Sellers-like, was planning to organize a company with a capital of fifteen hundred million dollars to control the carpet-weaving industries of the world. He wrote to Mr. Rogers about the great scheme, inviting the Standard Oil to "come in"; but the plan failed to bear the test of Mr. Rogers's investigation and was heard of no more.

Samuel Clemens's obligation to Henry Rogers was very great, but it was not quite the obligation that many supposed it to be. It was often asserted that the financier lent, even gave, the humorist large sums, and pointed out opportunities for speculation. No part of this statement is true. Mr. Rogers neither lent nor gave Mark Twain money, and never allowed him to speculate when he could prevent it. He sometimes invested Mark Twain's own funds for him, but he never bought for him a share of stock without money in hand to pay for it in full—money belonging to, and earned by, Clemens himself.

What Henry Rogers did give to Mark Twain was his priceless counsel and time—gifts more precious than any mere sum of money—favors that Mark Twain could accept without humiliation. He did accept them, and never ceased to be grateful. He rarely wrote without expressing his gratitude, and we get the size of Mark Twain's obligation when in one letter we read:

I have abundant peace of mind again—no sense of burden. Work is become a pleasure—it is not labor any longer.

MARK TWAIN PAYS HIS DEBTS

He wrote much and well, mainly magazine articles, including some of those chapters later gathered in his book on *Christian Science*. He reveled like a boy in his new freedom and fortunes, in the lavish honors paid him, in the rich circumstance of Viennese life. But always just beneath the surface were unforgetable sorrows. His face in repose was always sad. Once, after writing to Howells of his successes, he added:

All those things might move and interest one. But how desperately more I have been moved to-night by the thought of a little old copy in the nursery of *At the Back of the North Wind*. Oh, what happy days they were when that book was read, and how Susy loved it!

LIV

RETURN AFTER EXILE

NEWS came to Vienna of the death of Orion Clemens, at the age of seventy-two. Orion had died as he had lived—a gentle dreamer, always with a new plan. He had not been sick at all. One morning early he had seated himself at a table, with pencil and paper, and was putting down the details of his latest project, when death came— kindly, in the moment of new hope. He was a generous, upright man, beloved by all who understood him.

The Clemenses remained two winters in Vienna, spending the second at the Hôtel Krantz, where their rooms were larger and finer than at the Métropole, and even more crowded with notabilities. Their *salon* acquired the name of the "Second Embassy," and Mark Twain was, in fact, the most representative American in the Austrian capital. It became the fashion to consult him on every question of public interest, his comments, whether serious or otherwise, being always worth printing. When European disarmament was proposed, Editor William T. Stead, of the *Review of Reviews*, wrote for his opinion. He replied:

RETURN AFTER EXILE

Dear Mr. Stead,—The Tsar is ready to disarm. I am ready to disarm. Collect the others; it should not be much of a task now. Mark Twain.

He refused offers of many sorts. He declined ten thousand dollars for a tobacco indorsement, though he liked the tobacco well enough. He declined ten thousand dollars a year for five years to lend his name as editor of a humorous periodical. He declined another ten thousand for ten lectures, and another offer for fifty lectures at the same rate—that is, one thousand dollars per night. He could get along without these sums, he said, and still preserve some remnants of his self-respect.

It was May, 1899, when Clemens and his family left Vienna. They spent a summer in Sweden on account of the health of Jean Clemens, and located in London apartments—30 Wellington Court—for the winter. Then followed a summer at beautiful Dollis Hill, an old house where Gladstone had often visited, on a shady hilltop just outside of London. The city had not quite inclosed the place then, and there were spreading oaks, a pond with lily-pads, and wide spaces of grassy lawn. The place to-day is converted into a public garden called Gladstone Park. Writing to Twichell in mid-summer, Clemens said:

I am the only person who is ever in the house in the daytime, but I am working, and deep in the luxury of it. But there is one tremendous defect. Livy is all so enchanted with the place and so in love with it that she doesn't know how she is going to tear herself away from it.

289

However, there was one still greater attraction than Dollis Hill, and that was America—home. Mark Twain at sixty-five and a free man once more had decided to return to his native land. They closed Dollis Hill at the end of September, and October 6, 1900, sailed on the *Minnehaha* for New York, bidding good-by, as Mark Twain believed, and hoped, to foreign travel. Nine days later, to a reporter who greeted him on the ship, he said:

"If I ever get ashore I am going to break both of my legs so I can't get away again."

LV

NEW YORK tried to outdo Vienna and London in honoring Mark Twain. Every newspaper was filled with the story of his great fight against debt, and his triumph. "He had behaved like Walter Scott," writes Howells, "as millions rejoiced to know who had not known how Walter Scott behaved till they knew it was like Clemens." Clubs and societies vied with one another in offering him grand entertainments. Literary and lecture proposals poured in. He was offered at the rate of a dollar a word for his writing—he could name his own terms for lectures.

These sensational offers did not tempt him. He was sick of the platform. He made a dinner speech here and there—always an event—but he gave no lectures or readings for profit. His literary work he confined to a few magazines, and presently concluded an arrangement with Harper & Brothers for whatever he might write, the payment to be twenty (later thirty) cents per word. He arranged with the same firm for the publication of all his books, by this time collected in uniform edition. He wished his affairs to be settled as nearly as might be. His desire was freedom from care. Also he would have liked a period of quiet and rest, but that was impossible. He realized that the multitude of honors tendered him was in a sense a vast compliment which he could not entirely refuse. Howells writes that Mark Twain's countrymen "kept it up past all precedent," and in return Mark Twain tried to do his part. "His friends saw that he was wearing himself out," adds Howells, and certain it is that he grew thin and pale and had a hacking cough. Once to Richard Watson Gilder he wrote:

In bed with a chest cold and other company.

DEAR GILDER,—I can't. If I were a well man I could explain with this pencil, but in the cir——ces I will leave it all to your imagination.

Was it Grady that killed himself trying to do all the dining and speeching? No, old man, no, no!

Ever yours,   MARK.

In the various dinner speeches and other utterances made by Mark Twain at this time, his hearers recognized a new and great seriousness of purpose. It was not really new, only, perhaps, more emphasized. He still made them laugh, but he insisted on making them think, too. He preached a new gospel of patriotism—not the patriotism that means a boisterous cheering of the Stars and Stripes wherever unfurled, but the patriotism that proposes to keep the Stars and Stripes clean and worth shouting for. In one place he said:

We teach the boys to atrophy their independence. We teach them to take their patriotism at second hand; to

A PROPHET AT HOME

shout with the largest crowd without examining into the
right or wrong of the matter—exactly as boys under
monarchies are taught, and have always been taught.

He protested against the blind allegiance of monarchies. He was seldom "with the largest crowd"
himself. Writing much of our foreign affairs, then
in a good deal of a muddle, he assailed so fearlessly
and fiercely measures which he held to be unjust
that he was caricatured as an armed knight on a
charger and as Huck Finn with a gun.

But he was not always warlike. One of the
speeches he made that winter was with Col. Henry
Watterson, a former Confederate soldier, at a Lincoln birthday memorial at Carnegie Hall. "Think
of it!" he wrote Twichell, "two old rebels function-
ing there; I as president and Watterson as orator
of the day. Things have changed somewhat in
these forty years, thank God!"

The Clemens household did not go back to Hartford. During their early years abroad it had been
Mrs. Clemens's dream to return and open the
beautiful home, with everything the same as before.
The death of Susy had changed all this. The
mother had grown more and more to feel that she
could not bear the sorrow of Susy's absence in the
familiar rooms. After a trip which Clemens himself
made to Hartford, he wrote, "I realize that if we
ever enter the house again to live, our hearts will
break."

So they did not go back. Mrs. Clemens had seen
it for the last time on that day when the carriage
waited while she went back to take a last look into

20   293

the vacant rooms. They had taken a house at 14 West Tenth Street for the winter, and when summer came they went to a log cabin on Saranac Lake, which they called "The Lair." Here Mark Twain wrote *A Double-barreled Detective Story*, a not very successful burlesque of Sherlock Holmes. But most of the time that summer he loafed and rested, as was his right. Once during the summer he went on a cruise with H. H. Rogers, Speaker "Tom" Reed, and others on Mr. Rogers's yacht.

LVI

HONORED BY MISSOURI

THE family did not return to New York. They took a beautiful house at Riverdale on the Hudson—the old Appleton homestead. Here they established themselves and settled down for American residence. They would have bought the Appleton place, but the price was beyond their reach.

It was in the autumn of 1901 that Mark Twain settled in Riverdale. In June of the following year he was summoned West to receive the degree of LL.D. from the university of his native state. He made the journey a sort of last general visit to old associations and friends. In St. Louis he saw Horace Bixby, fresh, wiry, and capable as he had been forty-five years before. Clemens said:

"I have become an old man. You are still thirty-five."

They went over to the rooms of the pilots' association, where the river-men gathered in force to celebrate his return. Then he took train for Hannibal.

He spent several days in Hannibal and saw Laura Hawkins—Mrs. Frazer, and a widow now—and John Briggs, an old man, and John RoBards, who had worn the golden curls and the medal for good conduct. They drove him to the old house on Hill Street, where once he had lived and set type; photographers were there and photographed him standing at the front door.

"It all seems so small to me," he said, as he looked through the house. "A boy's home is a big place to him. I suppose if I should come back again ten years from now it would be the size of a bird-house." He did not see "Huck"—Tom Blankenship had not lived in Hannibal for many years. But he was driven to all the familiar haunts—to Lover's Leap, the cave, and the rest; and Sunday afternoon, with John Briggs, he walked over Holliday's Hill—the "Cardiff Hill" of *Tom Sawyer*. It was just such a day as the one when they had damaged a cooper shop and so nearly finished the old negro driver. A good deal more than fifty years had passed since then, and now here they were once more—Tom Sawyer and Joe Harper—two old men, the hills still fresh and green, the river rippling in the sun. Looking across to the Illinois shore and the green islands where they had played, and to Lover's Leap on the south, the man who had been Sam Clemens said:

"John, that is one of the loveliest sights I ever saw. Down there is the place we used to swim, and yonder is where a man was drowned, and there's where the steamboat sank. Down there on Lover's Leap is where the Millerites put on their robes one night to go to heaven. None of them went that night, but I suppose most of them have gone now."

HONORED BY MISSOURI

John Briggs said, "Sam, do you remember the day we stole peaches from old man Price, and one of his bow-legged niggers came after us with dogs, and how we made up our minds we'd catch that nigger and drown him?"

And so they talked on of this thing and that, and by and by drove along the river, and Sam Clemens pointed out the place where he swam it and was taken with a cramp on the return.

"Once near the shore I thought I would let down," he said, "but was afraid to, knowing that if the water was deep I was a goner, but finally my knee struck the sand and I crawled out. That was the closest call I ever had."

They drove by a place where a haunted house had stood. They drank from a well they had always known—from the bucket, as they had always drunk —talking, always talking, touching with lingering fondness that most beautiful and safest of all our possessions—the past.

"Sam," said John, when they parted, "this is probably the last time we shall meet on earth. God bless you. Perhaps somewhere we shall renew our friendship."

"John," was the answer, "this day has been worth a thousand dollars to me. We were like brothers once, and I feel that we are the same now. Good-by, John. I'll try to meet you—somewhere."

Clemens left next day for Columbia, where the university is located. At each station a crowd had gathered to cheer and wave as the train pulled in and to offer him flowers. Sometimes he tried to say a few words, but his voice would not come. This was more than even Tom Sawyer had dreamed.

Certainly there is something deeply touching in the recognition of one's native State; the return of the boy who has set out unknown to battle with life and who is called back to be crowned is unlike any other home-coming—more dramatic, more moving. Next day at the university Mark Twain, summoned before the crowded assembly-hall to receive his degree, stepped out to the center of the stage and paused. He seemed in doubt as to whether he should make a speech or only express his thanks for the honor received. Suddenly and without signal the great audience rose and stood in silence at his feet. He bowed but he could not speak. Then the vast assembly began a peculiar chant, spelling out slowly the word M-i-s-s-o-u-r-i, with a pause between each letter. It was tremendously impressive.

Mark Twain was not left in doubt as to what was required of him when the chant ended. The audience demanded a speech—a speech, and he made them one—such a speech as no one there would forget to his dying day.

Back in St. Louis, he attended the rechristening of the St. Louis harbor boat; it had been previously called the *St. Louis*, but it was now to be called the *Mark Twain*.

LVII

THE CLOSE OF A BEAUTIFUL LIFE

LIFE which had begun very cheerfully at Riverdale ended sadly enough. In August, at York
Harbor, Maine, Mrs. Clemens's health failed and
she was brought home an invalid, confined almost
entirely to her room. She had been always the life,
the center, the mainspring of the household. Now
she must not even be consulted—hardly visited.
On her bad days—and they were many—Clemens,
sad and anxious, spent most of his time lingering
about her door, waiting for news, or until he was
permitted to see her for a brief moment. In his
memorandum-book of that period he wrote:

Our dear prisoner is where she is through overwork—
day and night devotion to the children and me. We did
not know how to value it. We know now.

And on the margin of a letter praising him for
what he had done for the world's enjoyment, and
for his triumph over debt, he wrote:

Livy never gets her share of those applauses, but it is
because the people do not know. Yet she is entitled to
the lion's share.

She improved during the winter, but very slowly. Her husband wrote in his diary:

Feb. 2, 1903—Thirty-third wedding anniversary. I was allowed to see Livy five minutes this morning, in honor of the day.

Mrs. Clemens had always remembered affectionately their winter in Florence of ten years before, and she now expressed the feeling that if she were in Florence again she would be better. The doctors approved, and it was decided that she should be taken there as soon as she was strong enough to travel. She had so far improved by June that they journeyed to Elmira, where in the quiet rest of Quarry Farm her strength returned somewhat and the hope of her recovery was strong.

Mark Twain wrote a story that summer in Elmira, in the little octagonal study, shut in now by trees and overgrown with vines. *A Dog's Tale*, a pathetic plea against vivisection, was the last story written in the little retreat that had seen the beginning of *Tom Sawyer* twenty-nine years before.

There was a feeling that the stay in Europe was this time to be permanent. On one of the first days of October Clemens wrote in his note-book:

To-day I place flowers on Susy's grave—for the last time, probably—and read the words, "Good night, dear heart, good night, good night."

They sailed on the 24th, by way of Naples and Genoa, and were presently installed in the Villa Reale di Quarto, a fine old Italian palace, in an

ancient garden looking out over Florence toward
Vallombrosa and the Chianti hills. It was a beautiful spot, though its aging walls and cypresses and
matted vines gave it a rather mournful look. Mrs.
Clemens's health improved there for a time, in spite
of dull, rainy, depressing weather; so much so that
in May, when the warmth and sun came back,
Clemens was driving about the country, seeking a
villa that he might buy for a home.

On one of these days—it was a Sunday in early
June, the 5th—when he had been out with Jean,
and had found a villa which he believed would fill
all their requirements, he came home full of enthusiasm and hope, eager to tell the patient about the
discovery. Certainly she seemed better. A day or
two before she had been wheeled out on the terrace
to enjoy the wonder of early Italian summer.

He found her bright and cheerful, anxious to hear
all their plans for the new home. He stayed with
her alone through the dinner hour, and their talk
was as in the old days. Summoned to go at last, he
chided himself for staying so long; but she said
there was no harm and kissed him, saying, "You
will come back?" and he answered, "Yes, to say
good night," meaning at half-past nine, as was the
permitted custom. He stood a moment at the door,
throwing kisses to her, and she returned them, her
face bright with smiles.

He was so full of hope—they were going to be
happy again. Long ago he had been in the habit of
singing jubilee songs to the children. He went up-
stairs now to the piano and played the chorus and

sang "Swing Low, Sweet Chariot," and "My Lord He Calls Me." He stopped then, but Jean, who had come in, asked him to go on. Mrs. Clemens, from her room, heard the music and said to Katy Leary:

"He is singing a good-night carol to me."

The music ceased presently. A moment later she asked to be lifted up. Almost in that instant life slipped away without a sound.

Clemens, just then coming to say good-night, saw a little group gathered about her bed, and heard Clara ask:

"Katy, is it true? Oh, Katy, *is* it true?"

In his note-book that night he wrote:

At a quarter-past nine this evening she that was the life of my life passed to the relief and the peace of death, after twenty-two months of unjust and unearned suffering. I first saw her thirty-seven years ago, and now I have looked upon her face for the last time. . . . I was full of remorse for things done and said in these thirty-four years of married life that have hurt Livy's heart.

And to Howells a few days later:

To-day, treasured in her worn, old testament, I found a dear and gentle letter from you dated Far Rockaway, September 12, 1896, about our poor Susy's death. I am tired and old; I wish I were with Livy.

They brought her to America; and from the house, and the rooms, where she had been made a bride bore her to a grave beside Susy and little Langdon.

LVIII

MARK TWAIN AT SEVENTY

IN a small cottage belonging to Richard Watson
Gilder, at Tyringham, Massachusetts, Samuel
Clemens and his daughters tried to plan for the future. Mrs. Clemens had always been the directing
force—they were lost without her. They finally took
a house in New York City, No. 21 Fifth Avenue, at the
corner of Ninth Street, installed the familiar furnishings, and tried once more to establish a home. The
house was handsome within and without—a proper
residence for a venerable author and sage—a suitable
setting for Mark Twain. But it was lonely for him.
It lacked soul—comfort that would reach the heart.
He added presently a great Æolian orchestrelle, with
a variety of music for his different moods. Sometimes he played it himself, though oftener his secretary played to him. He went out little that winter—seeing only a few old and intimate friends.
His writing, such as it was, was of a serious nature,
protests against oppression and injustice in a variety of forms. Once he wrote a "War Prayer,"
supposed to have been made by a mysterious,
white-robed stranger who enters a church during
those ceremonies that precede the marching of the

nation's armies to battle. The minister had prayed for victory, a prayer which the stranger interprets as a petition that the enemy's country be laid waste, its soldiers be torn by shells, its people turned out roofless, to wander through their desolated land in rags and hunger. It was a scathing arraignment of war, a prophecy, indeed, which to-day has been literally fulfilled. He did not print it, because then it would have been regarded as sacrilege.

When summer came again, in a beautiful house at Dublin, New Hampshire, on the Monadnock slope, he seemed to get back into the old swing of work, and wrote that pathetic story, *A Horse's Tale*. Also *Eve's Diary*, which, under its humor, is filled with tenderness, and he began a wildly fantastic tale entitled *Three Thousand Years Among the Microbes*, a satire in which Gulliver is outdone. He never finished it. He never *could* finish it, for it ran off into amazing by-paths that led nowhere, and the tale was lost. Yet he always meant to get at it again some day and make order out of chaos.

Old friends were dying, and Mark Twain grew more and more lonely. "My section of the procession has but a little way to go," he wrote when the great English actor Henry Irving died. Charles Henry Webb, his first publisher, John Hay, Bret Harte, Thomas B. Reed, and, indeed, most of his earlier associates were gone. When an invitation came from San Francisco to attend a California reunion he replied that his wandering days were over and that it was his purpose to sit by the fire for the rest of his life. And in another letter:

3,000 YEARS
AMONG the MICROBES
By a microbe
=
WITH NOTES
added by the Same Hand
7,000 years Later
=

Translated from the Original
Microbic
by

Mark Twain

MARK TWAIN'S SUGGESTED TITLE-PAGE FOR HIS MICROBE BOOK

I have done more for San Francisco than any other of its old residents. Since I left there, it has increased in population fully 300,000. I could have done more—I could have gone earlier—it was suggested.

A choice example, by the way, of Mark Twain's best humor, with its perfectly timed pause, and the

305

afterthought. Most humorists would have been content to end with the statement, "I could have gone earlier." Only Mark Twain could have added that final exquisite touch—"it was suggested."

Mark Twain was nearing seventy. With the 30th of November (1905) he would complete the scriptural limitation, and the president of his publishing-house, Col. George Harvey, of Harper's, proposed a great dinner for him in celebration of his grand maturity. Clemens would have preferred a small assembly in some snug place, with only his oldest and closest friends. Colonel Harvey had a different view. He had given a small, choice dinner to Mark Twain on his sixty-seventh birthday; now it must be something really worth while—something to outrank any former literary gathering. In order not to conflict with Thanksgiving holidays, the 5th of December was selected as the date. On that evening, two hundred American and English men and women of letters assembled in Delmonico's great banquet-hall to do honor to their chief. What an occasion it was! The tables of gay diners and among them Mark Twain, his snow-white hair a gleaming beacon for every eye. Then, by and by, presented by William Dean Howells, he rose to speak. Instantly the brilliant throng was on its feet, a shouting billow of life, the white handkerchiefs flying foam-like on its crest. It was a supreme moment! The greatest one of them all hailed by their applause as he scaled the mountain-top.

Never did Mark Twain deliver a more perfect

address than he gave that night. He began with the beginning, the meagerness of that little hamlet that had seen his birth, and sketched it all so quaintly and delightfully that his hearers laughed and shouted, though there was tenderness under it, and often the tears were just beneath the surface. He told of his habits of life, how he had reached seventy by following a plan of living that would probably kill anybody else; how, in fact, he believed he had no valuable habits at all. Then, at last, came that unforgetable close:

Threescore years and ten!

It is the scriptural statute of limitations. After that you owe no active duties; for you the strenuous life is over. You are a time-expired man, to use Kipling's military phrase: you have served your term, well or less well, and you are mustered out. You are become an honorary member of the republic, you are emancipated, compulsions are not for you, nor any bugle-call but "lights out." You pay the time-worn duty bills if you choose, or decline, if you prefer—and without prejudice—for they are not legally collectable.

The previous-engagement plea, which in forty years has cost you so many twinges, you can lay aside forever; on this side of the grave you will never need it again. If you shrink at thought of night, and winter, and the late home-comings from the banquet and the lights and laughter, through the deserted streets—a desolation which would not remind you now, as for a generation it did, that your friends are sleeping and you must creep in a-tiptoe and not disturb them, but would only remind you that you need not tiptoe, you can never disturb them more—if you shrink at the thought of these things you need only reply, "Your invitation honors me and pleases me because you still keep me in your remembrance, but I am seventy; seventy, and would nestle in the chimney-corner, and smoke my pipe, and read my book, and take my rest, wishing you well in all affection, and that when you, in your turn, shall arrive at Pier 70 you may step aboard your waiting ship with a reconciled spirit, and lay your course toward the sinking sun with a contented heart.

The tears that had been lying in wait were no longer kept back. If there were any present who did not let them flow without shame, who did not shout their applause from throats choked with sobs, they failed to mention the fact later.

Many of his old friends, one after another, rose to tell their love for him—Cable, Carnegie, Gilder, and the rest. Mr. Rogers did not speak, nor the Reverend Twichell, but they sat at his special table. Aldrich could not be there, but wrote a letter. A group of English authors, including Alfred Austin, Barrie, Chesterton, Dobson, Doyle, Hardy, Kipling, Lang, and others, joined in a cable. Helen Keller wrote:

And you are seventy years old? Or is the report exaggerated, like that of your death? I remember, when I saw you last, at the house of dear Mr. Hutton, in Princeton, you said:

"If a man is a pessimist before he is forty-eight, he knows too much. If he is an optimist after he is forty-eight, he knows too little."

Now we *know* you are an optimist, and nobody would dare to accuse one on the "seven-terraced summit" of

MARK TWAIN AT SEVENTY

knowing little. So probably you are not seventy, after all, but only forty-seven!

Helen Keller was right. Mark Twain was never a pessimist in his heart.

LIX

MARK TWAIN ARRANGES FOR HIS BIOGRAPHY

IT was at the beginning of 1906—a little more
than a month after the seventieth-birthday dinner
—that the writer of these chapters became personally associated with Mark Twain. I had met him
before, and from time to time he had returned a
kindly word about some book I had written and
inconsiderately sent him, for he had been my literary hero from childhood. Once, indeed, he had
allowed me to use some of his letters in a biography
I was writing of Thomas Nast; he had been always
an admirer of the great cartoonist, and the permission was kindness itself. Before the seating at the
birthday dinner I happened to find myself for a
moment alone with Mark Twain and remembered
to thank him in person for the use of the letters; a
day or two later I sent him a copy of the book.
I did not expect to hear from it again.

It was a little while after this that I was asked to
join in a small private dinner to be given to Mark
Twain at the Players, in celebration of his being
made an honorary member of that club—there being
at the time only one other member of this class, Sir
Henry Irving. I was in the Players a day or two

310

before the event, and David Munro, of *The North American Review*, a man whose gentle and kindly nature made him "David" to all who knew him, greeted me joyfully, his face full of something he knew I would wish to hear.

He had been chosen, he said, to propose the Players' dinner to Mark Twain, and had found him propped up in bed, and beside him a copy of the Nast book. I suspect now that David's generous heart prompted Mark Twain to speak of the book, and that his comment had lost nothing in David's eager retelling. But I was too proud and happy to question any feature of the precious compliment, and Munro—always most happy in making others happy—found opportunity to repeat it, and even to improve upon it—usually in the presence of others—several times during the evening.

The Players' dinner to Mark Twain was given on the evening of January 3, 1906, and the picture of it still remains clear to me. The guests, assembled around a single table in the private dining-room, did not exceed twenty-five in number. Brander Matthews presided, and the knightly Frank Millet, who would one day go down on the *Titanic*, was there, and Gilder and Munro and David Bispham and Robert Reid, and others of their kind. It so happened that my seat was nearly facing the guest of the evening, who by a custom of the Players is placed at the side and not at the distant end of the long table. Regarding him at leisure, I saw that he seemed to be in full health. He had an alert, rested look; his complexion had the tints of a miniature painting. Lit by the soft glow of the shaded candles, outlined against the richness of the shadowed walls, he made a figure of striking beauty. I could not take my eyes from it, for it stirred in me the farthest memories. I saw the interior of a farm-house sitting-room in the Middle West where I had first heard the name of Mark Twain, and where night after night a group had gathered around the evening lamp to hear read aloud the story of the Innocents on their Holy Land pilgrimage, which to a boy of eight had seemed only a wonderful poem and fairy-tale. To Charles Harvey Genung, who sat next to me, I whispered something of this, and how during the thirty-six years since then no one had meant to me quite what Mark Twain had meant—in literature and, indeed, in life. Now here he was just across the table. It was a fairy-tale come true.

Genung said: "You should write his life."

It seemed to me no more than a pleasant remark, but he came back to it again and again, trying to encourage me with the word that Munro had brought back concerning the biography of Nast. However, nothing of what he said had kindled any spark of hope. I put him off by saying that certainly some one of longer and closer friendship and larger experience had been selected for the work. Then the speaking began, and the matter went out of my mind. Later in the evening, when we had left our seats and were drifting about the table, I found a chance to say a word to our guest concerning his *Joan of Arc*, which I had recently re-read. To my happiness, he told me that long-ago incident—the stray leaf from Joan's life, blown to him by the wind—which had led to his interest in all literature. Then presently I was with Genung again and he was still insisting that I write the life of Mark Twain. It may have been his faithful urging, it may have been the quick sympathy kindled by the name of Joan of Arc; whatever it was, in the instant of bidding good-by to our guest I was prompted to add:

"May I call to see you, Mr. Clemens, some day?" And something—to this day I do not know what— prompted him to answer:

"Yes, come soon."

Two days later, by appointment with his secretary, I arrived at 21 Fifth Avenue, and waited in the library to be summoned to his room. A few moments later I was ascending the long stairs, wondering why I had come on so useless an errand, trying to think up an excuse for having come at all.

He was propped up in bed—a regal bed, from a dismantled Italian palace—delving through a copy of *Huckleberry Finn*, in search of a paragraph concerning which some unknown correspondent had inquired. He pushed the cigars toward me, commenting amusingly on this correspondent and on letter-writing in general. By and by, when there came a lull, I told him what so many thousands had told him before—what his work had meant to me, so long ago, and recalled my childish impressions of that large black-and-gilt book with its wonderful pictures and adventures—*The Innocents Abroad*. Very likely he was willing enough to let me change the subject presently and thank him for the kindly word which David Munro had brought. I do not remember what was his comment, but I suddenly found myself saying that out of his encouragement had grown a hope (though certainly it was less), that I might some day undertake a book about himself. I expected my errand to end at this point, and his silence seemed long and ominous.

He said at last that from time to time he had himself written chapters of his life, but that he had always tired of the work and put it aside. He added that he hoped his daughters would one day collect his letters, but that a biography—a detailed story of a man's life and effort—was another matter. I think he added one or two other remarks, then all at once, turning upon me those piercing agate-blue eyes, he said:

"When would you like to begin?"

There was a dresser, with a large mirror, at the end of the room. I happened to catch my reflection in it, and I vividly recollect saying to it, mentally: "This is not true; it is only one of many similar dreams." But even in a dream one must asnwer, and I said:

"Whenever you like. I can begin now."

He was always eager in any new undertaking.

"Very good," he said, "the sooner, then, the better. Let's begin while we are in the humor. The longer you postpone a thing of this kind, the less likely you are ever to get at it."

This was on Saturday; I asked if Tuesday, January 9, would be too soon to start. He agreed that

Tuesday would do, and inquired as to my plan of work. I suggested bringing a stenographer to make notes of his life-story as he could recall it, this record to be supplemented by other material—letters, journals, and what not. He said:

"I think I should enjoy dictating to a stenographer with some one to prompt me and act as audience. The room adjoining this was fitted up for my study. My manuscript and notes and private books and many of my letters are there, and there are a trunkful or two of such things in the attic. I seldom use the room myself. I do my writing and reading in bed. I will turn that room over to you for this work. Whatever you need will be brought to you. We can have the dictations here in the morning, and you can put in the rest of the day to suit yourself. You can have a key and come and go as you please."

That was always his way. He did nothing by halves. He got up and showed me the warm luxury of the study, with its mass of material—disordered, but priceless.

I have no distinct recollections of how I came away, but presently, back at the Players, I was confiding the matter to Charles Harvey Genung, who said he was not surprised; but I think he was.

LX

WORKING WITH MARK TWAIN

IT was true, after all; and on Tuesday morning, January 9, 1906, I was on hand with a capable stenographer, ready to begin. Clemens, meantime, had developed a new idea: he would like to add, he said, the new dictations to his former beginnings, completing an autobiography which was to be laid away and remain unpublished for a hundred years. He would pay the stenographer himself, and own the notes, allowing me, of course, free use of them as material for my book. He did not believe that he could follow the story of his life in its order of dates, but would find it necessary to wander around, picking up the thread as memory or fancy prompted. I could suggest subjects and ask questions. I assented to everything, and we set to work immediately.

As on my former visit, he was in bed when we arrived, though clad now in a rich Persian dressing-gown, and propped against great, snowy pillows. A small table beside him held his pipes, cigars, papers, also a reading-lamp, the soft light of which brought out his brilliant coloring and the gleam of his snowy hair. There was daylight, too, but it was dull winter daylight, from the north, while the walls of the room were a deep, unreflecting red.

He began that morning with some memories of the Comstock mine; then he dropped back to his childhood, closing at last with some comment on matters quite recent. How delightful it was—his quaint, unhurried fashion of speech, the unconscious habits of his delicate hands, the play of his features as his fancies and phrases passed through his mind and were accepted or put aside. We were watching one of the great literary creators of his time in the very process of his architecture. Time did not count. When he finished, at last, we were all amazed to find that more than two hours had slipped away.

"And how much I have enjoyed it," he said. "It is the ideal plan for this kind of work. Narrative writing is always disappointing, The moment you pick up a pen you begin to lose the spontaneity of the personal relation, which contains the very essence of interest. With short-hand dictation one can talk as if he were at his own dinner-table— always an inspiring place. I expect to dictate all the rest of my life, if you good people are willing to come and listen to it."

The dictations thus begun continued steadily from week to week, with increasing charm. We never knew what he was going to talk about, and it was seldom that *he* knew until the moment of beginning. But it was always fascinating, and I felt myself the most fortunate biographer in the world, as indeed I was.

It was not all smooth sailing, however. In the course of time I began to realize that these marvelous dictated chapters were not altogether history, but were often partly, or even entirely, imaginary. The creator of Tom Sawyer and Huck Finn had been embroidering old incidents or inventing new ones too long to stick to history now, to be able to separate the romance in his mind from the reality of the past. Also, his memory of personal events had become inaccurate. He realized this, and once said, in his whimsical, gentle way:

"When I was younger I could remember anything, whether it happened or not; but I am getting old, and soon I shall remember only the latter."

Yet it was his constant purpose to stick to fact, and especially did he make no effort to put himself in a good light. Indeed, if you wanted to know the worst of Mark Twain you had only to ask him for it. He would give it to the last syllable, and he would improve upon it and pile up his sins, and sometimes the sins of others, without stint. Certainly the dictations were precious, for they revealed character as nothing else could; but as material for history they often failed to stand the test of the documents in the next room—the letters, note-books, agreements, and the like—from which I was gradually rebuilding the structure of the years.

In the talks that we usually had when the dictations were ended and the stenographer had gone I got much that was of great value. It was then that I usually made those inquiries which we had planned in the beginning, and his answers, coming quickly and without reflection, gave imagination less play. Sometimes he would touch some point of special interest and walk up and down, philosophizing, or commenting upon things in general, in a manner not always complimentary to humanity and its progress.

I seldom asked him a question during the dictation—or interrupted in any way, though he had asked me to stop him when I found him repeating or contradicting himself, or misstating some fact known to me. At first I lacked the courage to point out a mistake at the moment, and cautiously mentioned the matter when he had finished. Then he would be likely to say:

"Why didn't you stop me? Why did you let me go on making a donkey of myself when you could have saved me?"

So then I used to take the risk of getting struck by lightning, and nearly always stopped him in time. But if it happened that I upset his thought, the thunderbolt was apt to fly. He would say:

"Now you've knocked everything out of my head."

Then, of course, I was sorry and apologized, and in a moment the sky was clear again. There was generally a humorous complexion to the dictations, whatever the subject. Humor was his natural breath of life, and rarely absent.

Perhaps I should have said sooner that he smoked continuously during the dictations. His cigars were of that delicious fragrance which belongs to domestic tobacco. They were strong and inexpensive, and it was only his early training that made him prefer them. Admiring friends used to send him costly, imported cigars, but he rarely touched them, and they were smoked by visitors. He often smoked a pipe, and preferred it to be old and violent. Once when he had bought a new, expensive briar-root, he handed it to me, saying:

"I'd like to have you smoke that a year or two, and when it gets so you can't stand it, maybe it will suit me."

LXI

DICTATIONS AT DUBLIN, N. H.

FOLLOWING his birthday dinner, Mark Twain had become once more the "Belle of New York," and in a larger way than ever before. An editorial in the *Evening Mail* referred to him as a kind of joint Aristides, Solon, and Themistocles of the American metropolis, and added:

Things have reached a point where, if Mark Twain is not at a public meeting or banquet, he is expected to console it with one of his inimitable letters of advice and encouragement.

He loved the excitement of it, and it no longer seemed to wear upon him. Scarcely an evening passed that he did not go out to some dinner or gathering where he had promised to speak. In April, for the benefit of the Robert Fulton Society, he delivered his farewell lecture—the last lecture, he said, where any one would have to pay to hear him. It was at Carnegie Hall, and the great place was jammed. As he stood before that vast, shouting audience, I wondered if he was remembering that night, forty years before in San Francisco, when his lecture career had begun. We hoped he might speak of it, but he did not do so.

THE BOYS' LIFE OF MARK TWAIN

In May the dictations were transferred to Dublin, New Hampshire, to the long veranda of the Upton House, on the Monadnock slope. He wished to continue our work, he said; so the stenographer and

MARK TWAIN AND ANDREW CARNEGIE AT A SIMPLIFIED SPELLING DINNER (BY CESARE)

myself were presently located in the village, and drove out each morning, to sit facing one of the rarest views in all New England, while he talked of everything and anything that memory or fancy suggested. We had begun in his bedroom, but the glorious outside was too compelling.

The long veranda was ideal. He was generally ready when we arrived, a luminous figure in white flannels, pacing up and down before a background of sky and forest, blue lake, and distant hills. When it stormed we would go inside to a bright fire. The dictation ended, he would ask his secretary to play the orchestrelle, which at great expense had been freighted up from New York. In that high situation, the fire and the music and the stormbeat seemed to lift us very far indeed from reality. Certain symphonies by Beethoven, an impromptu by Schubert, and a nocturne by Chopin were the selections he cared for most,[1] though in certain moods he asked for the Scotch melodies.

There was a good deal of social life in Dublin, but the dictations were seldom interrupted. He became lonely, now and then, and paid a brief visit to New York, or to Mr. Rogers in Fairhaven, but he always returned gladly, for he liked the rest and quiet, and the dictations gave him employment. A part of his entertainment was a trio of kittens which he had rented for the summer—rented because then they would not lose ownership and would find home and protection in the fall. He named the kittens Sackcloth and Ashes—Sackcloth being a black-and-white kit, and Ashes a joint name owned by the two others, who were gray and exactly alike. All summer long these merry little creatures played up

[1] His special favorites were Schubert's Op. 142, part 2, and Chopin's Op. 37, part 2.

and down the wide veranda, or chased butterflies and grasshoppers down the clover slope, offering Mark Twain never-ending amusement. He loved to see them spring into the air after some insect, miss it, tumble back, and quickly jump up again with a surprised and disappointed expression.

In spite of his resolve not to print any of his autobiography until he had been dead a hundred years, he was persuaded during the summer to allow certain chapters of it to be published in *The North American Review*. With the price received, thirty thousand dollars, he announced he was going to build himself a country home at Redding, Connecticut, on land already purchased there, near a small country place of my own. He wished to have a fixed place to go each summer, he said, and his thought was to call it "Autobiography House."

LXII

A NEW ERA OF BILLIARDS

WITH the return to New York I began a period of closer association with Mark Twain. Up to that time our relations had been chiefly of a literary nature. They now became personal as well.

It happened in this way: Mark Twain had never outgrown his love for the game of billiards, though he had not owned a table since the closing of the Hartford house, fifteen years before. Mrs. Henry Rogers had proposed to present him with a table for Christmas, but when he heard of the plan, boy-like, he could not wait, and hinted that if he had the table "right now" he could begin to use it sooner. So the table came—a handsome combination affair, suitable to all games—and was set in place. That morning when the dictation ended he said:

"Have you any special place to lunch, to-day?"

I replied that I had not.

"Lunch here," he said, "and we'll try the new billiard-table."

I acknowledged that I had never played more than a few games of pool, and those very long ago.

"No matter," he said "the poorer you play the better I shall like it."

So I remained for luncheon, and when it was over we began the first game ever played on the "Christmas" table. He taught me a game in which caroms and pockets both counted, and he gave me heavy odds. He beat me, but it was a riotous, rollicking game, the beginning of a closer relation between us. We played most of the afternoon, and he suggested that I "come back in the evening and play some more." I did so, and the game lasted till after midnight. I had beginner's luck—"nigger luck," as he called it—and it kept him working feverishly to win. Once when I had made a great fluke—a carom followed by most of the balls falling into the pockets, he said:

"When you pick up that cue this table drips at every pore."

The morning dictations became a secondary interest. Like a boy, he was looking forward to the afternoon of play, and it seemed never to come quickly enough to suit him. I remained regularly for luncheon, and he was inclined to cut the courses short that we might the sooner get up-stairs for billiards. He did not eat the midday meal himself, but he would come down and walk about the dining-room, talking steadily that marvelous, marvelous talk which little by little I trained myself to remember, though never with complete success. He was only killing time, and I remember once, when he had been earnestly discussing some deep question, he suddenly noticed that the luncheon was ending.

"Now," he said, "we will proceed to more serious matters—it's your—shot."

My game improved with practice, and he reduced my odds. He was willing to be beaten, but not too often. We kept a record of the games, and he went to bed happier if the tally-sheet showed a balance in his favor.

He was not an even-tempered player. When the game went steadily against him he was likely to become critical, even fault-finding, in his remarks. Then presently he would be seized with remorse and become over-gentle and attentive, placing the balls as I knocked them into the pockets, hurrying to render this service. I wished he would not do it. It distressed me that he should humble himself. I was willing that he should lose his temper, that he should be even harsh if he felt so inclined—his age, his position, his genius gave him special privileges. Yet I am glad, as I remember it now, that the other side revealed itself, for it completes the sum of his humanity. Once in a burst of exasperation he made such an onslaught on the balls that he landed a couple of them on the floor. I gathered them up and we went on playing as if nothing had happened, only he was very gentle and sweet, like a summer meadow when the storm has passed by. Presently he said:

"This is a most amusing game. When you play badly it amuses me, and when I play badly and lose my temper it certainly must amuse you."

It was but natural that friendship should grow under such conditions. The disparity of our ages and gifts no longer mattered. The pleasant land of play is a democracy where such things do not count.

We celebrated his seventy-first birthday by playing billiards all day. He invented a new game for the occasion, and added a new rule for it with almost every shot. It happened that no other member of the family was at home—ill-health had banished every one, even the secretary. Flowers, telegrams, and congratulations came, and a string of callers. He saw no one but a few intimate friends.

We were entirely alone for dinner, and I felt the great honor of being his only guest on such an occasion. On that night, a year before, the flower of his profession had assembled to do him honor. Once between the courses, when he rose, as was his habit, to walk about, he wandered into the drawing-room, and, seating himself at the orchestrelle, began to play the beautiful "Flower Song" from Faust. It was a thing I had not seen him do before, and I never saw him do it again.

He was in his loveliest humor all that day and evening, and at night when we stopped playing he said:

"I have never had a pleasanter day at this game."

I answered: "I hope ten years from to-night we shall be playing it."

"Yes," he said, "still playing the best game on earth."

LXIII

LIVING WITH MARK TWAIN

I ACCOMPANIED him on a trip he made to Washington in the interest of copyright. Speaker "Uncle Joe" Cannon lent us his private room in the Capitol, and there all one afternoon Mark Twain received Congressmen, and in an atmosphere blue with cigar-smoke preached the gospel of copyright. It was a historic trip, and for me an eventful one, for it was on the way back to New York that Mark Twain suggested that I take up residence in his home. There was a room going to waste, he said, and I would be handier for the early and late billiard sessions. I accepted, of course.

Looking back, now, I see pretty vividly three quite distinct pictures. One of them, the rich, red interior of the billiard-room, with the brilliant green square in the center on which the gay balls are rolling, and bent over it his luminous white figure in the instant of play. Then there is the long lighted drawing-room, with the same figure stretched on a couch in the corner, drowsily smoking while the rich organ tones summon for him scenes and faces which the others do not see. Sometimes he rose, pacing the length of the parlors, but oftener he lay among the cushions, the light flooding his white hair and dress, heightening his brilliant coloring. He had taken up the fashion of wearing white altogether at this time. Black, he said, reminded him of his funerals.

The third picture is that of the dinner-table—always beautifully laid, and always a shrine of wisdom when he was there. He did not always talk, but he often did, and I see him clearest, his face alive with interest, presenting some new angle of thought in his vivid, inimitable speech. These are pictures that will not fade from my memory. How I wish the marvelous things he said were like them! I preserved as much of them as I could, and in time trained myself to recall portions of his exact phrasing. But even so they seemed never quite as he had said them. They lacked the breath of his personality. His dinner-table talk was likely to be political, scientific, philosophic. He often discussed aspects of astronomy, which was a passion with him. I could succeed better with the billiard-room talk—that was likely to be reminiscent, full of anecdotes. I kept a pad on the window-sill, and made notes while he was playing. At one time he told me of his dreams.

"There is never a month passes," he said, "that I do not dream of being in reduced circumstances and obliged to go back to the river to earn a living. Usually in my dream I am just about to start into a black shadow without being able to tell whether it is Selma Bluff, or Hat Island, or only a black wall of night. Another dream I have is being compelled to go back to the lecture platform. In it I am always getting up before an audience, with nothing to say, trying to be funny, trying to make the audience laugh, realizing I am only making silly jokes. Then the audience realizes it, and pretty soon they commence to get up and leave. That dream always ends by my standing there in the semi-darkness talking to an empty house."

He did not return to Dublin the next summer, but took a house at Tuxedo, nearer New York. I did not go there with him, for in the spring it was agreed that I should make a pilgrimage to the Mississippi and the Pacific coast to see those few still remaining who had known Mark Twain in his youth. John Briggs was alive, also Horace Bixby, "Joe" Goodman, Steve and Jim Gillis, and there were a few others.

It was a trip taken none too soon. John Briggs, a gentle-hearted old man who sat by his fire and through one afternoon told me of the happy days along the river-front from the cave to Holliday's Hill, did not reach the end of the year. Horace Bixby, at eighty-one, was still young, and piloting a government snag-boat. Neither was Joseph Goodman old, by any means, but Jim Gillis was near his end, and Steve Gillis was an invalid, who said:

"Tell Sam I'm going to die pretty soon, but that I love him; that I've loved him all my life, and I'll love him till I die."

LXIV

A DEGREE FROM OXFORD

ON my return I found Mark Twain elated: he
had been invited to England to receive the degree of Literary Doctor from the Oxford University.
It is the highest scholastic honorary degree; and to
come back, as I had, from following the early wanderings of the barefoot truant of Hannibal, only to
find him about to be officially knighted by the world's
most venerable institution of learning, seemed rather
the most surprising chapter even of his marvelous
fairy-tale. If Tom Sawyer had owned the magic
wand, he hardly could have produced anything as
startling as that.

He sailed on the 8th of June, 1907, exactly forty
years from the day he had sailed on the *Quaker City*
to win his greater fame. I did not accompany him.
He took with him a secretary to make notes, and my
affairs held me in America. He was absent six weeks,
and no attentions that England had ever paid him
before could compare with her lavish welcome during
this visit. His reception was really national. He
was banqueted by the greatest clubs of London,
he was received with special favor at the King's
garden party, he traveled by a royal train, crowds

gathering everywhere to see him pass. At Oxford when he appeared on the street the name Mark Twain ran up and down like a cry of fire, and the people came running. When he appeared on the stage at the Sheldonian Theater to receive his degree, clad in his doctor's robe of scarlet and gray, there arose a great tumult—the shouting of the undergraduates for the boy who had been Tom Sawyer and had played with Huckleberry Finn. The papers next day spoke of his reception as a "cyclone," surpassing any other welcome, though Rudyard Kipling was one of those who received degrees on that occasion, and General Booth and Whitelaw Reid, and other famous men.

Perhaps the most distinguished social honor paid to Mark Twain at this time was the dinner given him by the staff of London *Punch*, in the historic *Punch* editorial rooms on Bouverie Street. No other foreigner had ever been invited to that sacred board, where Thackeray had sat, and Douglas Jerrold and others of the great departed. *Punch* had already saluted him with a front-page cartoon, and at this dinner the original drawing was presented to him by the editor's little daughter, Joy Agnew.

The Oxford degree, and the splendid homage paid him by England at large, became, as it were, the crowning episode of Mark Twain's career. I think he realized this, although he did not speak of it— indeed, he had very little to say of the whole matter. I telephoned a greeting when I knew that he had arrived in New York, and was summoned to "come down and play billiards." I confess I went with a good deal of awe, prepared to sit in silence and listen to the tale of the returning hero. But when I arrived he was already in the billiard-room, knocking the balls about—his coat off, for it was a hot night. As I entered, he said:

"Get your cue—I've been inventing a new game."

That was all. The pageant was over, the curtain was rung down. Business was resumed at the old stand.

LXV

THE REMOVAL TO REDDING

THERE followed another winter during which I was much with Mark Twain, though a part of it he spent with Mr. Rogers in Bermuda, that pretty island resort which both men loved. Then came spring again, and June, and with it Mark Twain's removal to his newly built home, "Stormfield," at Redding, Connecticut.

The house had been under construction for a year. He had never seen it—never even seen the land I had bought for him. He even preferred not to look at any plans or ideas for decoration.

"When the house is finished and furnished, and the cat is purring on the hearth, it will be time enough for me to see it," he had said more than once.

He had only specified that the rooms should be large and that the billiard-room should be red. His billiard-rooms thus far had been of that color, and their memory was associated in his mind with enjoyment and comfort. He detested details of preparation, and then, too, he looked forward to the dramatic surprise of walking into a home that had been conjured into existence as with a word.

It was the 18th of June, 1908, that he finally took possession. The Fifth Avenue house was not dismantled, for it was the plan then to use Stormfield only as a summer place. The servants, however, with one exception, had been transferred to Redding, and Mark Twain and I remained alone, though not lonely, in the city house, playing billiards most of the time, and being as hilarious as we pleased, for there was nobody to disturb. I think he hardly mentioned the new home during that time. He had never seen even a photograph of the place, and I confess I had moments of anxiety, for I had selected the site and had been more or less concerned otherwise, though John Howells was wholly responsible for the building. I did not really worry, for I knew how beautiful and peaceful it all was.

The morning of the 18th was bright and sunny and cool. Mark Twain was up and shaved by six o'clock in order to be in time. The train did not leave until four in the afternoon, but our last billiards in town must begin early and suffer no interruption. We were still playing when, about three, word was brought up that the cab was waiting. Arrived at the station, a group collected, reporters and others, to speed him to his new home. Some of the reporters came along.

The scenery was at its best that day, and he spoke of it approvingly. The hour and a half required to cover the sixty miles' distance seemed short. The train porters came to carry out the bags. He drew from his pocket a great handful of silver.

"Give them something," he said; "give everybody liberally that does any service."

There was a sort of open-air reception in waiting —a varied assemblage of vehicles festooned with flowers had gathered to offer gallant country welcome. It was a perfect June evening, still and dream-like; there seemed a spell of silence on everything. The people did not cheer—they smiled and waved to the white figure, and he smiled and waved reply, but there was no noise. It was like a scene in a cinema.

His carriage led the way on the three-mile drive to the house on the hilltop, and the floral procession fell in behind. Hillsides were green, fields were white with daisies, dogwood and laurel shone among the trees. He was very quiet as we drove along. Once, with gentle humor, looking out over a white daisy-field, he said:

"That is buckwheat. I always recognize buckwheat when I see it. I wish I knew as much about other things as I know about buckwheat."

The clear-running brooks, a swift-flowing river, a tumbling cascade where we climbed a hill, all came in for his approval—then we were at the lane that led to his new home, and the procession behind dropped away. The carriage ascended still higher, and a view opened across the Saugatuck Valley, with its nestling village and church-spire and farmhouses, and beyond them the distant hills. Then came the house—simple in design, but beautiful— an Italian villa, such as he had known in Florence, adapted here to American climate and needs.

At the entrance his domestic staff waited to greet him, and presently he stepped across the threshold and stood in his own home for the first time in seventeen years. Nothing was lacking—it was as finished, as completely furnished, as if he had occupied it a lifetime. No one spoke immediately, but when his eyes had taken in the harmony of the place, with its restful, home-like comfort, and followed through the open French windows to the distant vista of treetops and farmsides and blue hills, he said, very gently:

"How beautiful it all is! I did not think it could be as beautiful as this." And later, when he had seen all of the apartments: "It is a perfect house—perfect, so far as I can see, in every detail. It might have been here always."

There were guests that first evening—a small home dinner-party—and a little later at the foot of the garden some fireworks were set off by neighbors inspired by Dan Beard, who had recently located in Redding. Mark Twain, watching the rockets that announced his arrival, said, gently:

"I wonder why they go to so much trouble for me. I never go to any trouble for anybody."

The evening closed with billiards, hilarious games, and when at midnight the cues were set in the rack no one could say that Mark Twain's first day in his new home had not been a happy one.

LXVI

LIFE AT STORMFIELD

MARK TWAIN loved Stormfield. Almost immediately he gave up the idea of going back to New York for the winter, and I think he never entered the Fifth Avenue house again. The quiet and undisturbed comfort of Stormfield came to him at the right time of life. His day of being the "Belle of New York" was over. Now and then he attended some great dinner, but always under protest. Finally he refused to go at all. He had much company during that first summer—old friends, and now and again young people, of whom he was always fond. The billiard-room he called "the aquarium," and a frieze of Bermuda fishes, in gay prints, ran around the walls. Each young lady visitor was allowed to select one of these as her patron fish and attach her name to it. Thus, as a member of the "aquarium club," she was represented in absence. Of course there were several cats at Stormfield, and these really owned the premises. The kittens scampered about the billiard-table after the balls, even when the game was in progress, giving all sorts of new angles to the shots. This delighted him, and he would not for anything have discommoded or removed one of those furry hazards.

My own house was a little more than half a mile away, our lands joining, and daily I went up to visit him—to play billiards or to take a walk across the fields. There was a stenographer in the neighborhood, and he continued his dictations, but not regularly. He wrote, too, now and then, and finished the little book called *Is Shakespeare Dead?*

Winter came. The walks were fewer, and there was even more company; the house was gay and the billiard games protracted. In February I made a trip to Europe and the Mediterranean, to go over some of his ground there. Returning in April, I found him somewhat changed. It was not that he had grown older, or less full of life, but only less active, less eager for gay company, and he no longer dictated, or very rarely. His daughter Jean, who had been in a health resort, was coming home to act as his secretary, and this made him very happy. We resumed our games, our talks, and our long walks across the fields. There were few guests, and we were together most of the day and evening. How beautiful the memory of it all is now! To me, of course, nothing can ever be like it again in this world.

Mark Twain walked slowly these days. Early in the summer there appeared indications of the heart trouble that less than a year later would bring the end. His doctor advised diminished smoking, and forbade the old habit of lightly skipping up and down stairs. The trouble was with the heart muscles, and at times there came severe deadly pains in his breast, but for the most part he did not suffer. He was allowed the walk, however, and once I showed him a part of his estate he had not seen before—a remote cedar hillside. On the way I pointed out a little corner of land which earlier he had given me to straighten our division line. I told him I was going to build a study on it and call it "Markland." I think the name pleased him. Later he said:

"If you had a place for that extra billiard-table of mine" (the Rogers table, which had been left in storage in New York), "I would turn it over to you."

I replied that I could adapt the size of my proposed study to fit the table, and he said:

"Now that will be very good. Then when I want exercise I can walk down and play billiards with you, and when you want exercise you can walk up and play billiards with me. You must build that study."

So it was planned, and the work was presently under way.

How many things we talked of! Life, death, the future—all the things of which we know so little and love so much to talk about. Astronomy, as I have said, was one of his favorite subjects. Neither of us had any real knowledge of the matter, which made its great facts all the more awesome. The thought that the nearest fixed star was twenty-five trillions of miles away—two hundred and fifty thousand times the distance to our own remote sun—gave him a sort of splendid thrill. He would figure out those appalling measurements of space, covering sheets of paper with his sums, but he was not a good mathematician, and the answers were generally wrong. Comets in particular interested him, and one day he said:

"I came in with Halley's comet in 1835. It is coming again next year, and I expect to go out with it. It will be the greatest disappointment of my life if I don't go out with Halley's comet."

He looked so strong, and full of color and vitality. One could not believe that his words held a prophecy. Yet the pains recurred with increasing frequency and severity; his malady, *angina pectoris*, was making progress. And how bravely he bore it all! He never complained, never bewailed. I have seen the fierce attack crumple him when we were at billiards, but he would insist on playing in his turn, bowed, his face white, his hand digging at his breast.

LXVII

THE DEATH OF JEAN

CLARA CLEMENS was married that autumn to Ossip Gabrilowitsch, the Russian pianist, and presently sailed for Europe, where they would make their home. Jean Clemens was now head of the house, and what with her various duties and poor health, her burden was too heavy. She had a passion for animal life of every kind, and in some farm-buildings at one corner of the estate had set up quite an establishment of chickens and domestic animals. She was fond of giving these her personal attention, and this, with her house direction and secretarial work, gave her little time for rest. I tried to relieve her of a share of the secretarial work, but she was ambitious and faithful. Still, her condition did not seem critical.

I stayed at Stormfield, now, most of the time— nights as well as days—for the dull weather had come and Mark Twain found the house rather lonely. In November he had an impulse to go to Bermuda, and we spent a month in the warm light of that summer island, returning a week before the Christmas holidays. And just then came Mark Twain's last great tragedy—the death of his daughter Jean.

The holidays had added heavily to Jean's labors.

Out of her generous heart she had planned gifts for everybody—had hurried to and from the city for her purchases, and in the loggia set up a beautiful Christmas tree. Meantime she had contracted a heavy cold. Her trouble was epilepsy, and all this was bad for her. On the morning of December 24, she died, suddenly, from the shock of a cold bath.

Below, in the loggia, drenched with tinsel, stood the tree, and heaped about it the packages of gifts which that day she had meant to open and put in place. Nobody had been overlooked.

Jean was taken to Elmira for burial. Her father, unable to make the winter journey, remained behind. Her cousin, Jervis Langdon, came for her.

It was six in the evening when she went away. A soft, heavy snow was falling, and the gloom of the short day was closing in. There was not the least noise, the whole world was muffled. The lanterns shone out the open door, and at an upper window, the light gleaming on his white hair, her father watched her going away from him for the last time. Later he wrote:

From my window I saw the hearse and the carriages wind along the road and gradually grow vague and spectral in the falling snow, and presently disappear. Jean was gone out of my life, and would not come back any more. The cousin she had played with when they were babies together—he and her beloved old Katy—were conducting her to her distant childhood home, where she will lie by her mother's side once more, in the company of Susy and Langdon.

344

LXVIII

DAYS IN BERMUDA

TEN days later Mark Twain returned to Bermuda, accompanied only by a valet. He had asked me if we would be willing to close our home for the winter and come to Stormfield, so that the place might be ready any time for his return. We came, of course, for there was no thought other than for his comfort. He did not go to a hotel in Bermuda, but to the home of Vice-Consul Allen, where he had visited before. The Allens were devoted to him and gave him such care as no hotel could offer.

Bermuda agreed with Mark Twain, and for a time there he gained in strength and spirits and recovered much of his old manner. He wrote me almost daily, generally with good reports of his health and doings, and with playful counsel and suggestions. Then, by and by, he did not write with his own hand, but through his newly appointed "secretary," Mr. Allen's young daughter, Helen, of whom he was very fond. The letters, however, were still gay. Once he said:

While the matter is in my mind I will remark that if you ever send me another letter which is not paged at the top I will write you with my own hand, so that I may use in utter freedom and without embarrassment the kind of words which alone can describe such a criminal.

He had made no mention so far of the pains in his breast, but near the end of March he wrote that he was coming home, if the breast pains did not "mend their ways pretty considerable. I do not want to die here," he said. "I am growing more and more particular about the place." A week later brought another alarming letter, also one from Mr. Allen, who frankly stated that matters had become very serious indeed. I went to New York and sailed the next morning, cabling the Gabrilowitsches to come without delay.

I sent no word to Bermuda that I was coming, and when I arrived he was not expecting me.

"Why," he said, holding out his hand, "you did not tell us you were coming?"

"No," I said, "it *is* rather sudden. I didn't quite like the sound of your last letters."

"But those were not serious. You shouldn't have come on my account."

I said then that I had come on my own account, that I had felt the need of recreation, and had decided to run down and come home with him.

"That's—very—good," he said, in his slow, gentle fashion. "*Now* I'm glad to see you."

His breakfast came in and he ate with appetite. I had thought him thin and pale, at first sight, but his color had come back now, and his eyes were bright. He told me of the fierce attacks of the pain, and how he had been given hypodermic injections, which he amusingly termed "hypnotic injunctions" and "the sub-cutaneous." From Mr. and Mrs. Allen I learned how slender had been his chances, and how uncertain were the days ahead. Mr. Allen had already engaged passage home for April 12th.

He seemed so little like a man whose days were numbered. On the afternoon of my arrival we drove out, as we had done on our former visit, and he discussed some of the old subjects in quite the old way. I had sold for him, for six thousand dollars, the farm where Jean had kept her animals, and he wished to use the money in erecting for her some sort of memorial. He agreed that a building to hold the library which he had already donated to the town of Redding would be appropriate and useful. He asked me to write at once to his lawyer and have the matter arranged.

We did not drive out again. The pains held off for several days, and he was gay and went out on the lawn, but most of the time he sat propped up in bed, reading and smoking. When I looked at him there, so full of vigor and the joy of life, I could not persuade myself that he would not outlive us all.

He had written very little in Bermuda—his last work being a chapter of amusing "Advice"—for me, as he confessed—what I was to do upon reaching the gate of which St. Peter is said to keep the key. As it is the last writing he ever did, and because it is characteristic, one or two paragraphs may be admitted here:

Upon arrival do not speak to St. Peter until spoken to. It is not your place to begin.

Do not begin any remark with "Say."

When applying for a ticket avoid trying to make conversation. If you *must* talk, let the weather alone. . . .

You can ask him for his autograph—there is no harm in that—but be careful and don't remark that it is one of the penalties of greatness. He has heard *that* before.

There were several pages of this counsel.

LXIX

THE RETURN TO REDDING

I SPENT most of each day with him, merely sitting by the bed and reading. I noticed when he slept that his breathing was difficult, and I could see that he did not improve, but often he was gay and liked the entire family to gather about and be merry. It was only a few days before we sailed that the severe attacks returned. Then followed bad nights; but respite came, and we sailed on the 12th, as arranged. The Allen home stands on the water, and Mr. Allen had chartered a tug to take us to the ship. We were obliged to start early, and the fresh morning breeze was stimulating. Mark Twain seemed in good spirits when we reached the *Oceana*, which was to take him home.

As long as I remember anything I shall remember the forty-eight hours of that homeward voyage. He was comfortable at first, and then we ran into the humid, oppressive air of the Gulf Stream, and he could not breathe. It seemed to me that the end might come at any moment, and this thought was in his own mind, but he had no dread, and his sense of humor did not fail. Once when the ship rolled and his hat fell from the hook and made the circuit of the cabin floor, he said:

"The ship is passing the hat."

I had been instructed in the use of the hypodermic needle, and from time to time gave him the "hypnotic injunction," as he still called it. But it did not afford him entire relief. He could remain in no position for any length of time. Yet he never complained and thought only of the trouble he might be making. Once he said:

"I am sorry for you, Paine, but I can't help it— I can't hurry this dying business."

And a little later:

"Oh, it is such a mystery, and it takes so long!"

Relatives, physicians, and news-gatherers were at the dock to welcome him. Revived by the cool, fresh air of the North, he had slept for several hours and was seemingly much better. A special compartment on the same train that had taken us first to Redding took us there now, his physicians in attendance. He did not seem to mind the trip or the drive home.

As we turned into the lane that led to Stormfield he said:

"Can we see where you have built your billiard-room?"

The gable of the new study showed among the trees, and I pointed it out to him.

"It looks quite imposing," he said.

Arriving at Stormfield, he stepped, unassisted, from the carriage to greet the members of the household, and with all his old courtliness offered each his

hand. Then in a canvas chair we had brought we
carried him up-stairs to his room—the big, beautiful
room that looked out to the sunset hills. This was
Thursday evening, April 14, 1910.

LXX

THE CLOSE OF A GREAT LIFE

MARK TWAIN lived just a week from that day and hour. For a time he seemed full of life, talking freely, and suffering little. Clara and Ossip Gabrilowitsch arrived on Saturday and found him cheerful, quite like himself. At intervals he read. Suetonius and Carlyle lay on the bed beside him, and he would pick them up and read a page or a paragraph. Sometimes when I saw him thus—the high color still in his face, the clear light in his eyes'— I said: "It is not reality. He is not going to die.'

But by Wednesday of the following week it was evident that the end was near. We did not know it then, but the mysterious messenger of his birth year, Halley's comet, became visible that night in the sky.[1]

On Thursday morning, the 21st, his mind was still fairly clear, and he read a little from one of the volumes on his bed. By Clara he sent word that he wished to see me, and when I came in he spoke of two unfinished manuscripts which he wished me to "throw away," as he briefly expressed it, for his words were few, now, and uncertain. I assured him

---

[1] See reference in Chapter lxvi.

that I would attend to the matter and he pressed my hand. It was his last word to me. During the afternoon, while Clara stood by him, he sank into a doze, and from it passed into a deeper slumber and did not heed us any more.

Through that peaceful spring afternoon the life-wave ebbed lower and lower. It was about half-past six, and the sun lay just on the horizon, when Dr. Quintard noticed that the breathing, which had gradually become more subdued, broke a little. There was no suggestion of any struggle. The noble head turned a little to one side, there was a fluttering sigh, and the breath that had been unceasing for seventy-four tumultuous years had stopped forever.

In the Brick Church, New York, Mark Twain—dressed in the white he loved so well—lay, with the nobility of death upon him, while a multitude of those who loved him passed by and looked at his face for the last time. Flowers in profusion were banked about him, but on the casket lay a single wreath which Dan Beard and his wife had woven from the laurel which grows on Stormfield hill. He was never more beautiful than as he lay there, and it was an impressive scene to see those thousands file by, regard him for a moment, gravely, thoughtfully, and pass on. All sorts were there, rich and poor; some crossed themselves, some saluted, some paused a little to take a closer look.

That night we went with him to Elmira, and next day he lay in those stately parlors that had seen his wedding-day, and where little Langdon and Susy had lain, and Mrs. Clemens, and then Jean, only a little while before.

The worn-out body had reached its journey's end; but his spirit had never grown old, and to-day, still young, it continues to cheer and comfort a tired world.

THE END

ALBERT BIGELOW PAINE

ALBERT BIGELOW PAINE was born July 10, 1861, in New Bedford, Massachusetts, but when he was only a year old his family went "west" to a farm near Bentonsport, Iowa. They moved again in 1865, this time to a farm in southern Illinois. His formal schooling was obtained from a rural school (where his Friday afternoon "compositions" gave him his first desire to write) and from an academy at Xenia, to which place they had moved in 1873. He left school in the early 'teens, having "gone through" the subjects offered: there was no question of continuing his education, for "in that day," as he said later, "we simpler people knew very little about going to college."

But he was fond of reading and his father was generous in providing books and magazines. And he was fond of writing, verses chiefly. When some of these were finally accepted by a New York family paper, he felt he was definitely launched upon a literary career. He continued his writing during the years that followed, even though for a number of those years he was wandering through the South making photographs, outdoor views for the most part. It may have been this gypsy existence that helped to develop in Mr. Paine those qualities which, years afterwards, made him a close companion of Mark Twain.

In 1895 he came to New York to live. It was here that he met Mark Twain and became his biographer. But before that he had attained literary prominence, "writing," as he says, "every sort of book, almost, and for readers of all ages." It was his life of Thomas Nast that led

355

directly to the Mark Twain book, but probably his best-known books are for children. His *Hollow Tree Stories* are delightful reading: Uncle Remus tales, without the dialect. Two of his more recent books, *Joan of Arc, Maid of France* and *The Girl in the White Armor* brought to Mr. Paine from the French government the decoration of the Legion d'Honneur.

The circumstances that led to his writing of the Twain biography and to his life with Twain are fully described in the *Boys' Life*. He spent four years in collecting the material for the biography and two years in writing it: this was the complete three-volume *Life*, from which he made the briefer edition. The high literary merit of the biography and the success it has won are due to a number of causes: the fascinating life Mark Twain had lived, the romance implicit in it, and his great popularity; the temperamental kinship between Twain and his biographer and the intimate life they led together; Mr. Paine's long and varied experience as a writer, which formed, as it were, an apprenticeship for the work on this book; the zeal and unflagging devotion of Mr. Paine to his task; and the simple, direct style of the book.

For a number of years Mr. Paine has lived abroad, chiefly in France. He loves France dearly, and, as he says, "life is quieter and freer there than elsewhere and less costly, both in money and nerve tissue." But he remains, of course, a loyal American citizen; and no matter what success he has attained as a writer on French subjects, it is through his biography of a great American that he is best known and will be longest remembered.